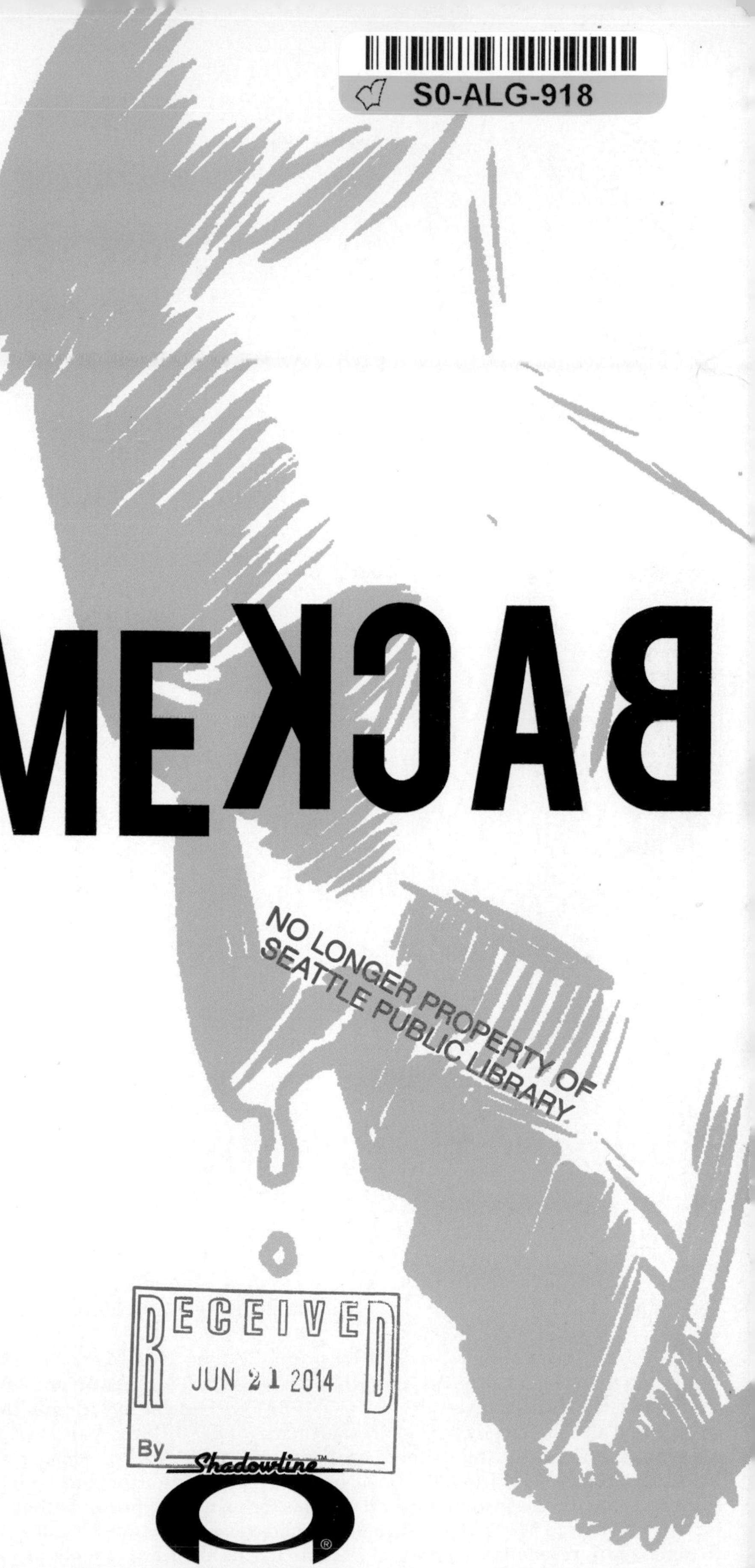

COMEBACK

Shadowline™
image®
www.ShadowlineOnline.com

COMEBACK TPB   First Printing: May, 2013   ISBN: 978-1-60706-737-

Published by Image Comics, Inc. Office of publication: 2001 Center St. Sixth Floor, Berkeley, CA 94704
Copyright © 2013 ED BRISSON and MICHAEL WALSH. Originally published in single magazine form a
COMEBACK #1-5. All rights reserved. COMEBACK™ (including all prominent characters featured herein)
its logo and all character likenesses are trademarks of ED BRISSON and MICHEL WALSH, unless otherwis
noted. Image Comics® and its logos are registered trademarks of Image Comics, Inc. Shadowline and it
logos are © and ™ 2013 Jim Valentino. No part of this publication may be reproduced or transmitted, in an
form or by any means (except for short excerpts for review purposes) without the express written permission
of Mr. Brisson or Mr. Walsh. All names, characters, events and locales in this publication are entirel
fictional. Any resemblance to actual persons (living or dead), events or places, without satiric intent, i
coincidental. PRINTED IN USA. For information regarding the CPSIA on this printed material call
203-595-3636 and provide reference # RICH – 486441. International Rights / Foreign Licensing -
foreignlicensing@imagecomics.com

WRITTEN AND LETTERED BY
ED BRISSON

ILLUSTRATED BY
MICHAEL WALSH

COLORED BY
JORDIE BELLAIRE

EDITED BY
LAURA TAVISHATI

COMMUNICATIONS
MARC LOMBARDI

PUBLISHER
JIM VALENTINO

IMAGE COMICS, INC.
Robert Kirkman - chief operating officer
Erik Larsen - chief financial officer
Todd McFarlane - president
Marc Silvestri - chief executive officer
Jim Valentino - vice-president

Eric Stephenson - publisher
Ron Richards - director of business development
Jennifer de Guzman - pr & marketing director
Branwyn Bigglestone - accounts manager
Emily Miller - accounting assistant
Jamie Parreno - marketing assistant
Jenna Savage - administrative assistant
Kevin Yuen - digital rights coordinator
Jonathan Chan - production manager
Drew Gill - art director
Tyler Shainline - print manager
Monica Garcia - production artist
Vincent Kukua - production artist
Jana Cook - production artist
www.imagecomics.com

follow #shadowline comics on FACEBOOK and TWITTER

ED

To Janet, for all her love and support.

MICHAEL

To Mom and Dad for supporting and believing in me from the very beginning. I wouldn't be here without you. To Caitlin, Shelby and Toni-Marie for your love.

JORDIE

To Declan who loves great comics and continuously supports new talent.

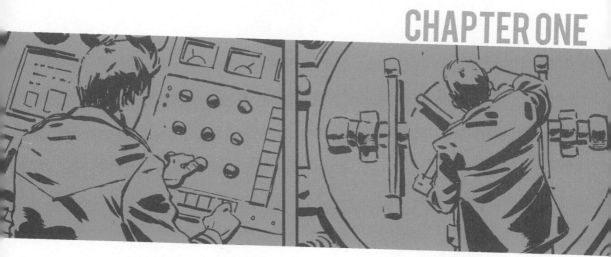

CHAPTER ONE

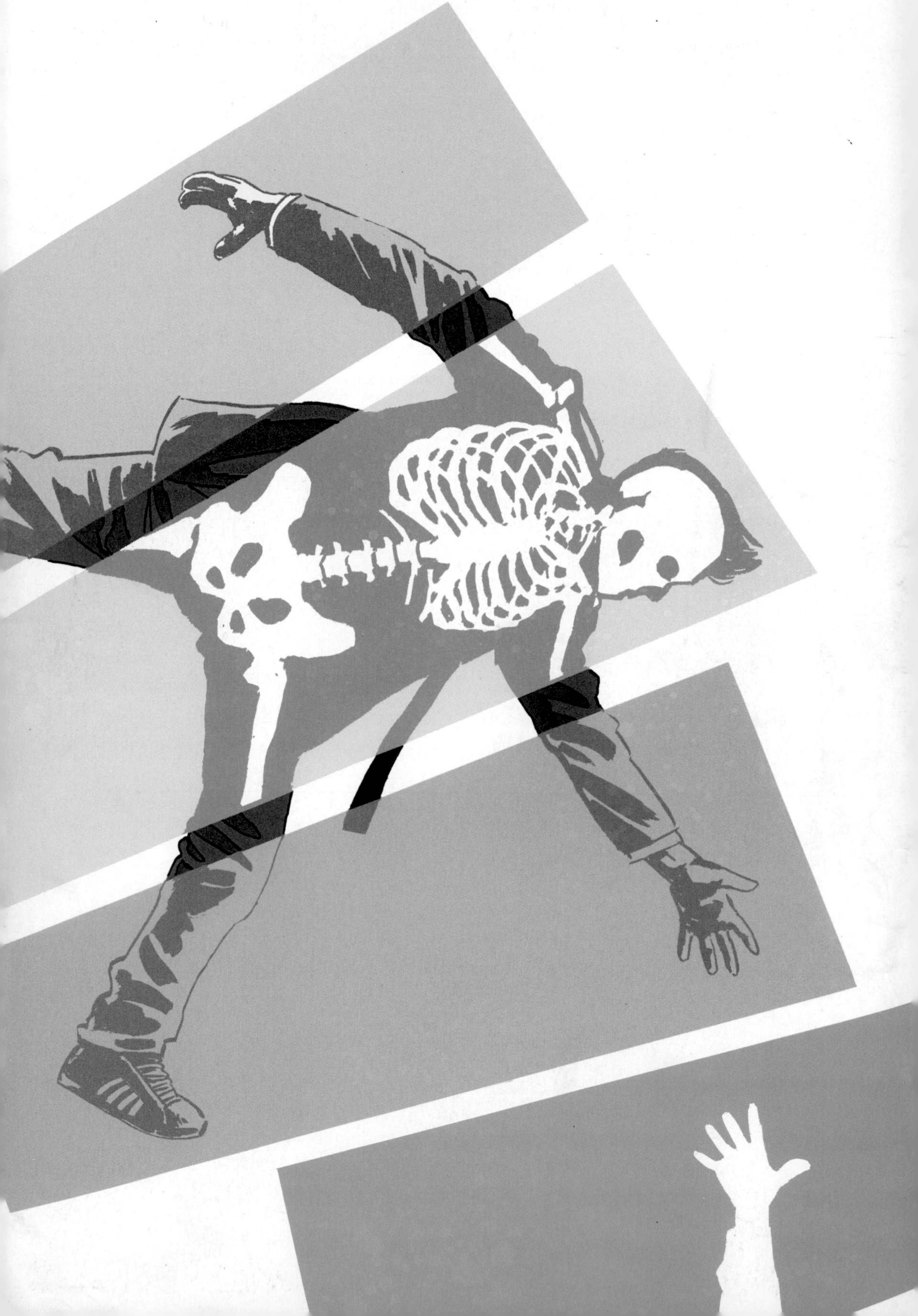

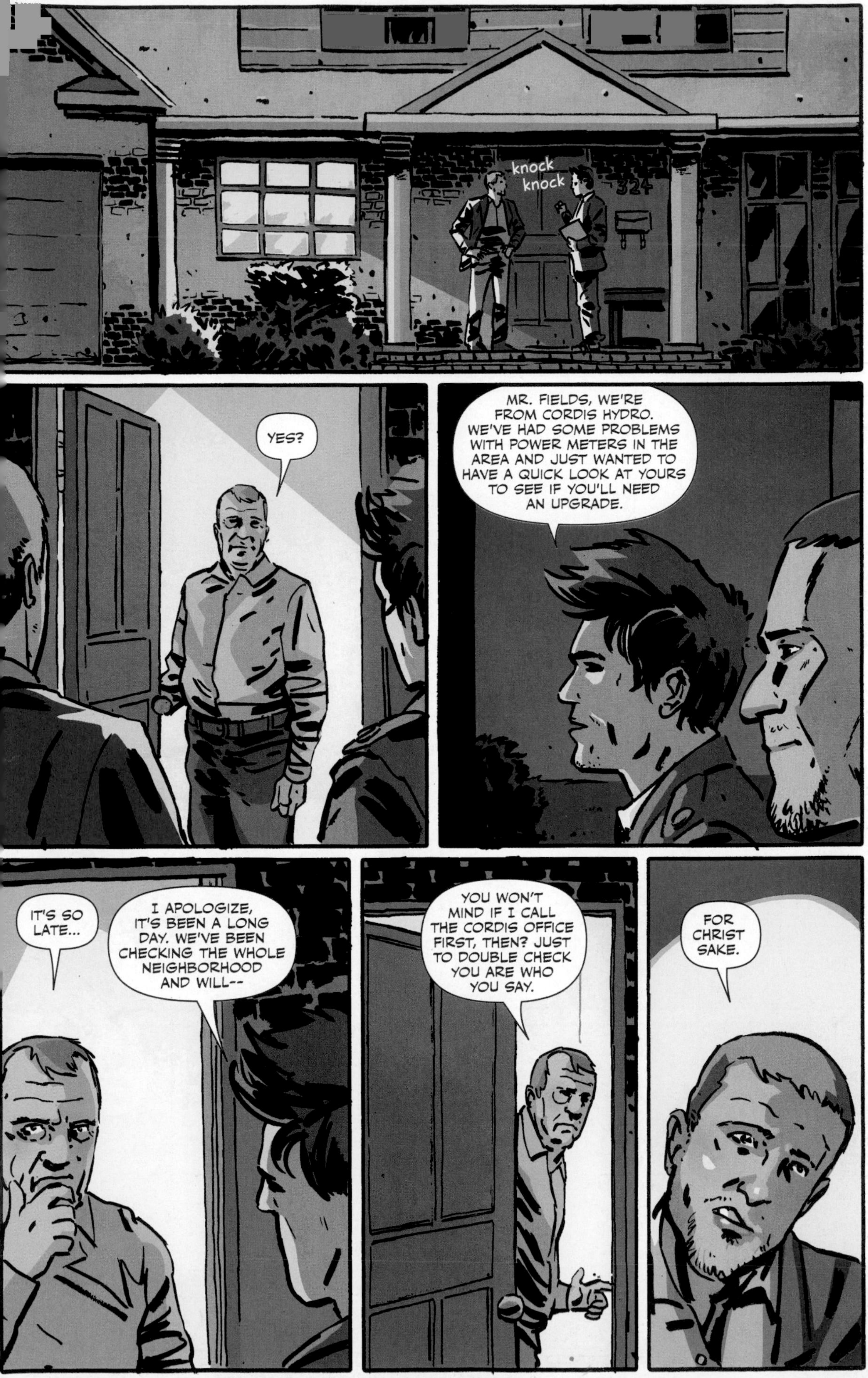
knock knock
YES?
MR. FIELDS, WE'RE FROM CORDIS HYDRO. WE'VE HAD SOME PROBLEMS WITH POWER METERS IN THE AREA AND JUST WANTED TO HAVE A QUICK LOOK AT YOURS TO SEE IF YOU'LL NEED AN UPGRADE.
IT'S SO LATE...
I APOLOGIZE, IT'S BEEN A LONG DAY. WE'VE BEEN CHECKING THE WHOLE NEIGHBORHOOD AND WILL--
YOU WON'T MIND IF I CALL THE CORDIS OFFICE FIRST, THEN? JUST TO DOUBLE CHECK YOU ARE WHO YOU SAY.
FOR CHRIST SAKE.

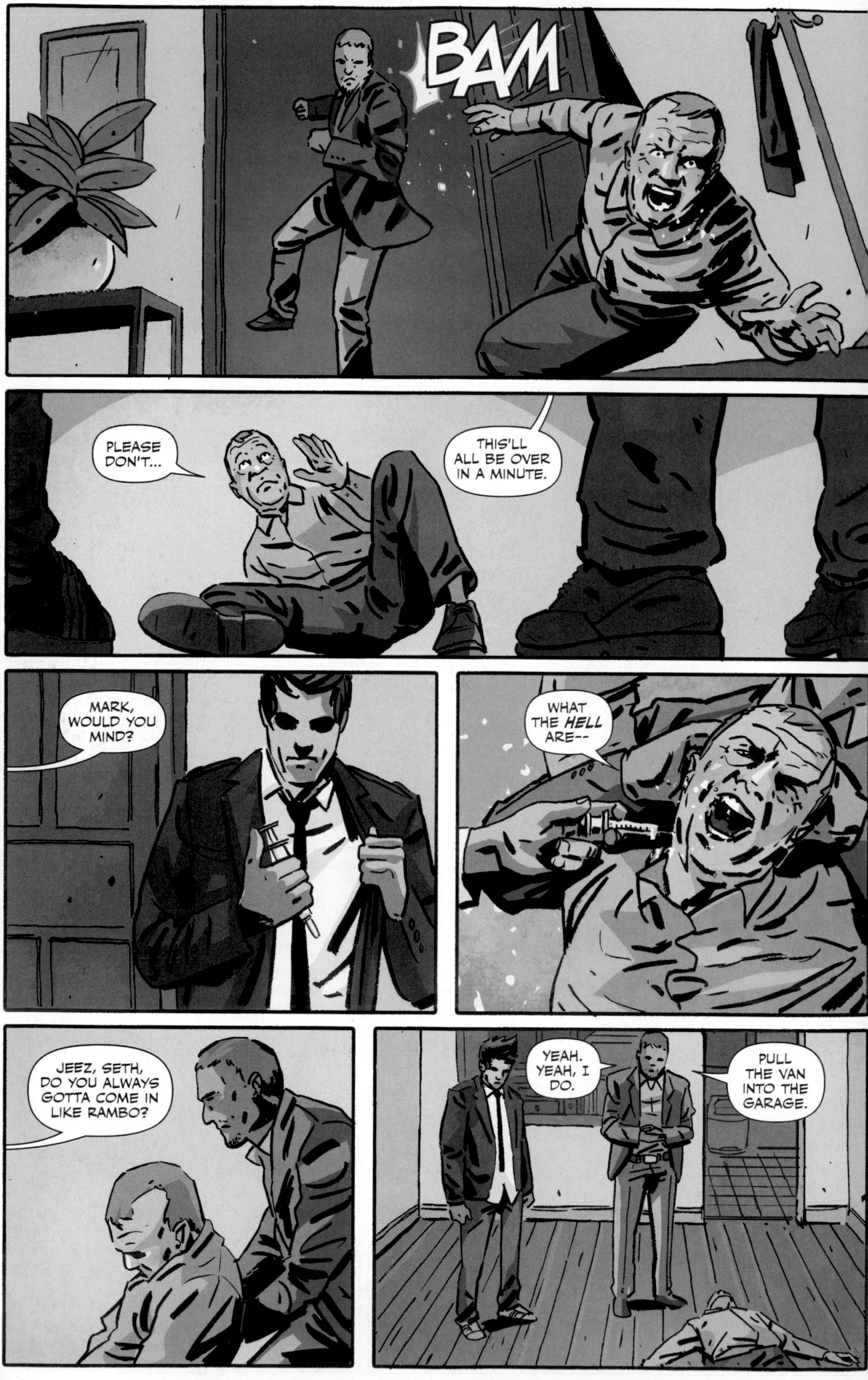
BAM
PLEASE DON'T...
THIS'LL ALL BE OVER IN A MINUTE.
MARK, WOULD YOU MIND?
WHAT THE *HELL* ARE--
JEEZ, SETH, DO YOU ALWAYS GOTTA COME IN LIKE RAMBO?
YEAH. YEAH, I DO.
PULL THE VAN INTO THE GARAGE.

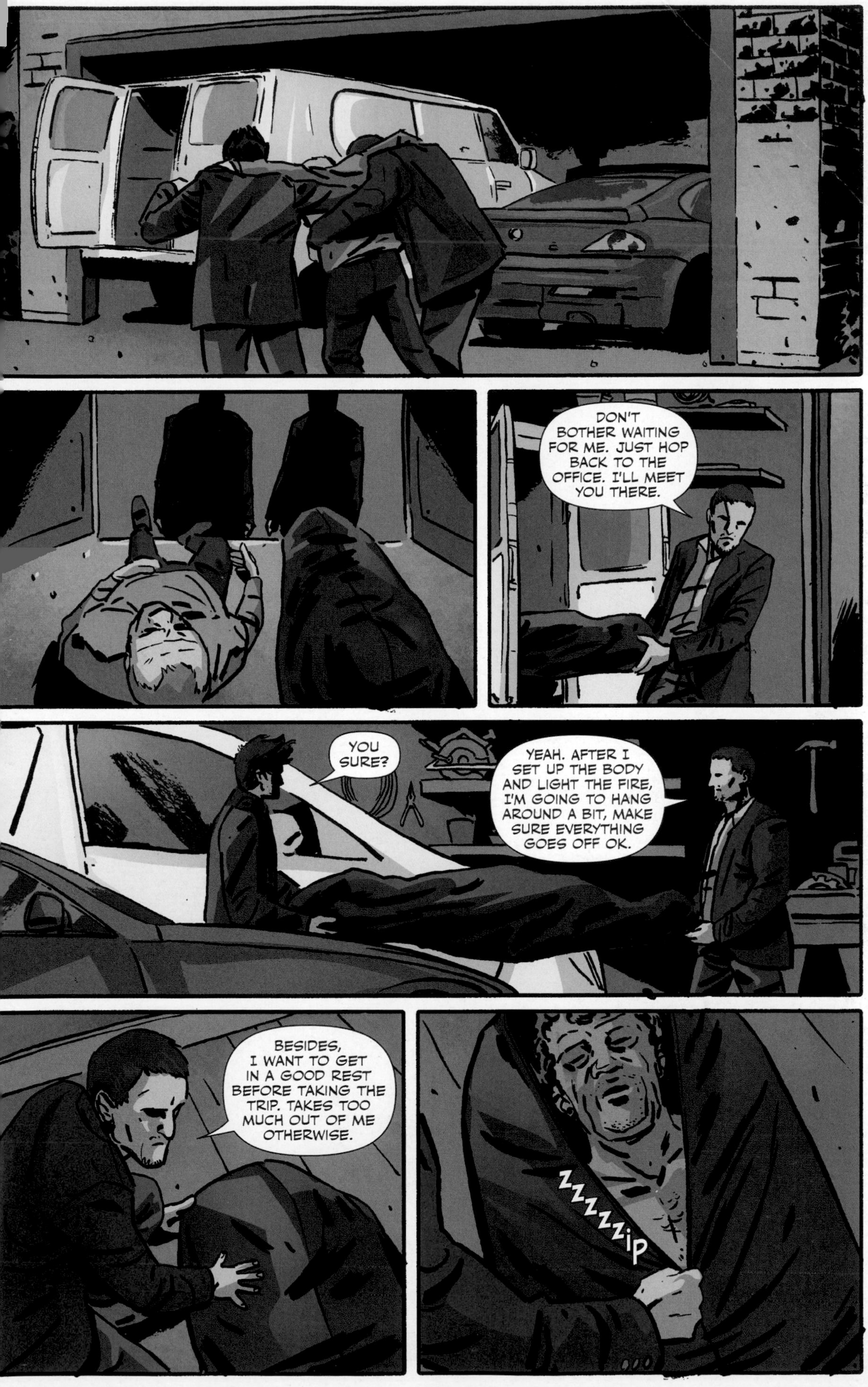
DON'T BOTHER WAITING FOR ME. JUST HOP BACK TO THE OFFICE. I'LL MEET YOU THERE.
YOU SURE?
YEAH. AFTER I SET UP THE BODY AND LIGHT THE FIRE, I'M GOING TO HANG AROUND A BIT, MAKE SURE EVERYTHING GOES OFF OK.
BESIDES, I WANT TO GET IN A GOOD REST BEFORE TAKING THE TRIP. TAKES TOO MUCH OUT OF ME OTHERWISE.
ZZZZZIP

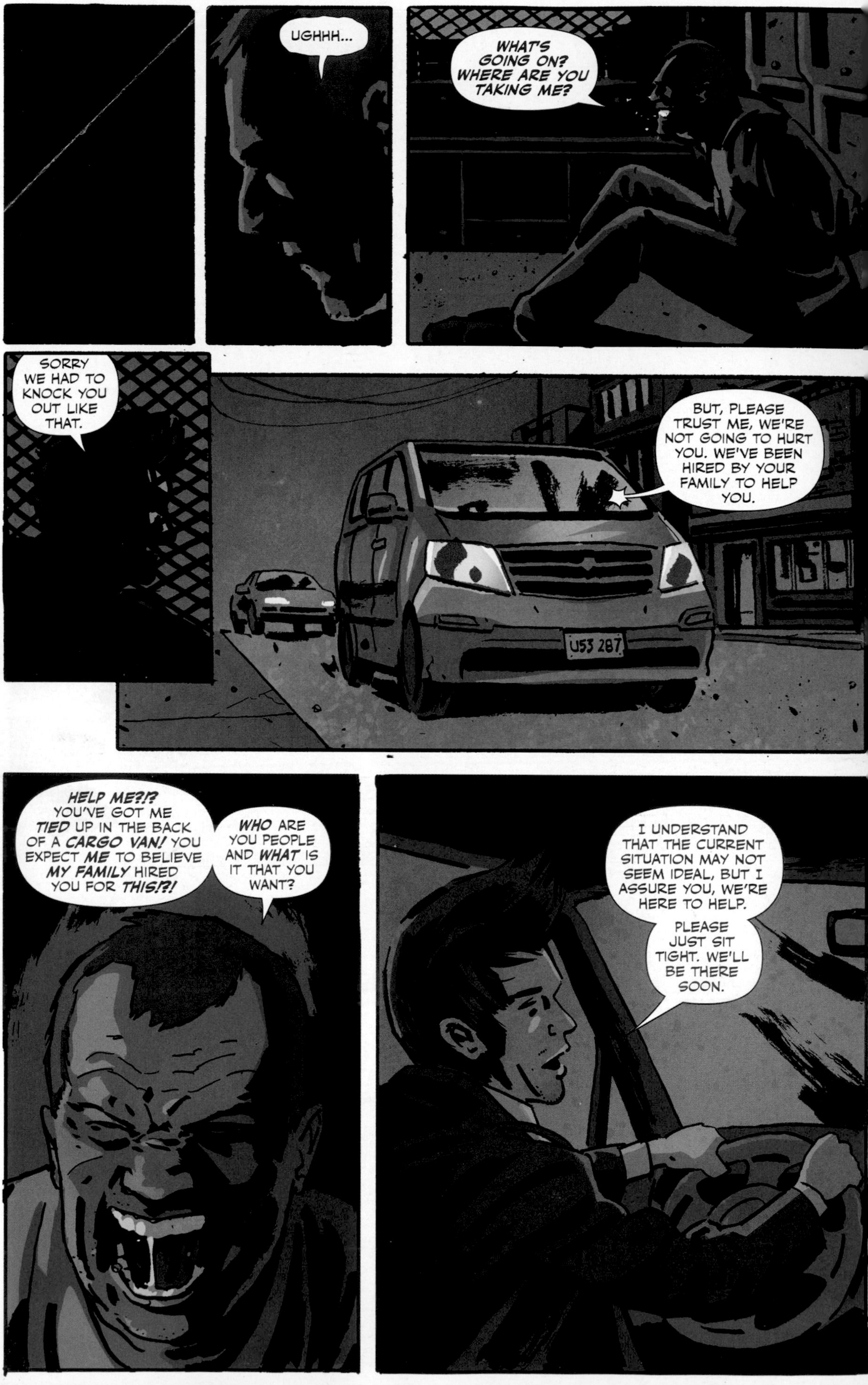
UGHHH...
WHAT'S GOING ON? WHERE ARE YOU TAKING ME?
SORRY WE HAD TO KNOCK YOU OUT LIKE THAT.
BUT, PLEASE TRUST ME, WE'RE NOT GOING TO HURT YOU. WE'VE BEEN HIRED BY YOUR FAMILY TO HELP YOU.
U53 287
HELP ME?!? YOU'VE GOT ME TIED UP IN THE BACK OF A CARGO VAN! YOU EXPECT ME TO BELIEVE MY FAMILY HIRED YOU FOR THIS!?!
WHO ARE YOU PEOPLE AND WHAT IS IT THAT YOU WANT?
I UNDERSTAND THAT THE CURRENT SITUATION MAY NOT SEEM IDEAL, BUT I ASSURE YOU, WE'RE HERE TO HELP.
PLEASE JUST SIT TIGHT. WE'LL BE THERE SOON.

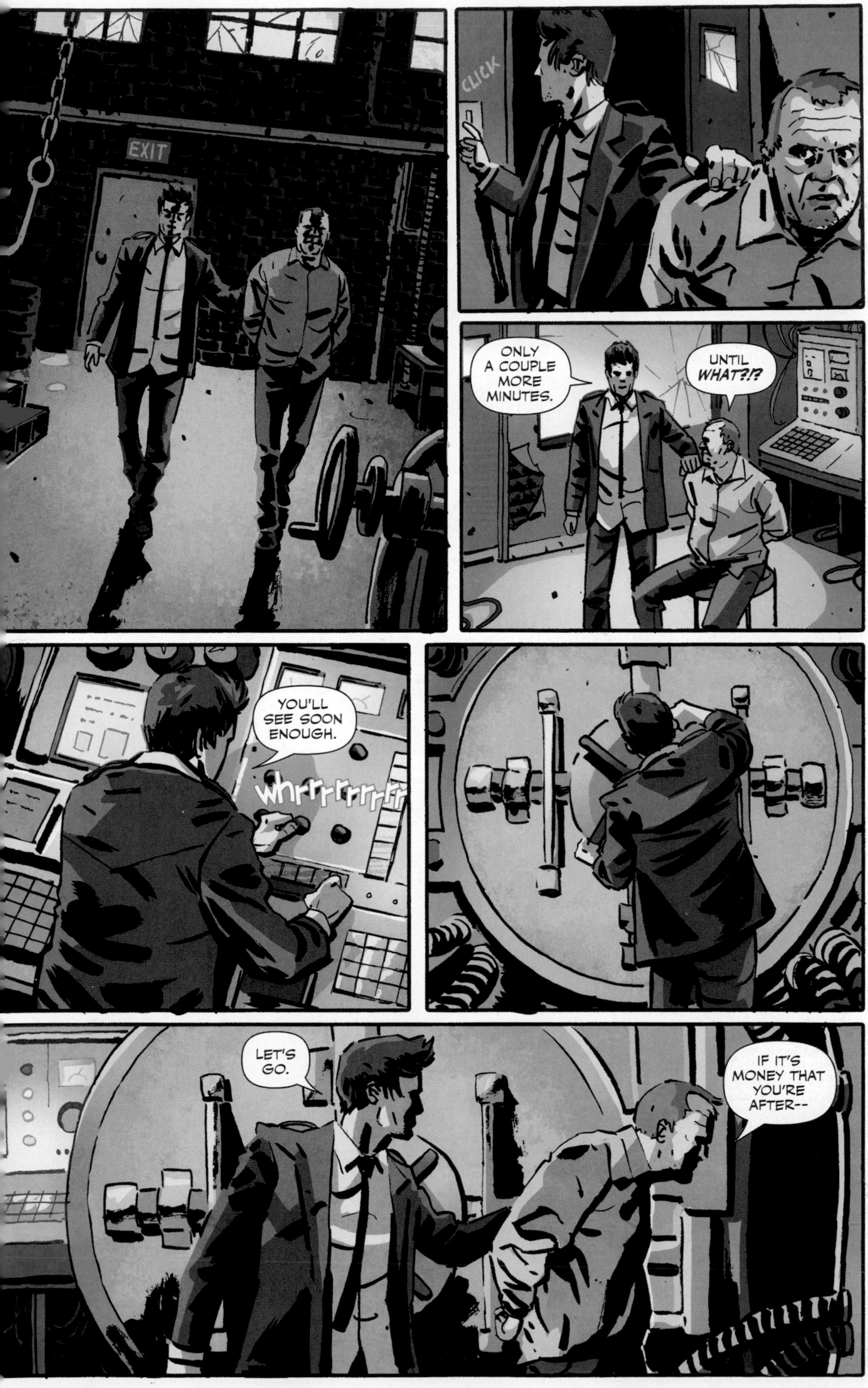
EXIT
CLICK
ONLY A COUPLE MORE MINUTES.
UNTIL *WHAT?!?*
YOU'LL SEE SOON ENOUGH.
whrrrrrrrrr
LET'S GO.
IF IT'S MONEY THAT YOU'RE AFTER--

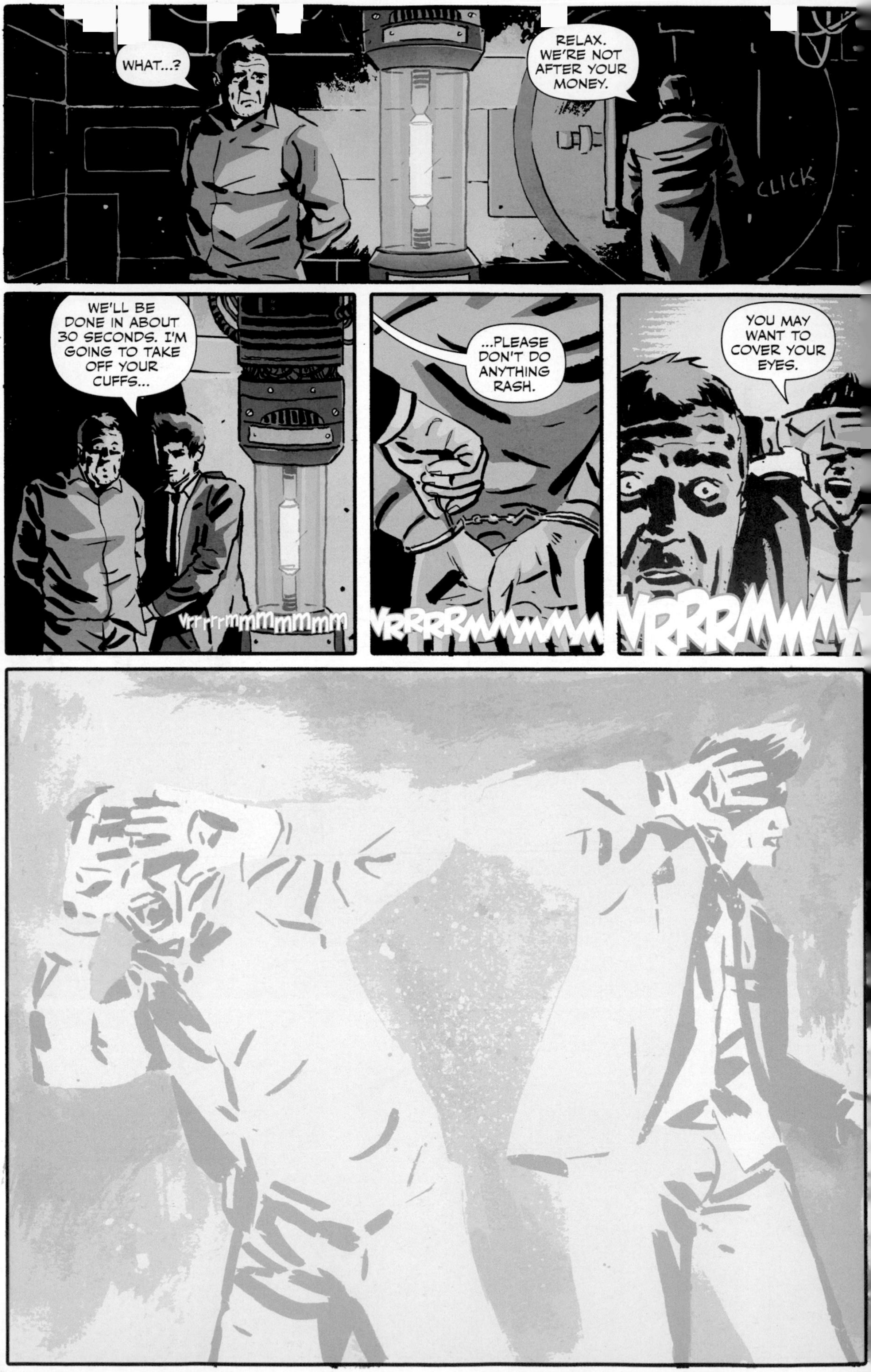
WHAT...?
RELAX. WE'RE NOT AFTER YOUR MONEY.
CLICK
WE'LL BE DONE IN ABOUT 30 SECONDS. I'M GOING TO TAKE OFF YOUR CUFFS...
VRRRRRMMMMMMMMM
...PLEASE DON'T DO ANYTHING RASH.
VRRRRMMMMMMMM
YOU MAY WANT TO COVER YOUR EYES.
VRRRMMMM

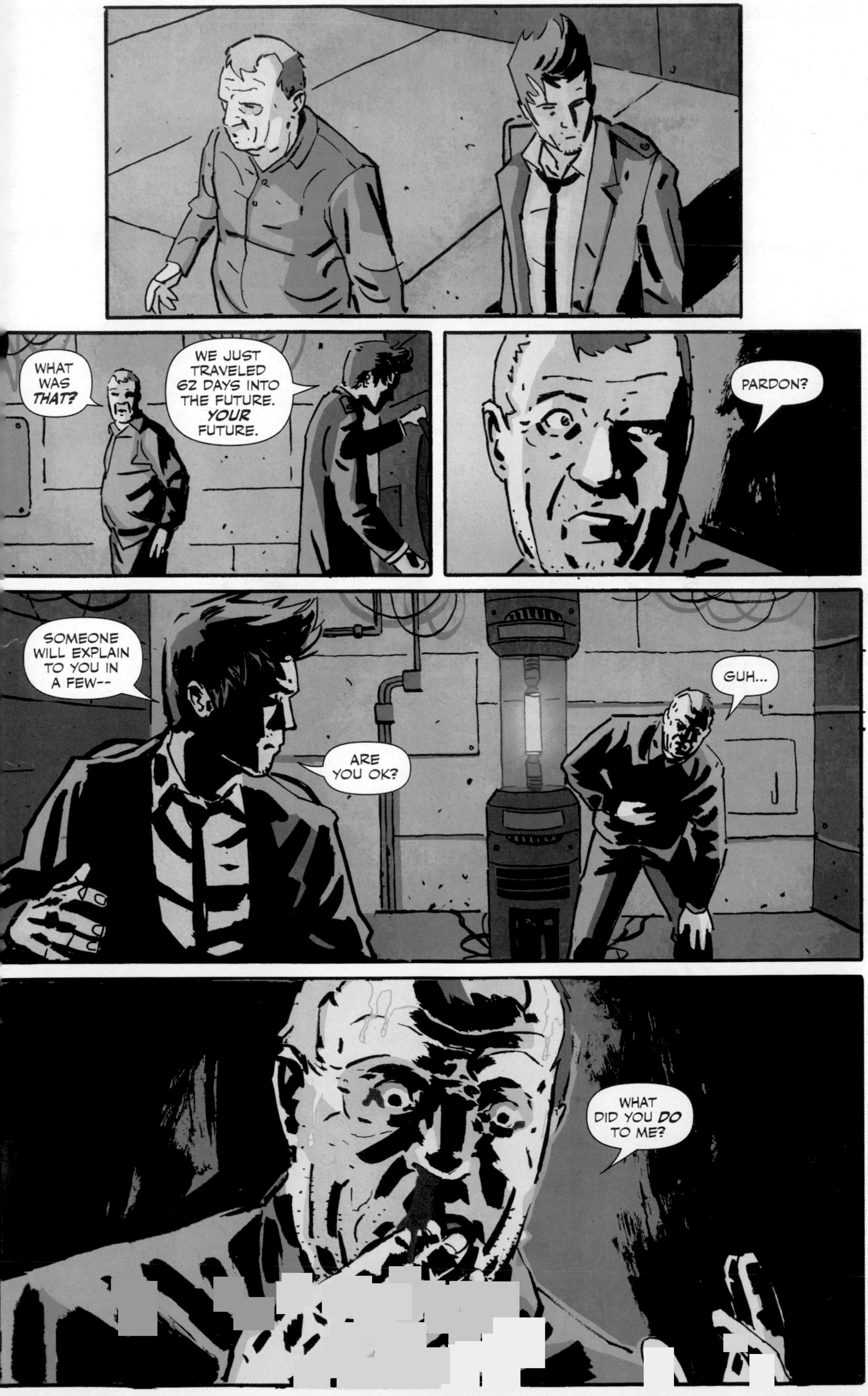
WHAT WAS THAT?
WE JUST TRAVELED 62 DAYS INTO THE FUTURE. YOUR FUTURE.
PARDON?
SOMEONE WILL EXPLAIN TO YOU IN A FEW--
ARE YOU OK?
GUH...
WHAT DID YOU DO TO ME?

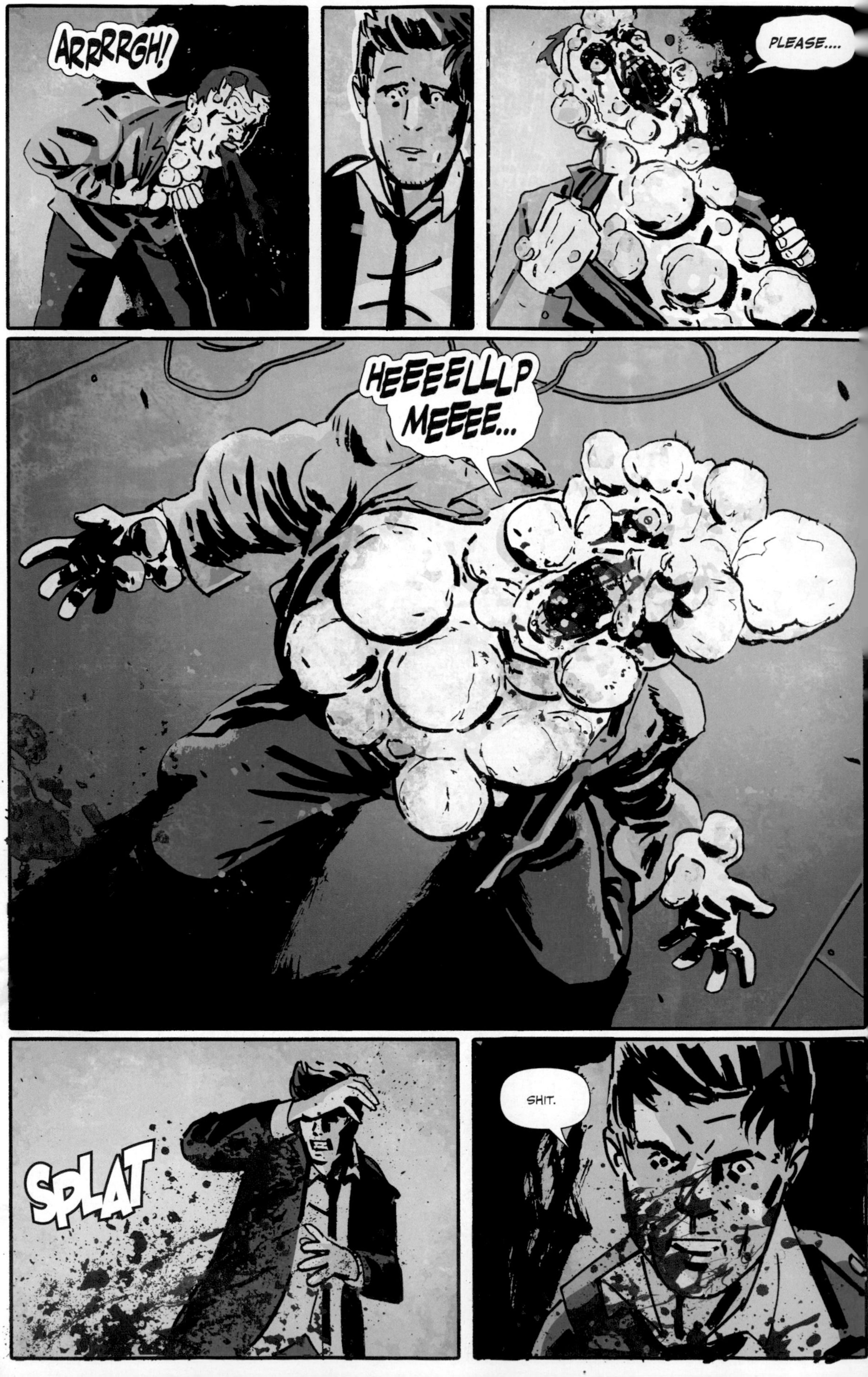
ARRRRGH!
PLEASE....
HEEEELLLP MEEEE...
SPLAT
SHIT.

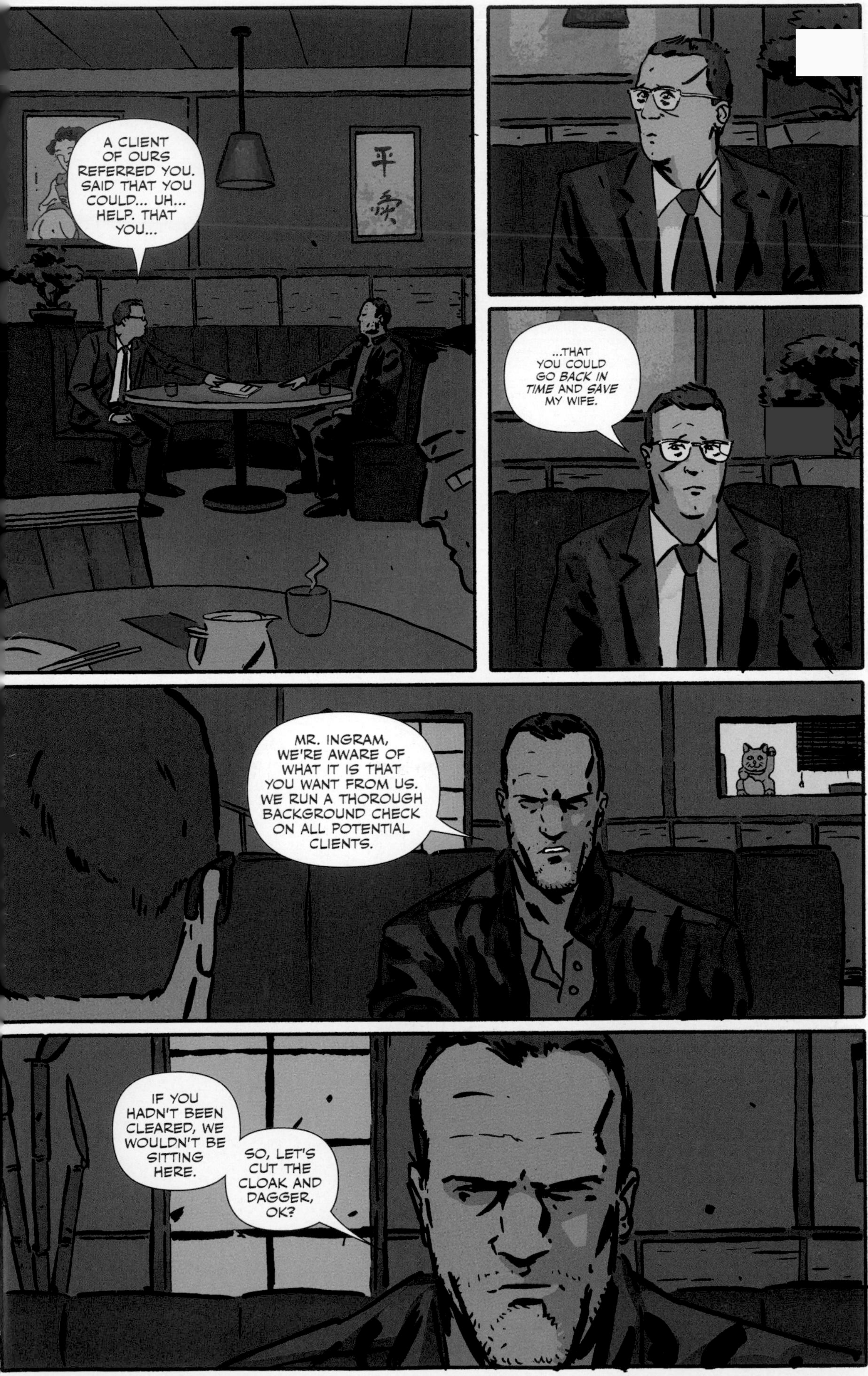
A CLIENT OF OURS REFERRED YOU. SAID THAT YOU COULD... UH... HELP. THAT YOU...
...THAT YOU COULD GO *BACK IN TIME* AND *SAVE* MY WIFE.
MR. INGRAM, WE'RE AWARE OF WHAT IT IS THAT YOU WANT FROM US. WE RUN A THOROUGH BACKGROUND CHECK ON ALL POTENTIAL CLIENTS.
IF YOU HADN'T BEEN CLEARED, WE WOULDN'T BE SITTING HERE.
SO, LET'S CUT THE CLOAK AND DAGGER, OK?

UNDERSTAND THAT THIS IS NOT A SIMPLE SNATCH AND GRAB OPERATION.

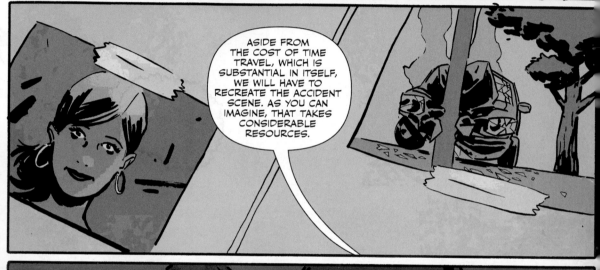

ASIDE FROM THE COST OF TIME TRAVEL, WHICH IS SUBSTANTIAL IN ITSELF, WE WILL HAVE TO RECREATE THE ACCIDENT SCENE. AS YOU CAN IMAGINE, THAT TAKES CONSIDERABLE RESOURCES.

WHATEVER THE COST! I HAVE THE MONEY--

WE KNOW THAT YOU DO, MR. INGRAM.

THERE'S LITTLE ABOUT YOU THAT WE DON'T KNOW.

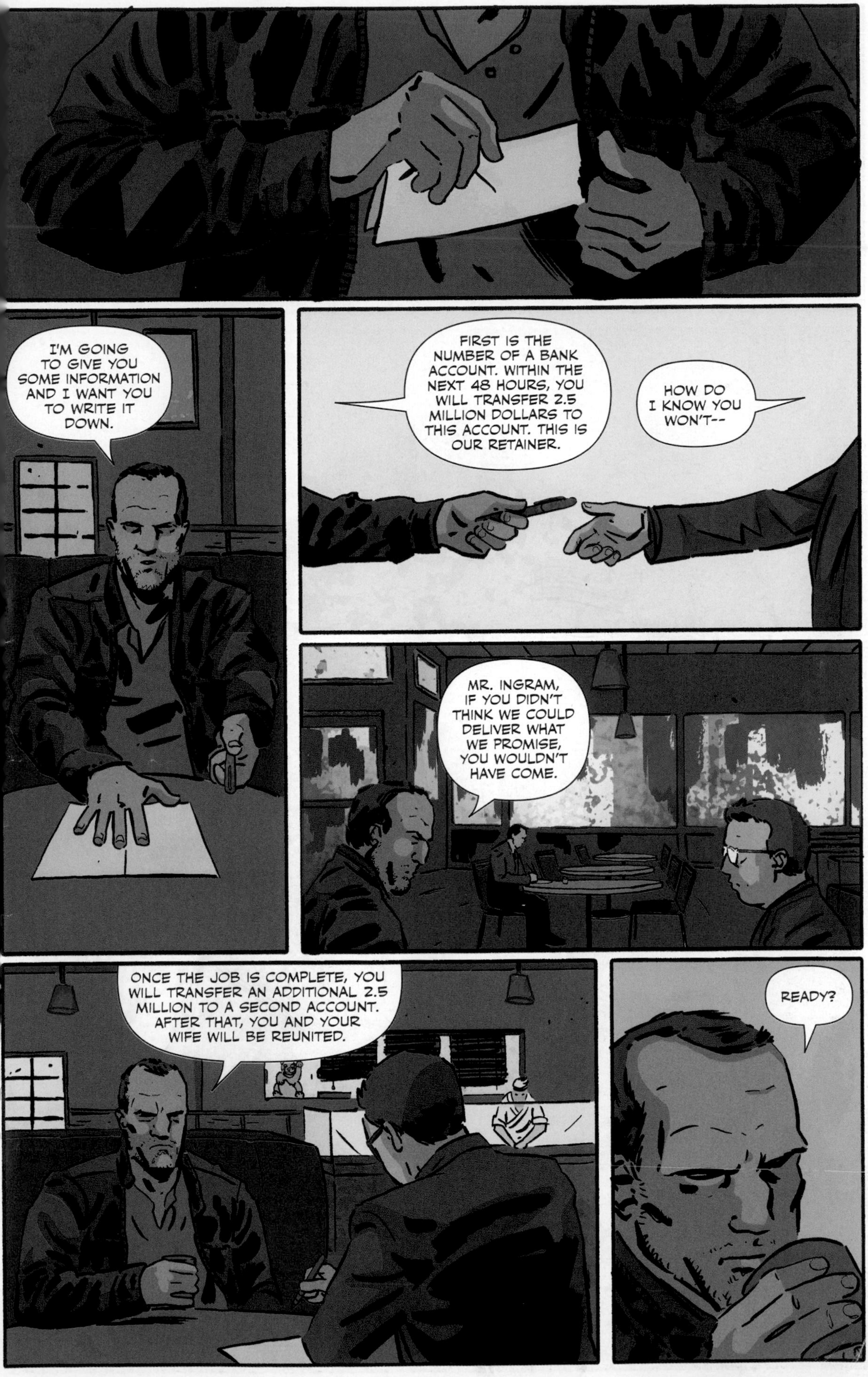
I'M GOING TO GIVE YOU SOME INFORMATION AND I WANT YOU TO WRITE IT DOWN.
FIRST IS THE NUMBER OF A BANK ACCOUNT. WITHIN THE NEXT 48 HOURS, YOU WILL TRANSFER 2.5 MILLION DOLLARS TO THIS ACCOUNT. THIS IS OUR RETAINER.
HOW DO I KNOW YOU WON'T--
MR. INGRAM, IF YOU DIDN'T THINK WE COULD DELIVER WHAT WE PROMISE, YOU WOULDN'T HAVE COME.
ONCE THE JOB IS COMPLETE, YOU WILL TRANSFER AN ADDITIONAL 2.5 MILLION TO A SECOND ACCOUNT. AFTER THAT, YOU AND YOUR WIFE WILL BE REUNITED.
READY?

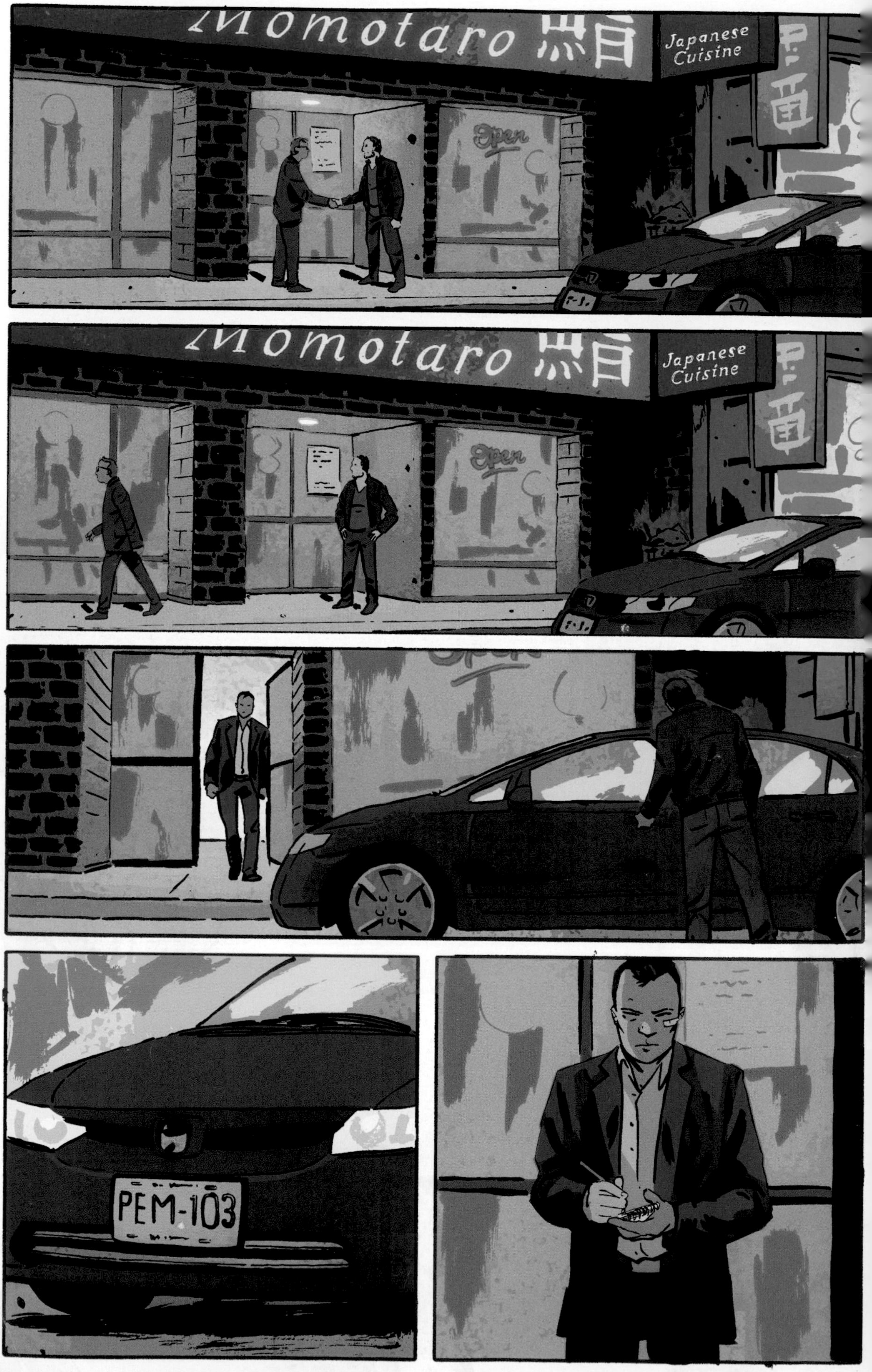
Momotaro
Japanese Cuisine
Open
Momotaro
Japanese Cuisine
Open
PEM-103

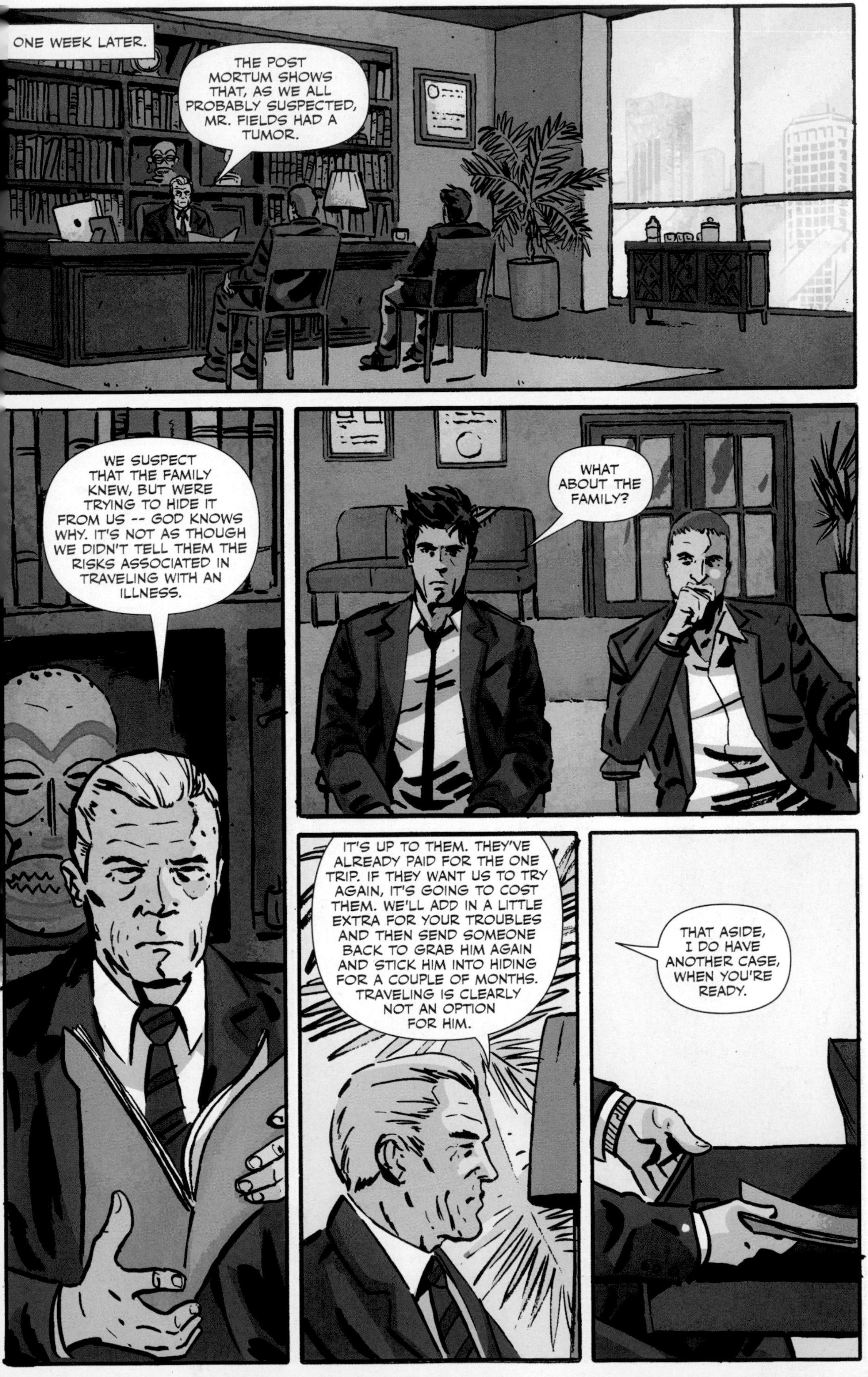
ONE WEEK LATER.
THE POST MORTUM SHOWS THAT, AS WE ALL PROBABLY SUSPECTED, MR. FIELDS HAD A TUMOR.
WE SUSPECT THAT THE FAMILY KNEW, BUT WERE TRYING TO HIDE IT FROM US -- GOD KNOWS WHY. IT'S NOT AS THOUGH WE DIDN'T TELL THEM THE RISKS ASSOCIATED IN TRAVELING WITH AN ILLNESS.
WHAT ABOUT THE FAMILY?
IT'S UP TO THEM. THEY'VE ALREADY PAID FOR THE ONE TRIP. IF THEY WANT US TO TRY AGAIN, IT'S GOING TO COST THEM. WE'LL ADD IN A LITTLE EXTRA FOR YOUR TROUBLES AND THEN SEND SOMEONE BACK TO GRAB HIM AGAIN AND STICK HIM INTO HIDING FOR A COUPLE OF MONTHS. TRAVELING IS CLEARLY NOT AN OPTION FOR HIM.
THAT ASIDE, I DO HAVE ANOTHER CASE, WHEN YOU'RE READY.

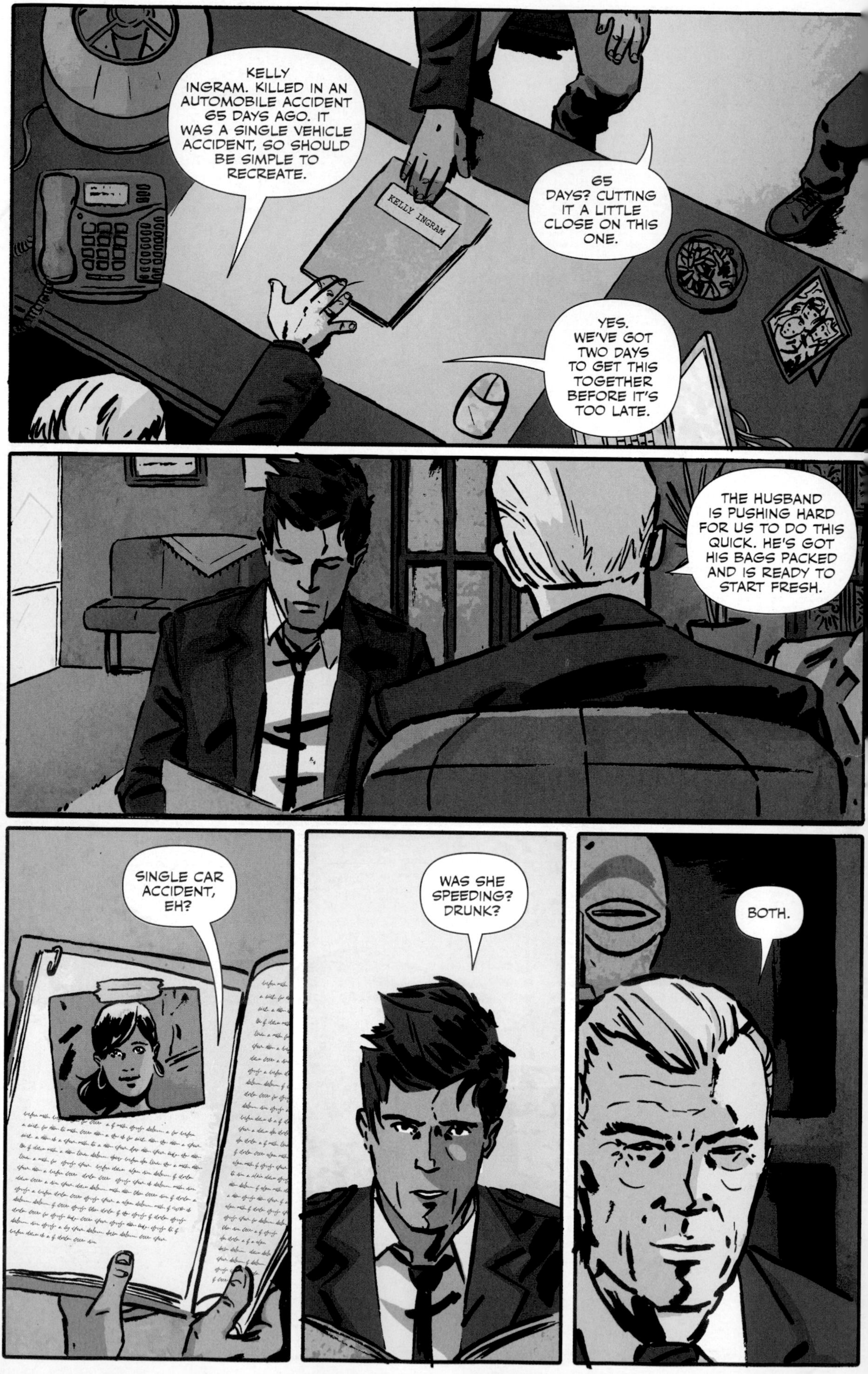
KELLY INGRAM
KELLY INGRAM. KILLED IN AN AUTOMOBILE ACCIDENT 65 DAYS AGO. IT WAS A SINGLE VEHICLE ACCIDENT, SO SHOULD BE SIMPLE TO RECREATE.
65 DAYS? CUTTING IT A LITTLE CLOSE ON THIS ONE.
YES. WE'VE GOT TWO DAYS TO GET THIS TOGETHER BEFORE IT'S TOO LATE.
THE HUSBAND IS PUSHING HARD FOR US TO DO THIS QUICK. HE'S GOT HIS BAGS PACKED AND IS READY TO START FRESH.
SINGLE CAR ACCIDENT, EH?
WAS SHE SPEEDING? DRUNK?
BOTH.

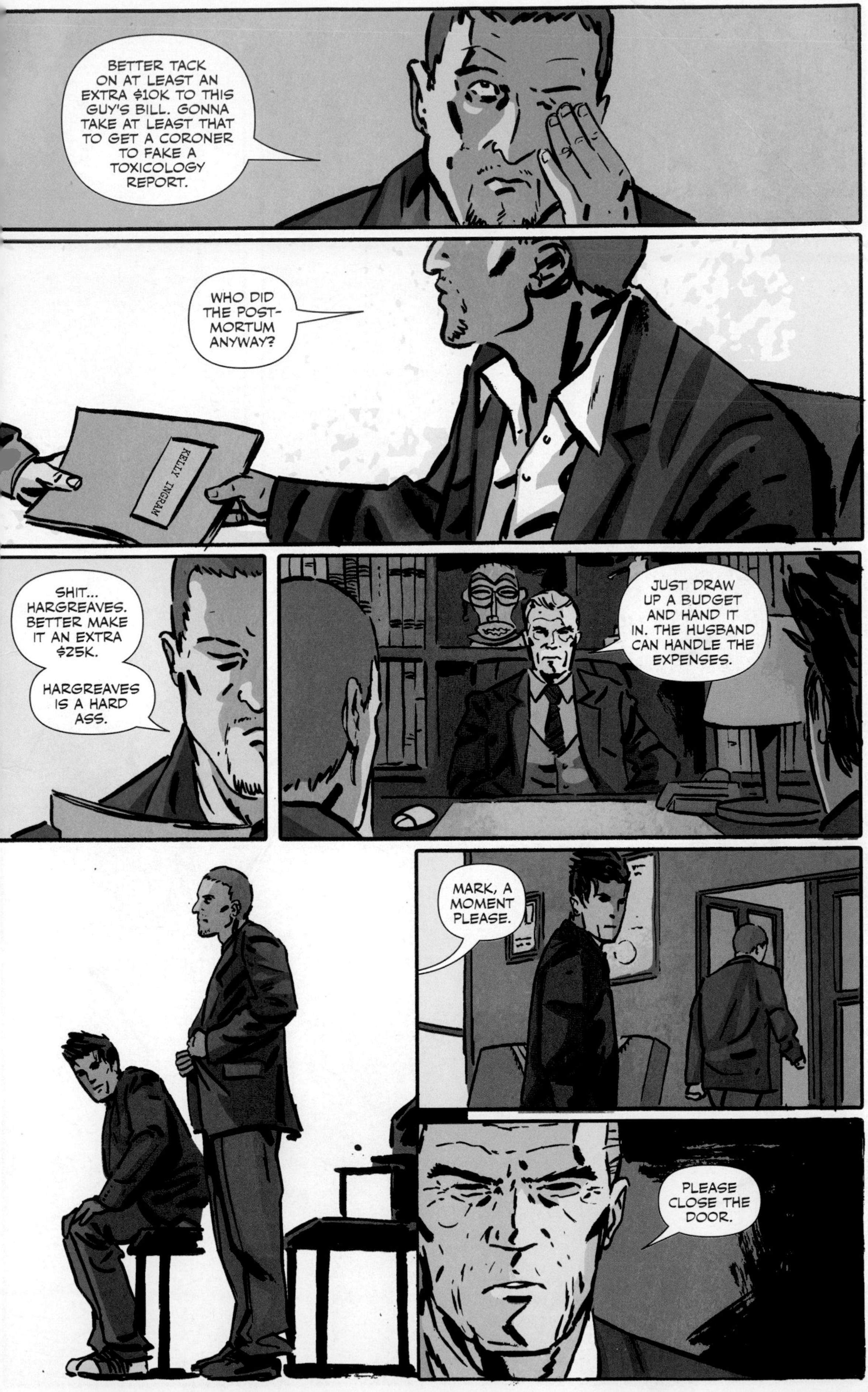
BETTER TACK ON AT LEAST AN EXTRA $10K TO THIS GUY'S BILL. GONNA TAKE AT LEAST THAT TO GET A CORONER TO FAKE A TOXICOLOGY REPORT.
WHO DID THE POST-MORTUM ANYWAY?
KELLY INGRAM
SHIT... HARGREAVES. BETTER MAKE IT AN EXTRA $25K.
HARGREAVES IS A HARD ASS.
JUST DRAW UP A BUDGET AND HAND IT IN. THE HUSBAND CAN HANDLE THE EXPENSES.
MARK, A MOMENT PLEASE.
PLEASE CLOSE THE DOOR.

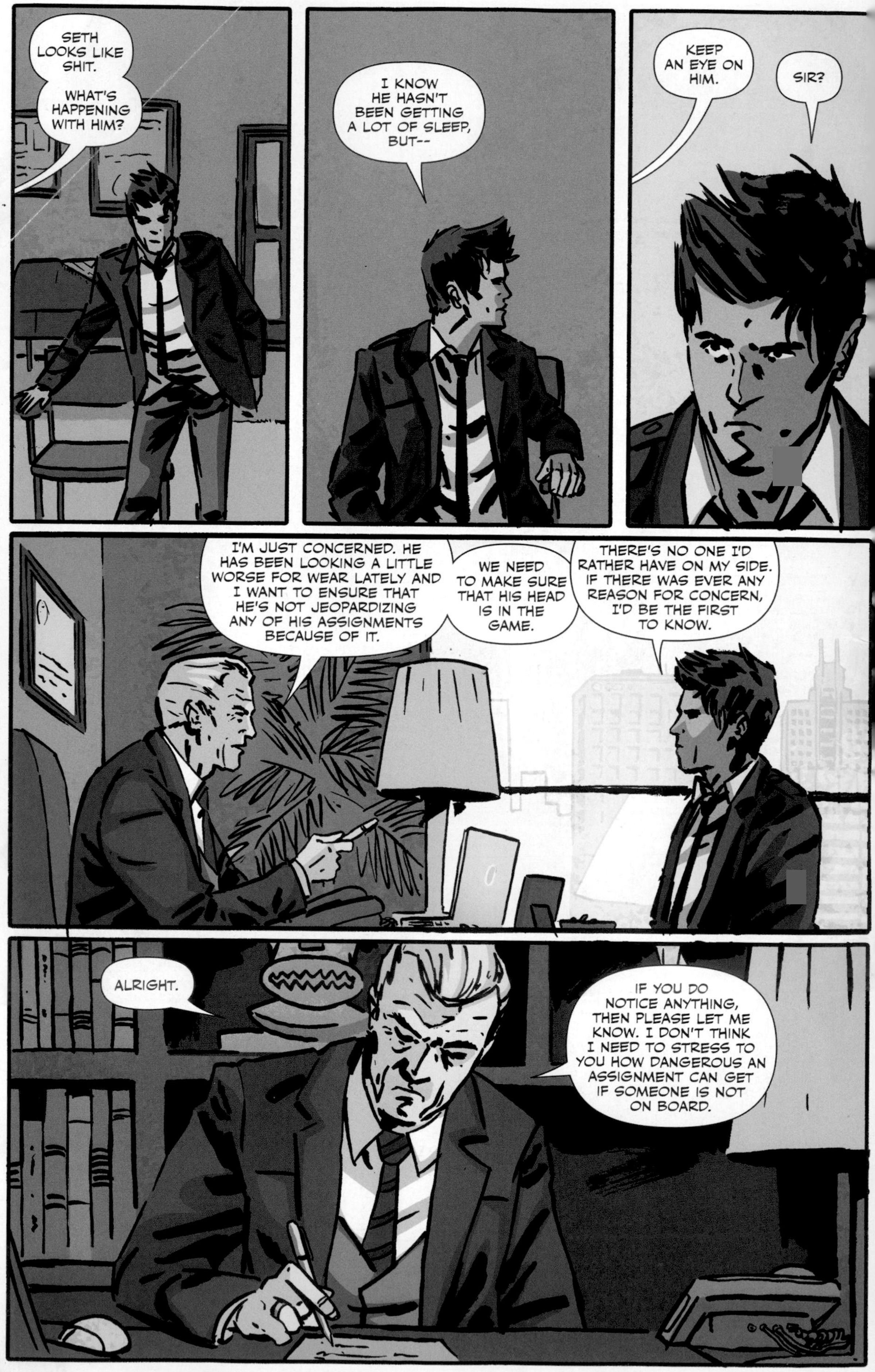
SETH LOOKS LIKE SHIT.
WHAT'S HAPPENING WITH HIM?
I KNOW HE HASN'T BEEN GETTING A LOT OF SLEEP, BUT--
KEEP AN EYE ON HIM.
SIR?
I'M JUST CONCERNED. HE HAS BEEN LOOKING A LITTLE WORSE FOR WEAR LATELY AND I WANT TO ENSURE THAT HE'S NOT JEOPARDIZING ANY OF HIS ASSIGNMENTS BECAUSE OF IT.
WE NEED TO MAKE SURE THAT HIS HEAD IS IN THE GAME.
THERE'S NO ONE I'D RATHER HAVE ON MY SIDE. IF THERE WAS EVER ANY REASON FOR CONCERN, I'D BE THE FIRST TO KNOW.
ALRIGHT.
IF YOU DO NOTICE ANYTHING, THEN PLEASE LET ME KNOW. I DON'T THINK I NEED TO STRESS TO YOU HOW DANGEROUS AN ASSIGNMENT CAN GET IF SOMEONE IS NOT ON BOARD.

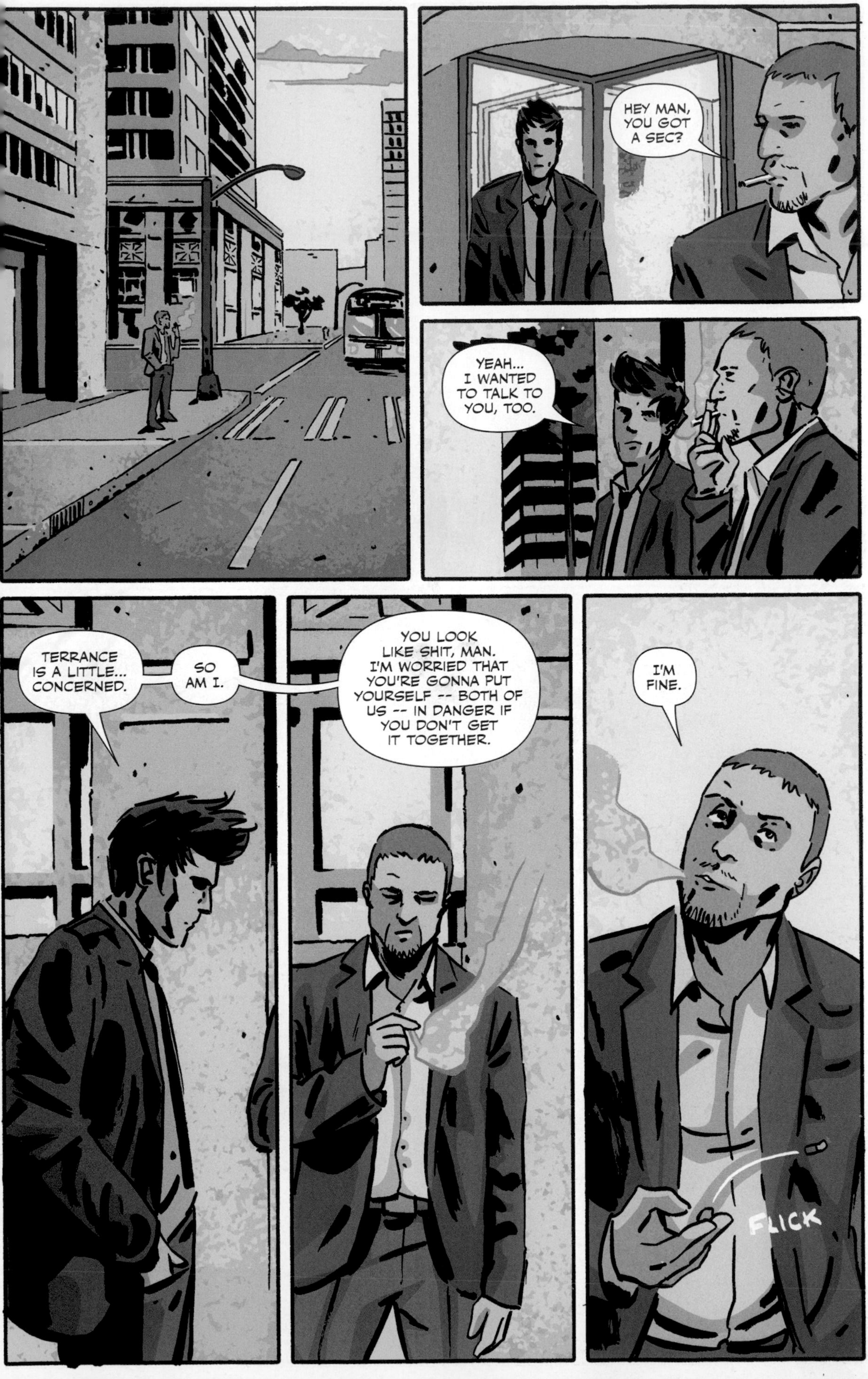
HEY MAN, YOU GOT A SEC?
YEAH... I WANTED TO TALK TO YOU, TOO.
TERRANCE IS A LITTLE... CONCERNED.
SO AM I.
YOU LOOK LIKE SHIT, MAN. I'M WORRIED THAT YOU'RE GONNA PUT YOURSELF -- BOTH OF US -- IN DANGER IF YOU DON'T GET IT TOGETHER.
I'M FINE.
FLICK

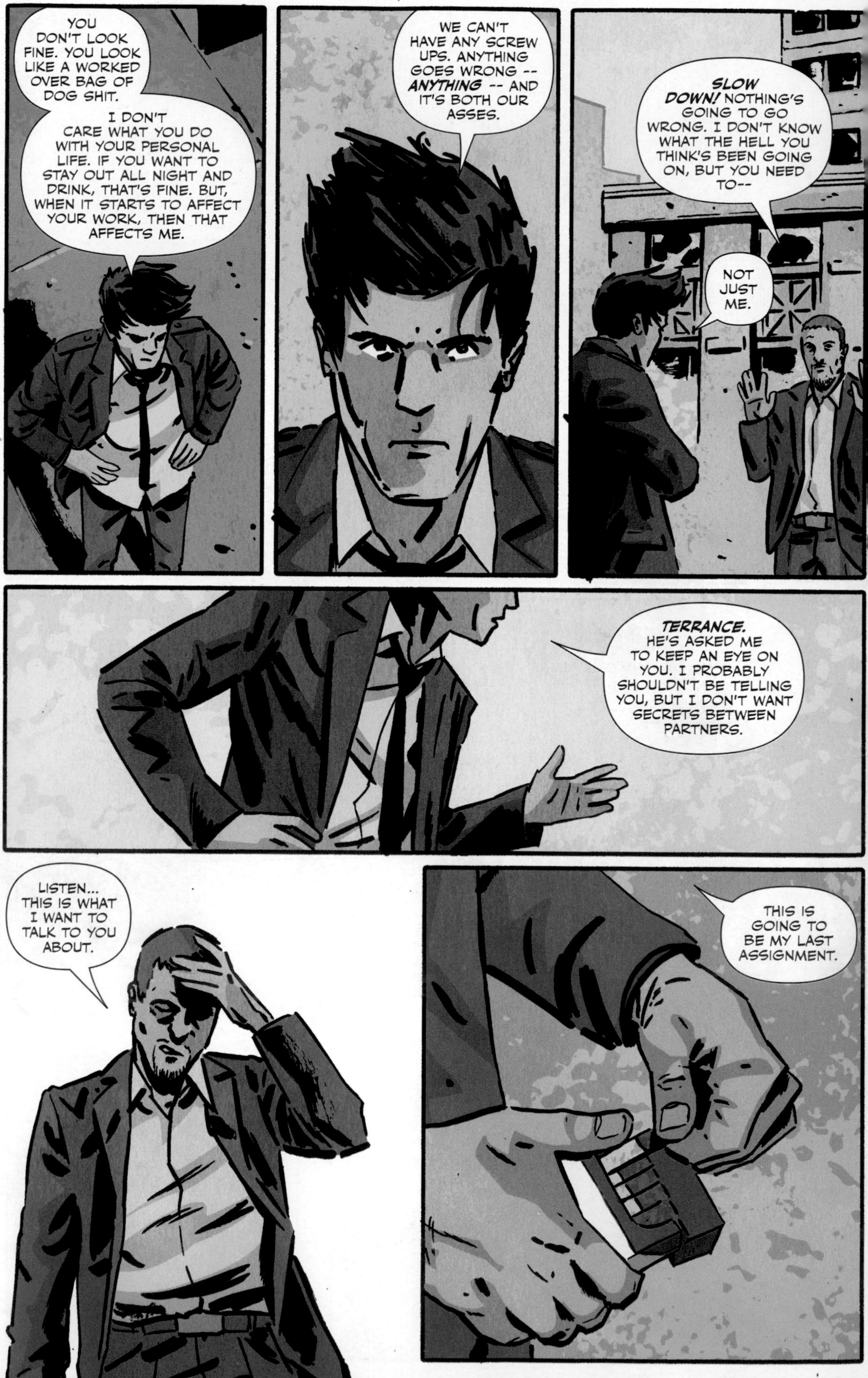
YOU DON'T LOOK FINE. YOU LOOK LIKE A WORKED OVER BAG OF DOG SHIT.
I DON'T CARE WHAT YOU DO WITH YOUR PERSONAL LIFE. IF YOU WANT TO STAY OUT ALL NIGHT AND DRINK, THAT'S FINE. BUT, WHEN IT STARTS TO AFFECT YOUR WORK, THEN THAT AFFECTS ME.
WE CAN'T HAVE ANY SCREW UPS. ANYTHING GOES WRONG -- *ANYTHING* -- AND IT'S BOTH OUR ASSES.
SLOW DOWN! NOTHING'S GOING TO GO WRONG. I DON'T KNOW WHAT THE HELL YOU THINK'S BEEN GOING ON, BUT YOU NEED TO--
NOT JUST ME.
TERRANCE. HE'S ASKED ME TO KEEP AN EYE ON YOU. I PROBABLY SHOULDN'T BE TELLING YOU, BUT I DON'T WANT SECRETS BETWEEN PARTNERS.
LISTEN... THIS IS WHAT I WANT TO TALK TO YOU ABOUT.
THIS IS GOING TO BE MY LAST ASSIGNMENT.

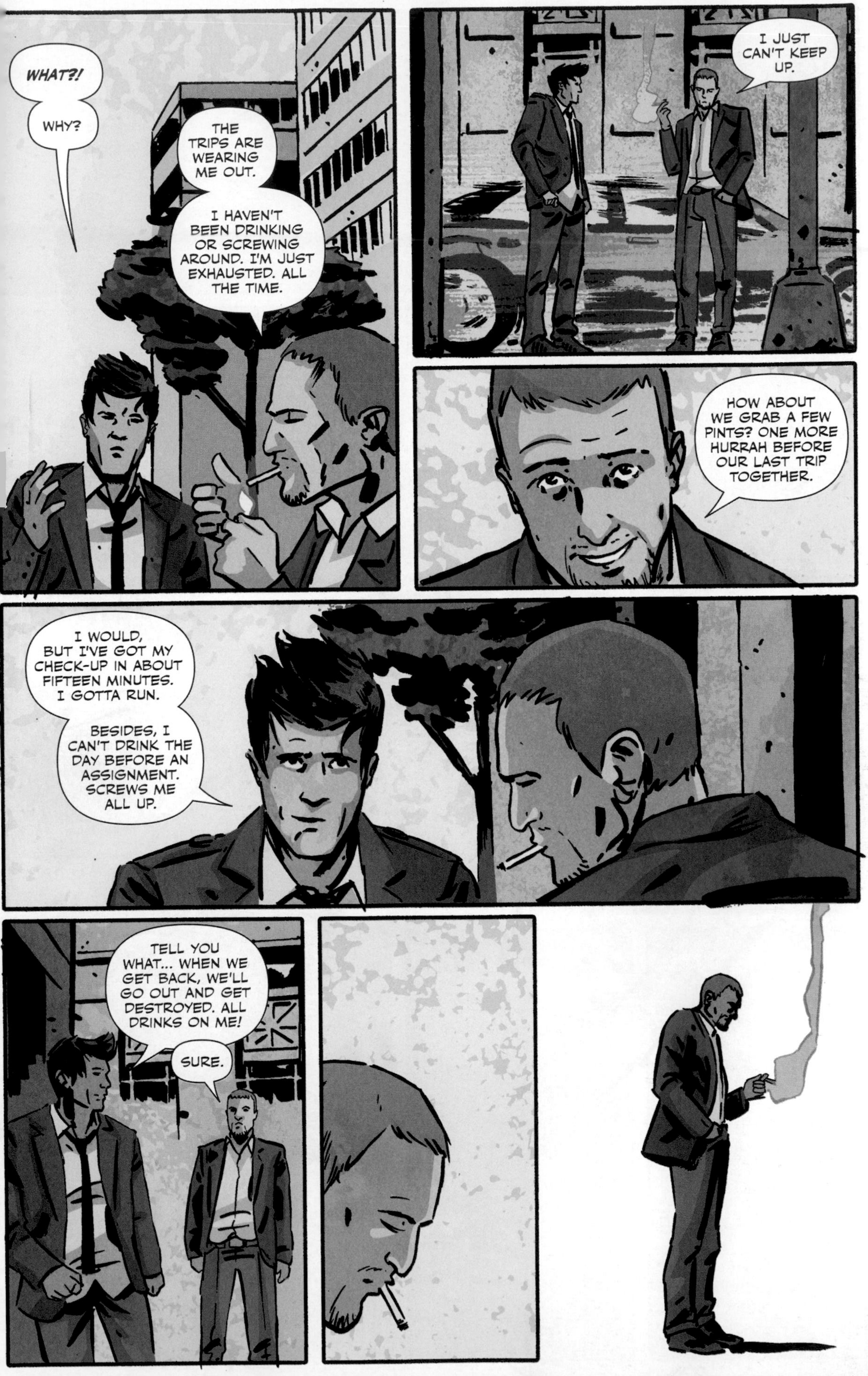
WHAT?!
WHY?
THE TRIPS ARE WEARING ME OUT.
I HAVEN'T BEEN DRINKING OR SCREWING AROUND. I'M JUST EXHAUSTED. ALL THE TIME.
I JUST CAN'T KEEP UP.
HOW ABOUT WE GRAB A FEW PINTS? ONE MORE HURRAH BEFORE OUR LAST TRIP TOGETHER.
I WOULD, BUT I'VE GOT MY CHECK-UP IN ABOUT FIFTEEN MINUTES. I GOTTA RUN.
BESIDES, I CAN'T DRINK THE DAY BEFORE AN ASSIGNMENT. SCREWS ME ALL UP.
TELL YOU WHAT... WHEN WE GET BACK, WE'LL GO OUT AND GET DESTROYED. ALL DRINKS ON ME!
SURE.

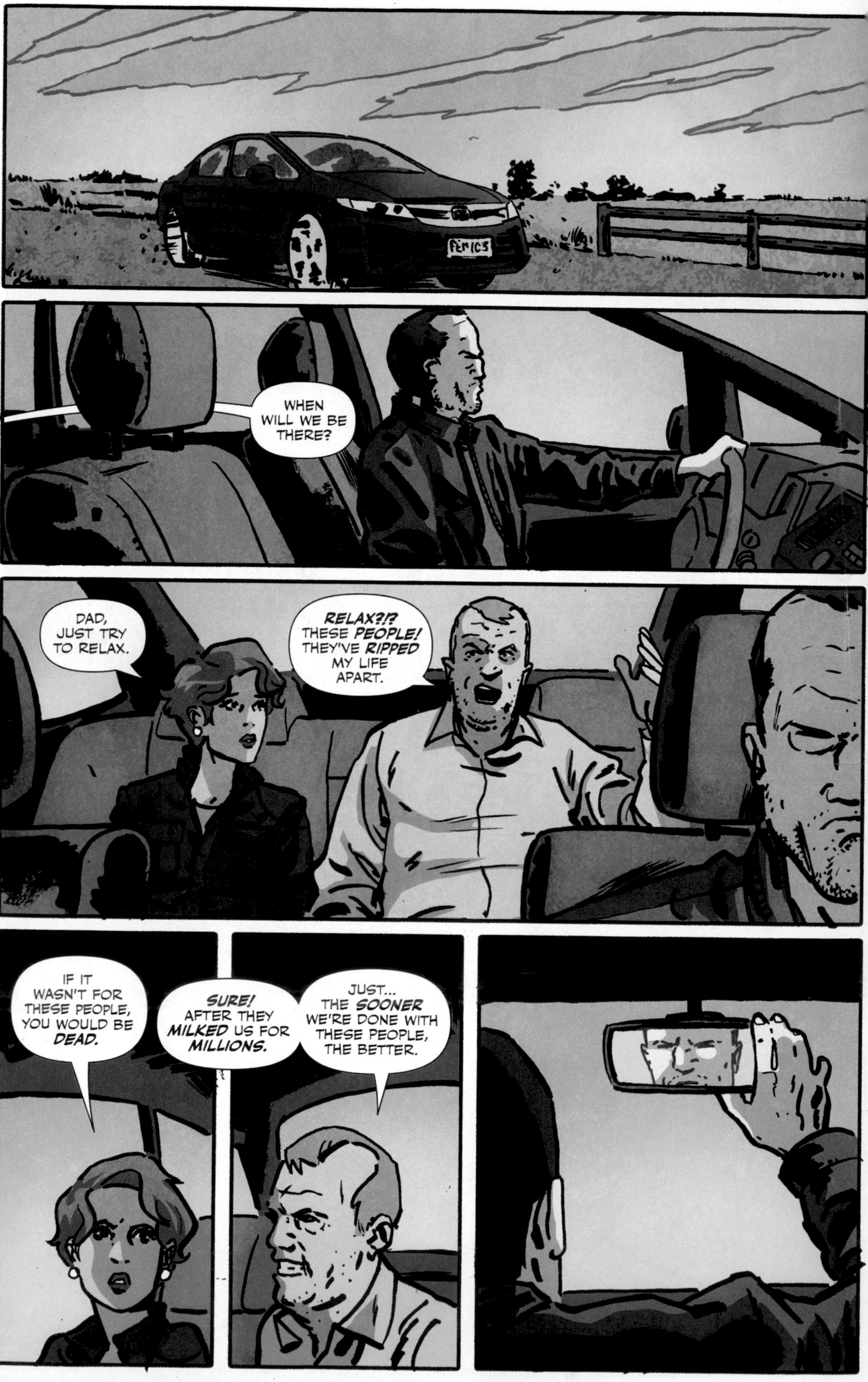
FENCES
WHEN WILL WE BE THERE?
DAD, JUST TRY TO RELAX.
RELAX?!? THESE PEOPLE! THEY'VE RIPPED MY LIFE APART.
IF IT WASN'T FOR THESE PEOPLE, YOU WOULD BE DEAD.
SURE! AFTER THEY MILKED US FOR MILLIONS.
JUST... THE SOONER WE'RE DONE WITH THESE PEOPLE, THE BETTER.

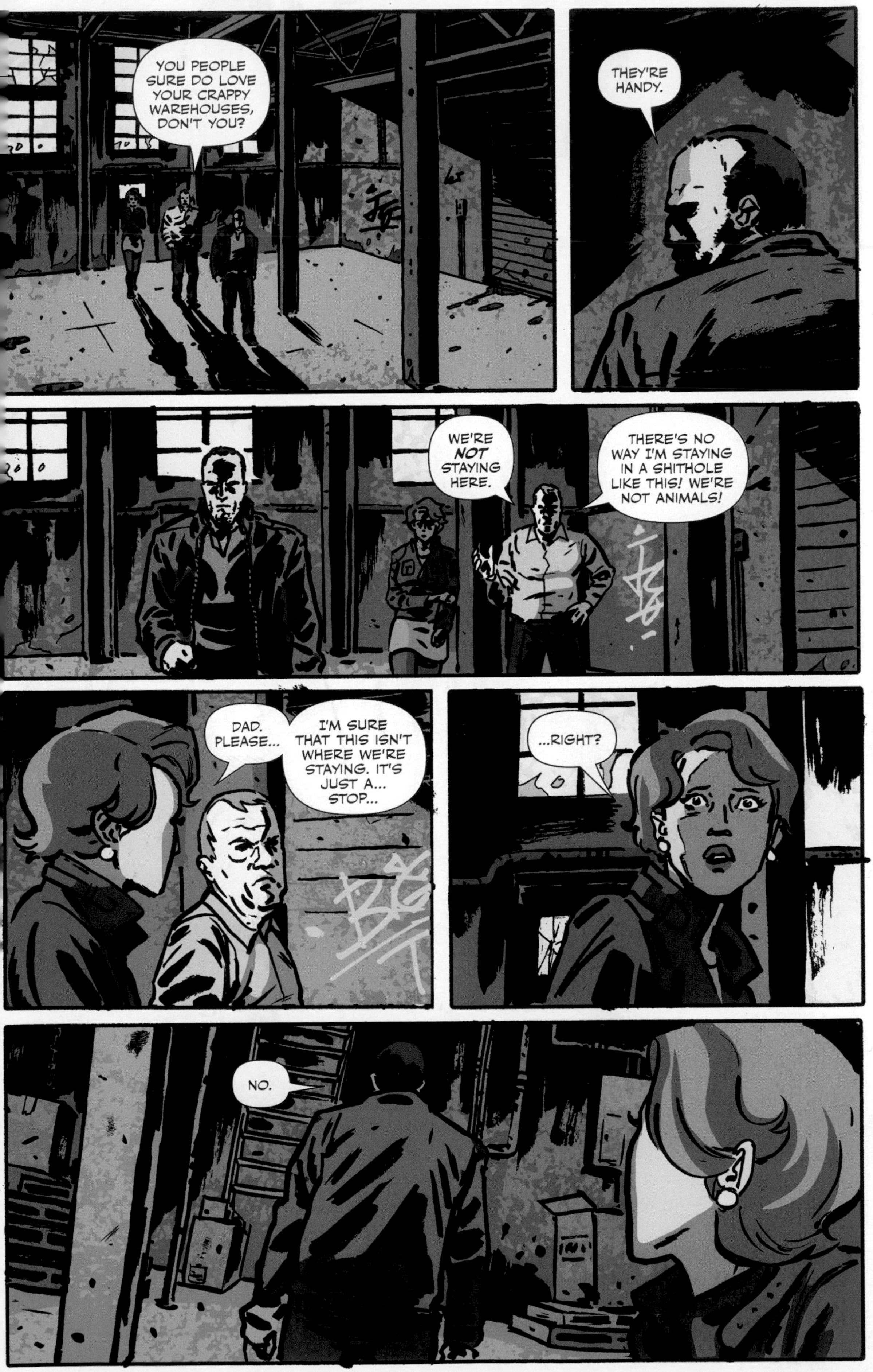
YOU PEOPLE SURE DO LOVE YOUR CRAPPY WAREHOUSES, DON'T YOU?
THEY'RE HANDY.
WE'RE NOT STAYING HERE.
THERE'S NO WAY I'M STAYING IN A SHITHOLE LIKE THIS! WE'RE NOT ANIMALS!
DAD. PLEASE...
I'M SURE THAT THIS ISN'T WHERE WE'RE STAYING. IT'S JUST A... STOP...
...RIGHT?
NO.

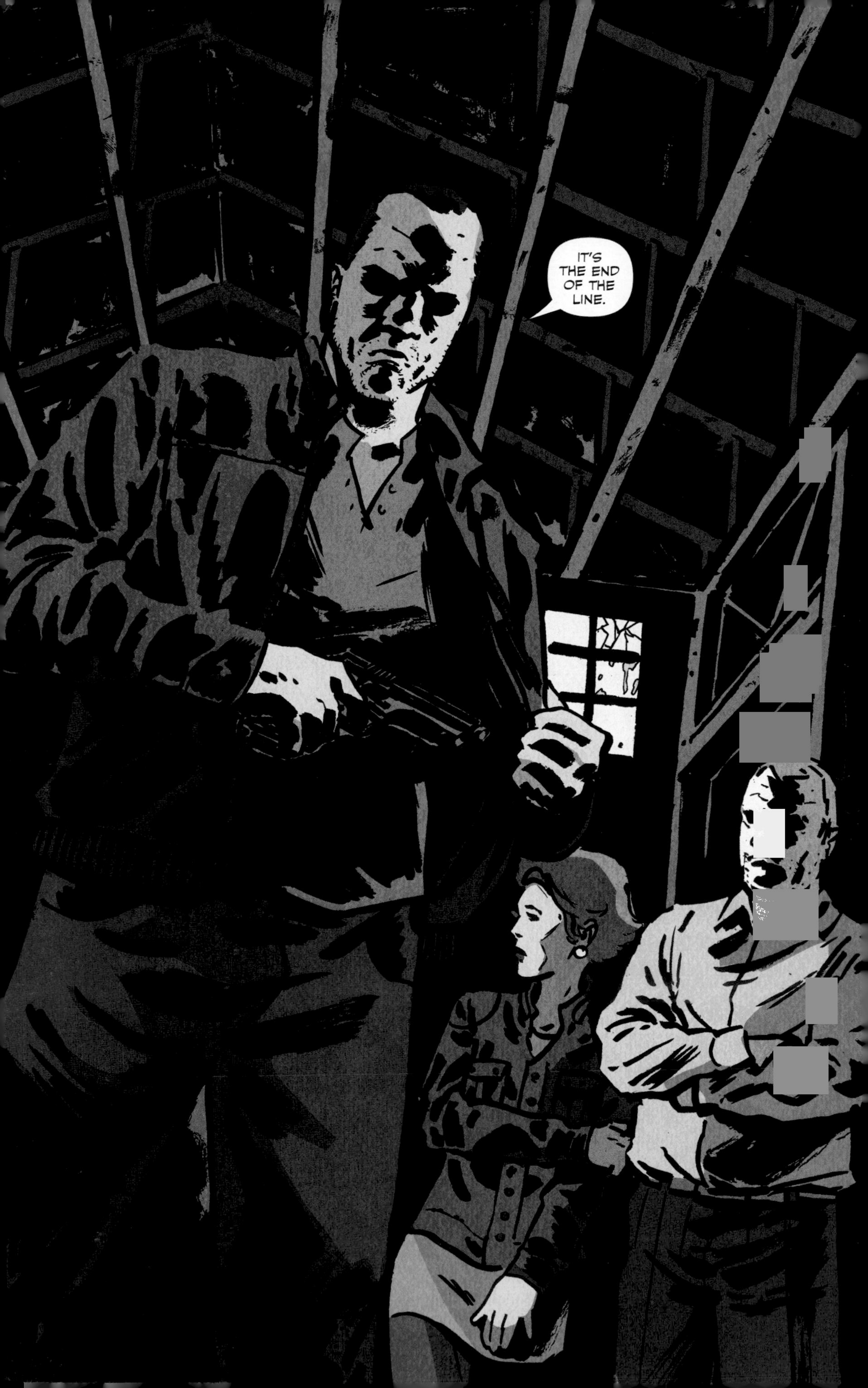
IT'S THE END OF THE LINE.

CHAPTER TWO

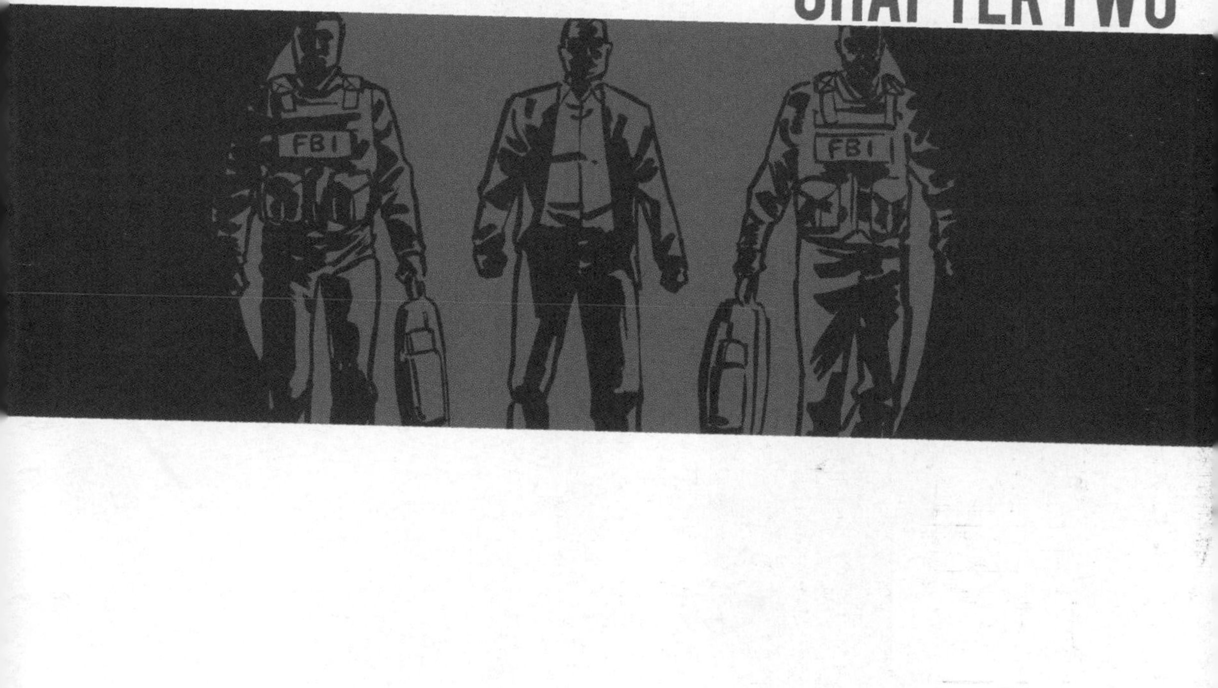
FBI
FBI

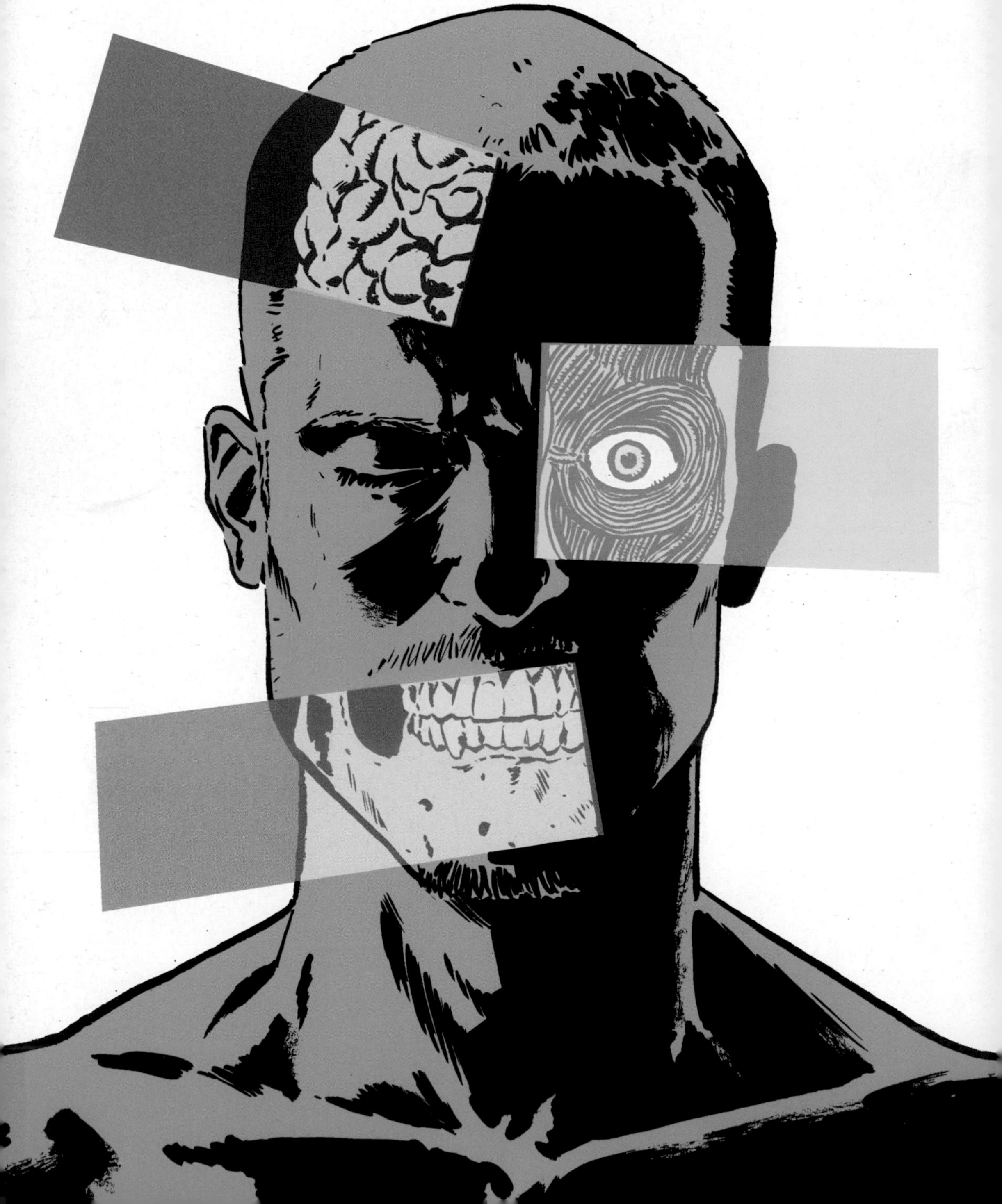

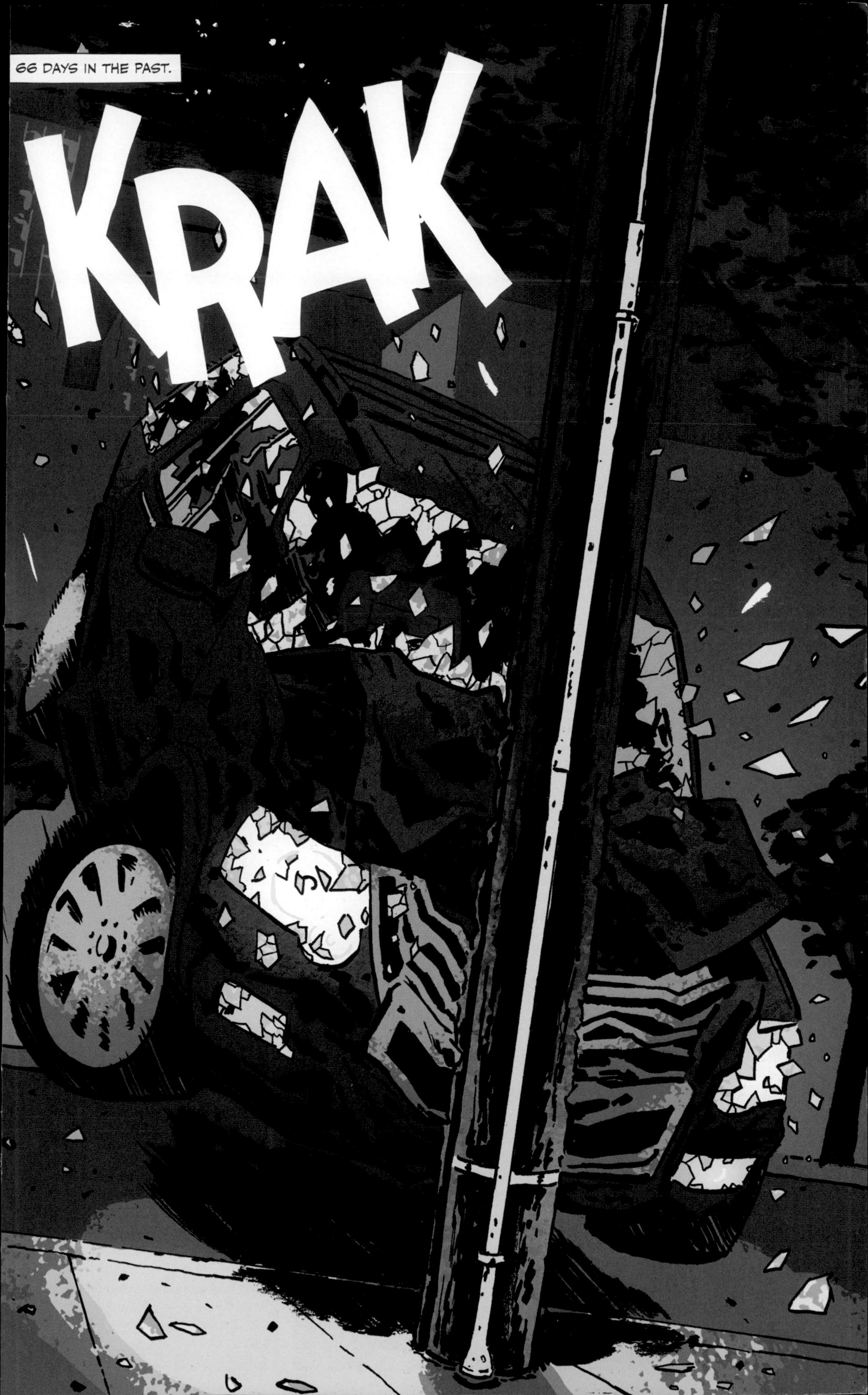
66 DAYS IN THE PAST.
KRAK

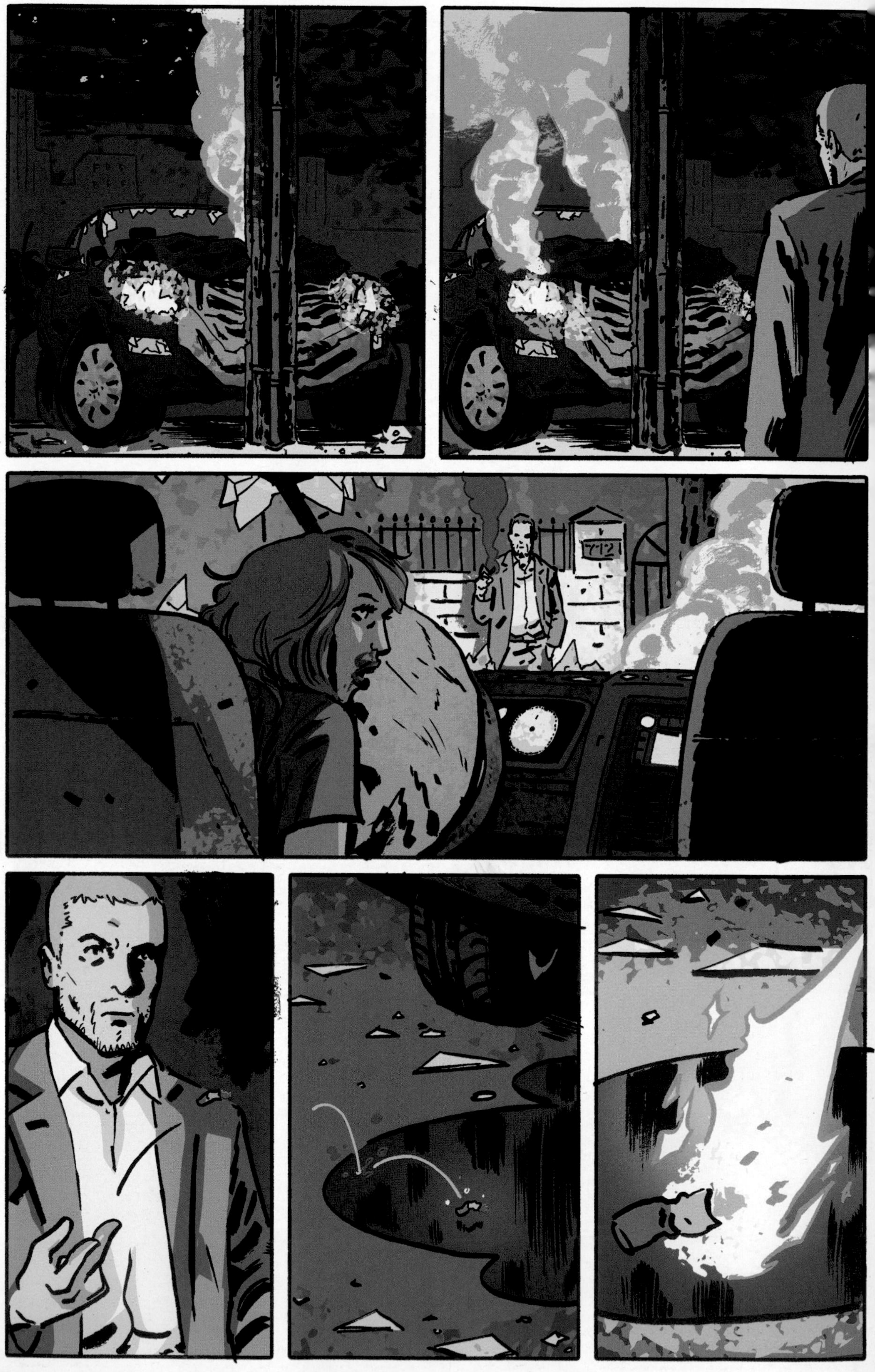

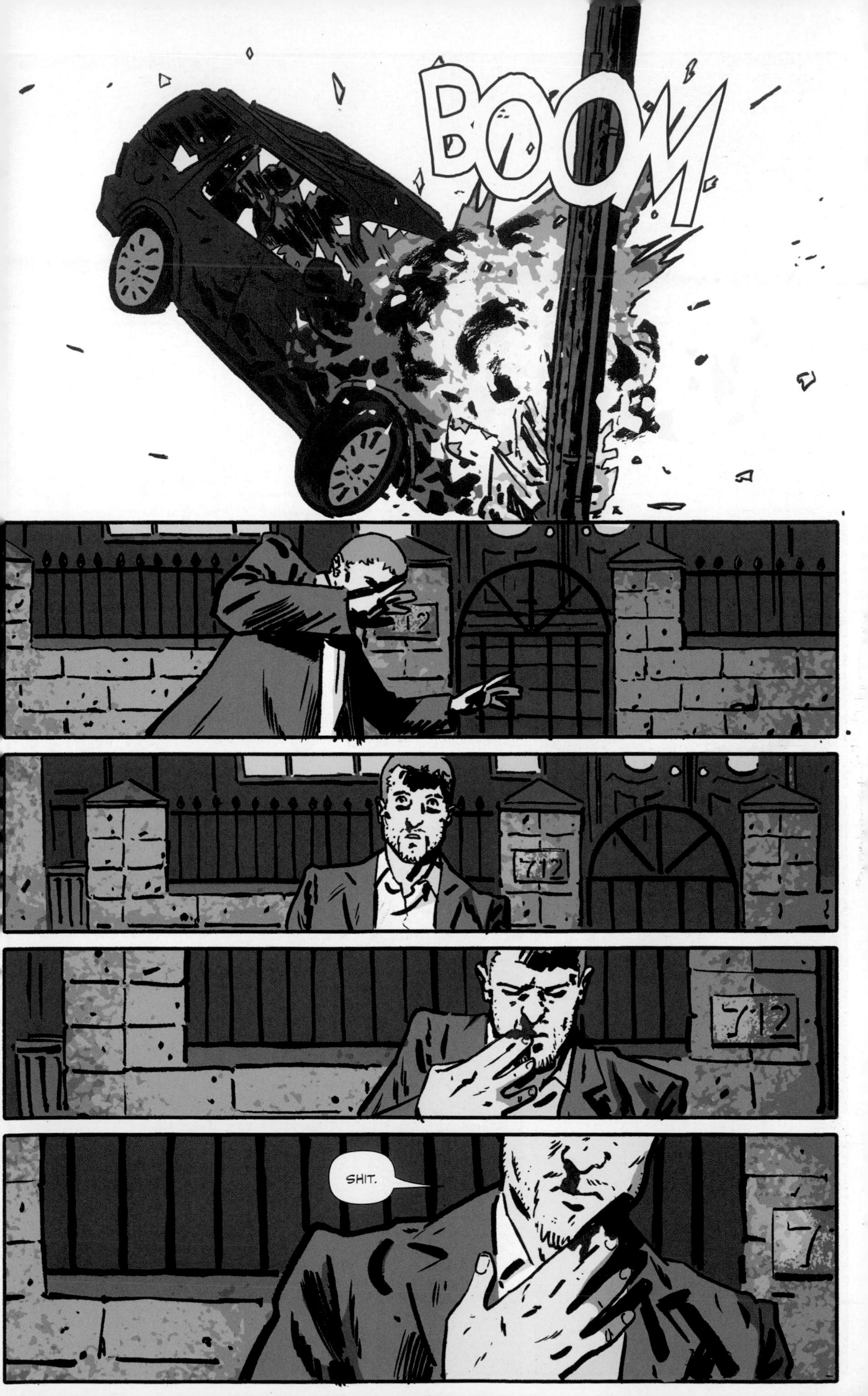
BOOM
712
712
712
SHIT.

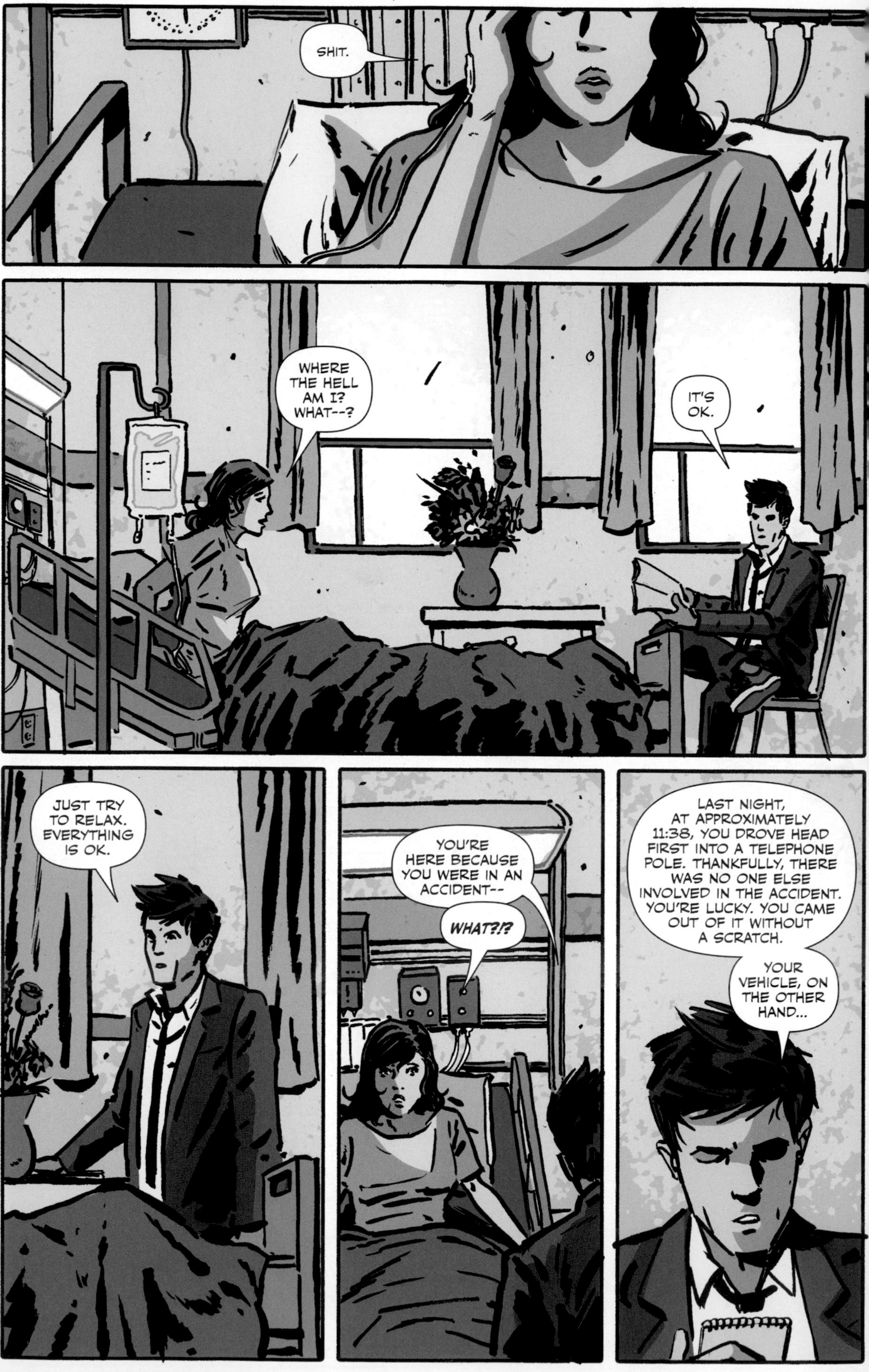
SHIT.
WHERE THE HELL AM I? WHAT--?
IT'S OK.
JUST TRY TO RELAX. EVERYTHING IS OK.
YOU'RE HERE BECAUSE YOU WERE IN AN ACCIDENT--
WHAT?!?
LAST NIGHT, AT APPROXIMATELY 11:38, YOU DROVE HEAD FIRST INTO A TELEPHONE POLE. THANKFULLY, THERE WAS NO ONE ELSE INVOLVED IN THE ACCIDENT. YOU'RE LUCKY. YOU CAME OUT OF IT WITHOUT A SCRATCH.
YOUR VEHICLE, ON THE OTHER HAND...

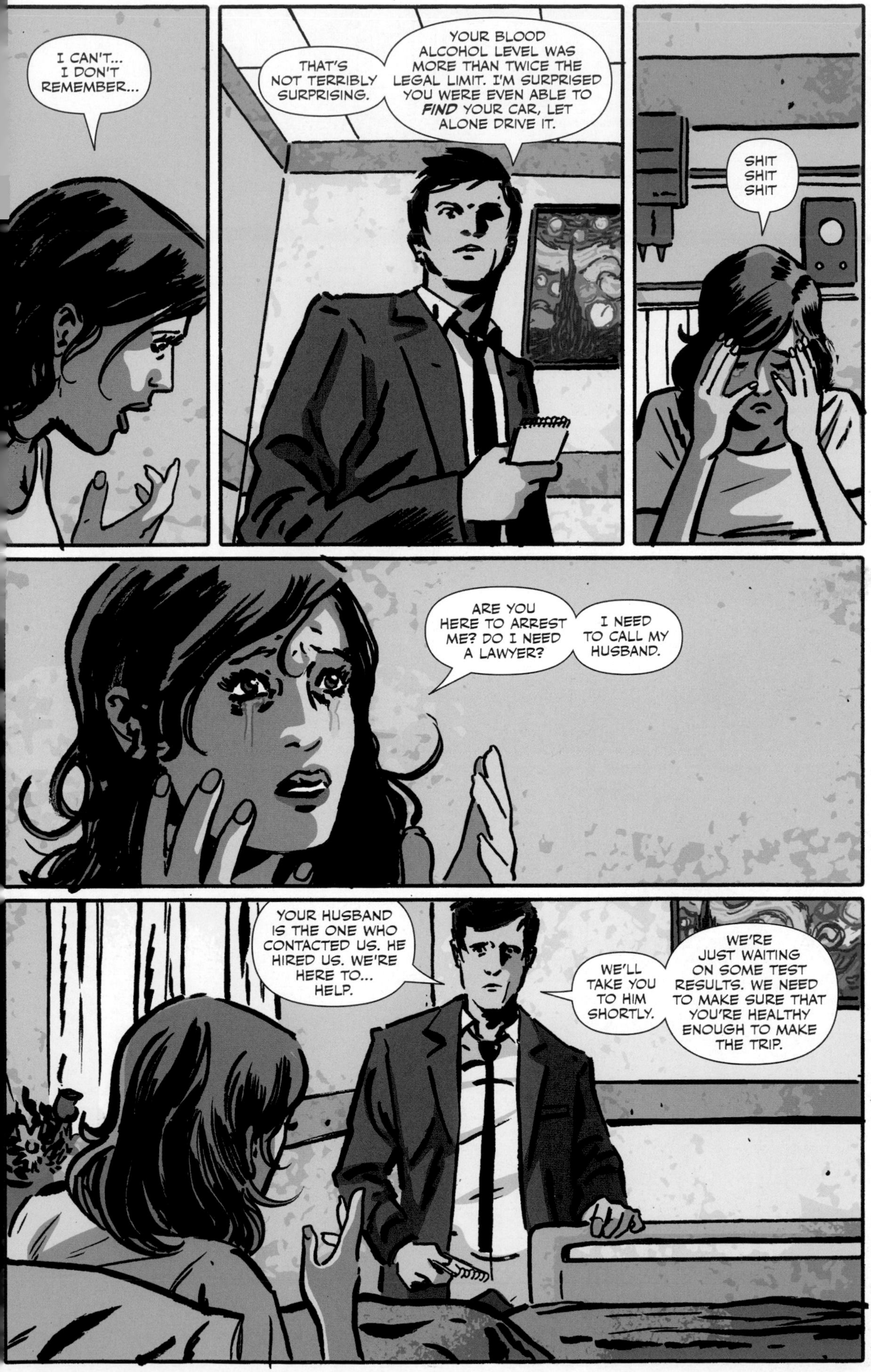
I CAN'T... I DON'T REMEMBER...
THAT'S NOT TERRIBLY SURPRISING.
YOUR BLOOD ALCOHOL LEVEL WAS MORE THAN TWICE THE LEGAL LIMIT. I'M SURPRISED YOU WERE EVEN ABLE TO *FIND* YOUR CAR, LET ALONE DRIVE IT.
SHIT SHIT SHIT
ARE YOU HERE TO ARREST ME? DO I NEED A LAWYER?
I NEED TO CALL MY HUSBAND.
YOUR HUSBAND IS THE ONE WHO CONTACTED US. HE HIRED US. WE'RE HERE TO... HELP.
WE'LL TAKE YOU TO HIM SHORTLY.
WE'RE JUST WAITING ON SOME TEST RESULTS. WE NEED TO MAKE SURE THAT YOU'RE HEALTHY ENOUGH TO MAKE THE TRIP.

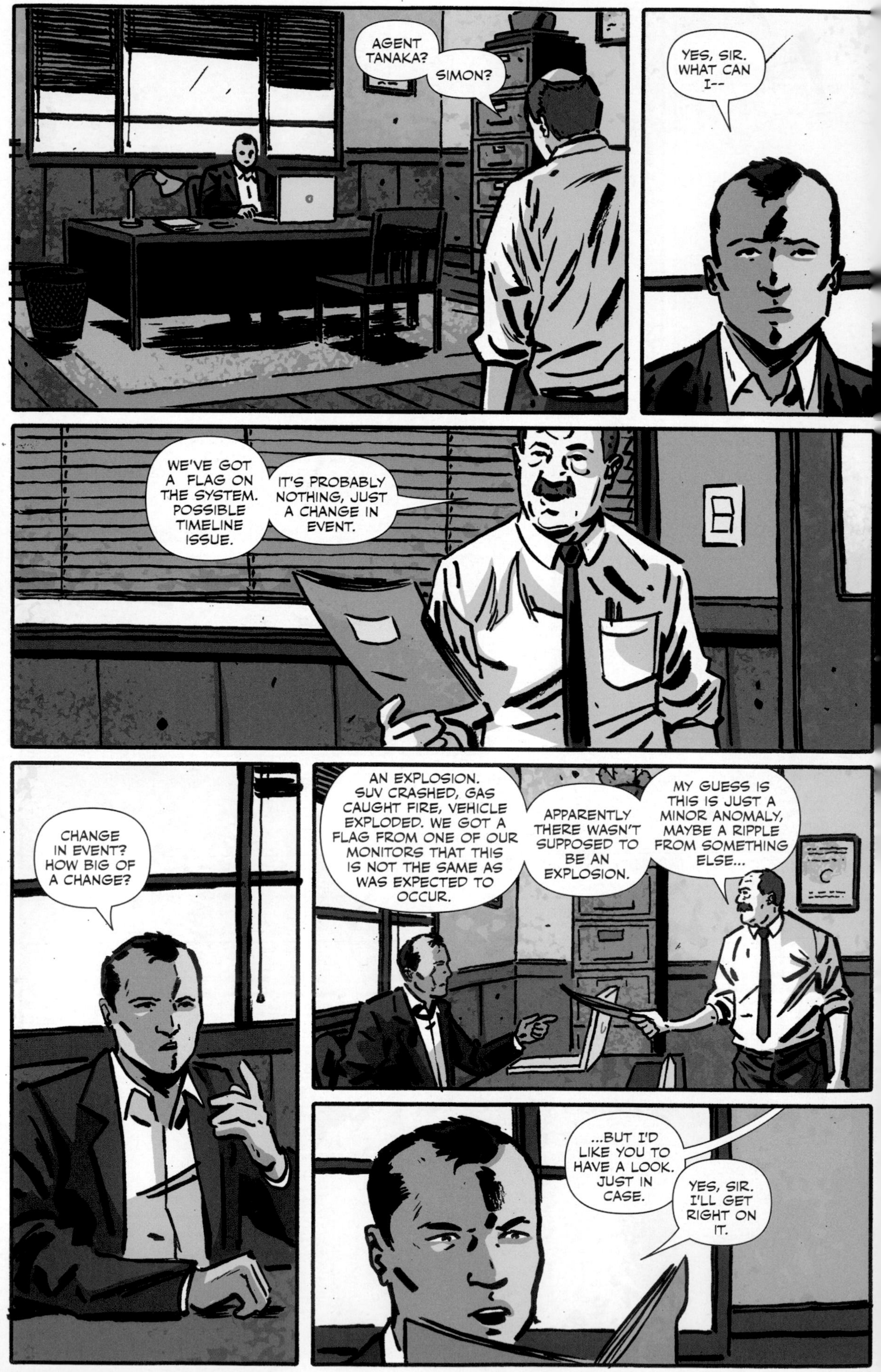
AGENT TANAKA?
SIMON?
YES, SIR. WHAT CAN I--
WE'VE GOT A FLAG ON THE SYSTEM. POSSIBLE TIMELINE ISSUE.
IT'S PROBABLY NOTHING, JUST A CHANGE IN EVENT.
CHANGE IN EVENT? HOW BIG OF A CHANGE?
AN EXPLOSION. SUV CRASHED, GAS CAUGHT FIRE, VEHICLE EXPLODED. WE GOT A FLAG FROM ONE OF OUR MONITORS THAT THIS IS NOT THE SAME AS WAS EXPECTED TO OCCUR.
APPARENTLY THERE WASN'T SUPPOSED TO BE AN EXPLOSION.
MY GUESS IS THIS IS JUST A MINOR ANOMALY, MAYBE A RIPPLE FROM SOMETHING ELSE...
...BUT I'D LIKE YOU TO HAVE A LOOK. JUST IN CASE.
YES, SIR. I'LL GET RIGHT ON IT.

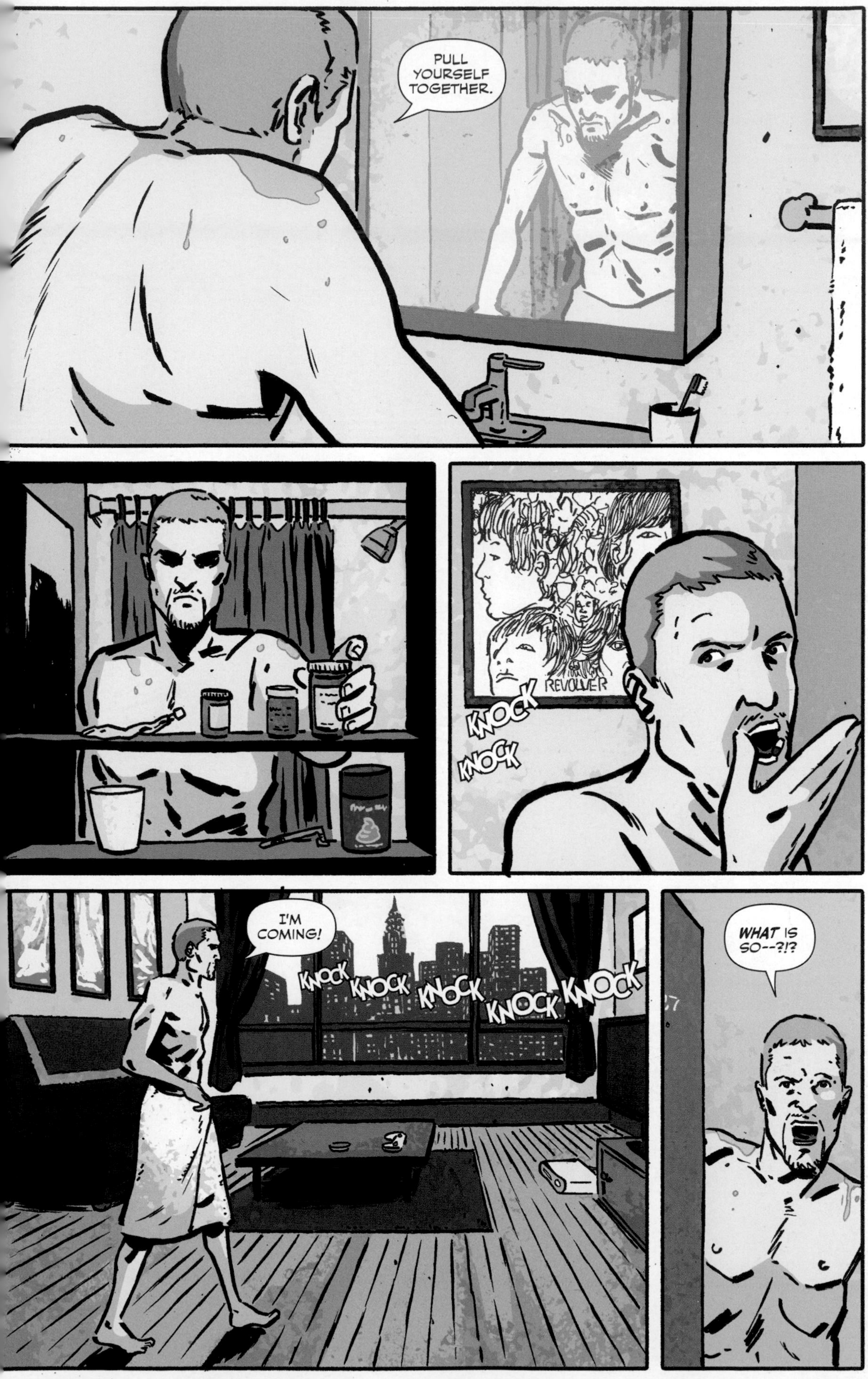
PULL YOURSELF TOGETHER.
REVOLVER
KNOCK
KNOCK
I'M COMING!
KNOCK KNOCK KNOCK KNOCK KNOCK
WHAT IS SO--?!?

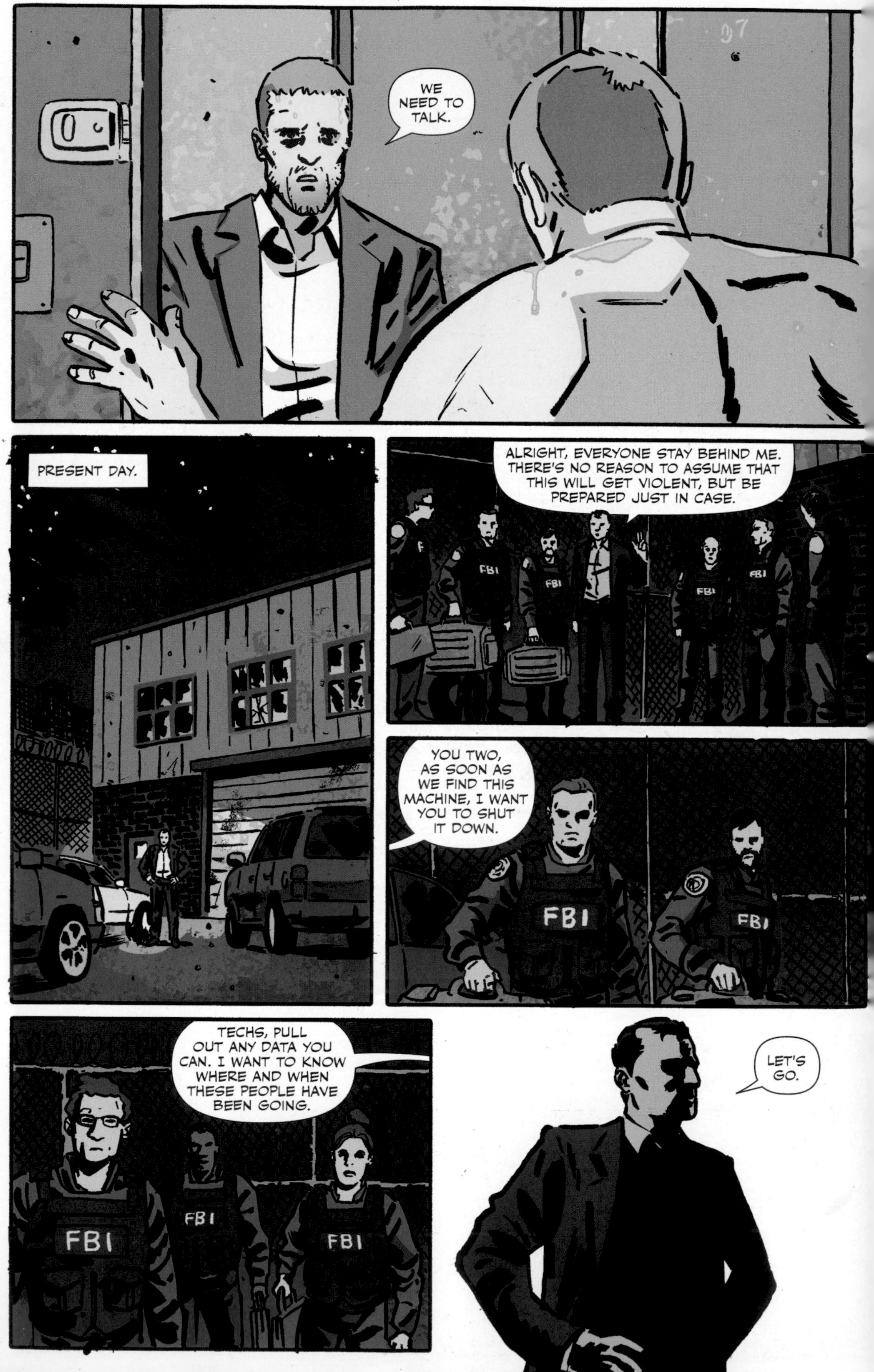
WE NEED TO TALK.
PRESENT DAY.
ALRIGHT, EVERYONE STAY BEHIND ME. THERE'S NO REASON TO ASSUME THAT THIS WILL GET VIOLENT, BUT BE PREPARED JUST IN CASE.
YOU TWO, AS SOON AS WE FIND THIS MACHINE, I WANT YOU TO SHUT IT DOWN.
TECHS, PULL OUT ANY DATA YOU CAN. I WANT TO KNOW WHERE AND WHEN THESE PEOPLE HAVE BEEN GOING.
LET'S GO.

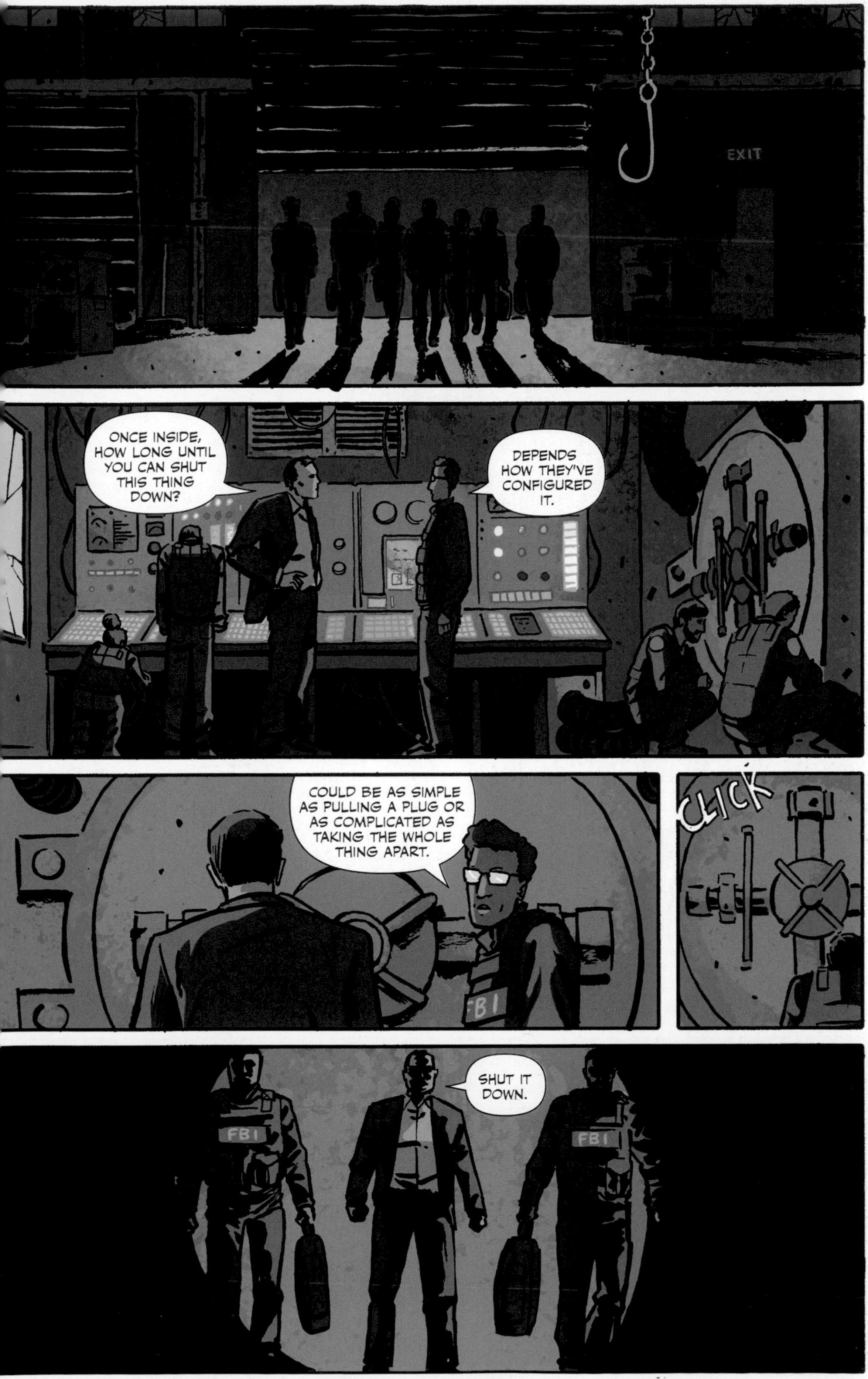
EXIT
ONCE INSIDE, HOW LONG UNTIL YOU CAN SHUT THIS THING DOWN?
DEPENDS HOW THEY'VE CONFIGURED IT.
COULD BE AS SIMPLE AS PULLING A PLUG OR AS COMPLICATED AS TAKING THE WHOLE THING APART.
FBI
CLICK
SHUT IT DOWN.
FBI
FBI

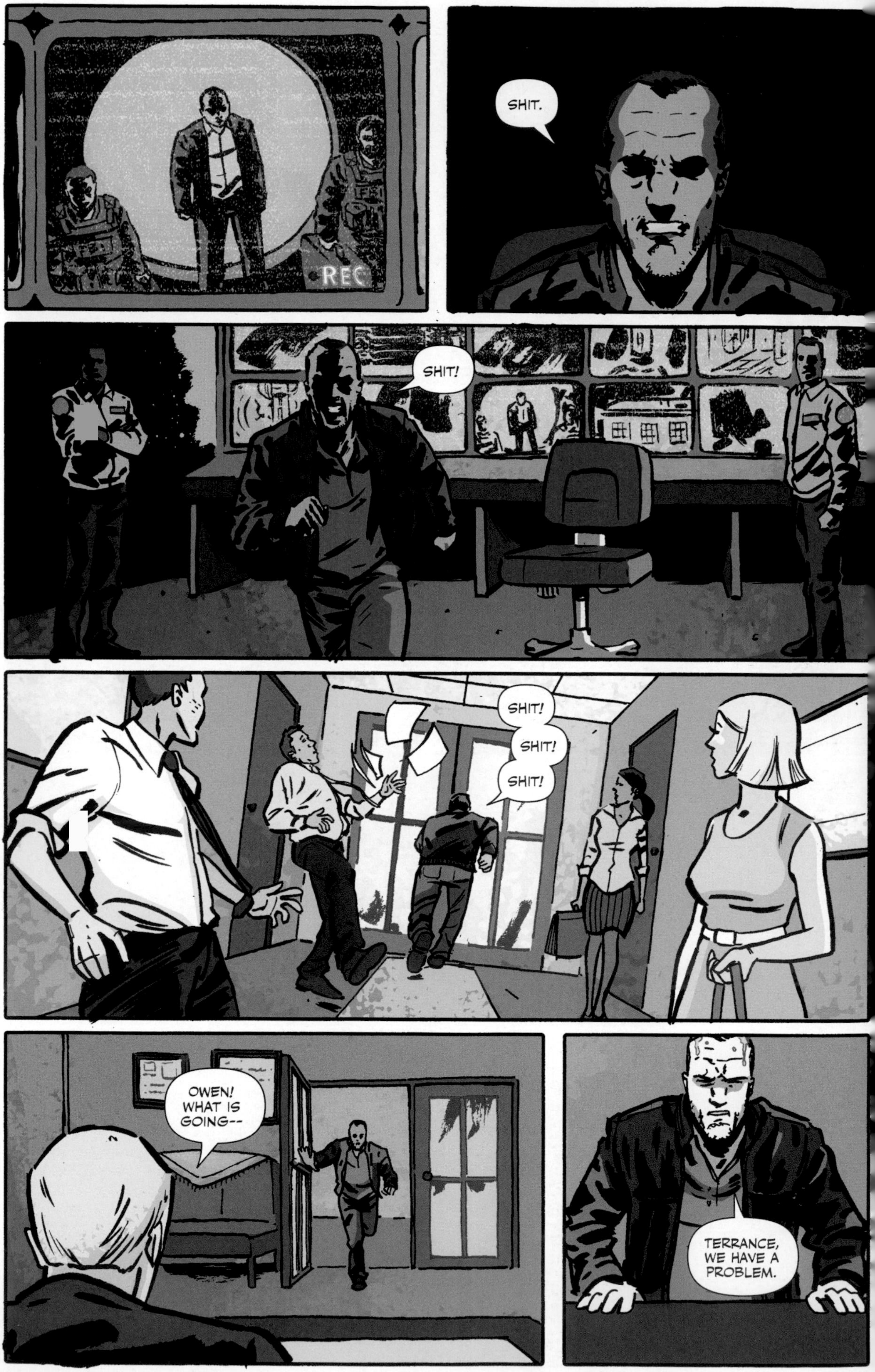
REC
SHIT.
SHIT!
SHIT!
SHIT!
SHIT!
OWEN! WHAT IS GOING--
TERRANCE, WE HAVE A PROBLEM.

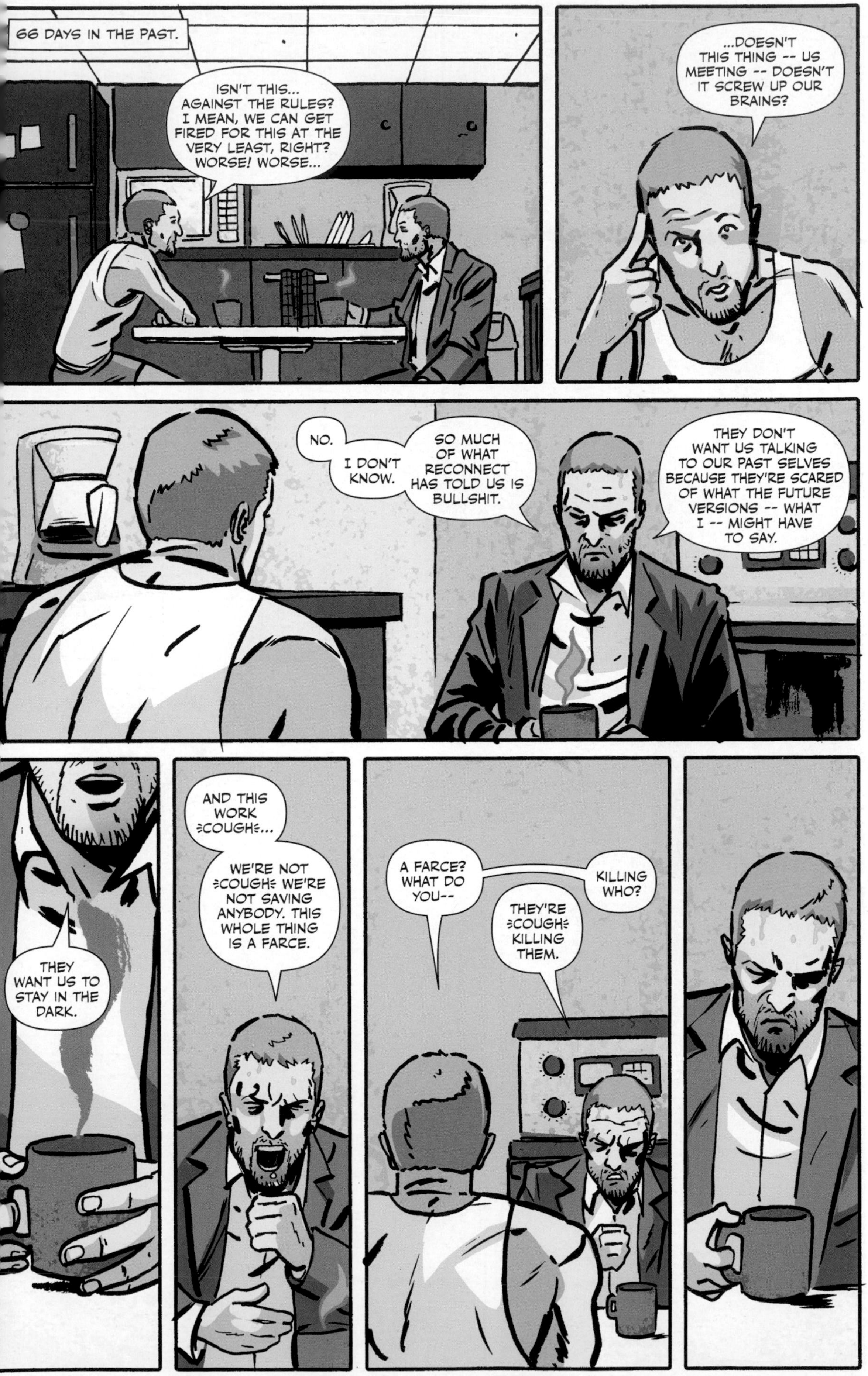
66 DAYS IN THE PAST.
ISN'T THIS... AGAINST THE RULES? I MEAN, WE CAN GET FIRED FOR THIS AT THE VERY LEAST, RIGHT? WORSE! WORSE...
...DOESN'T THIS THING -- US MEETING -- DOESN'T IT SCREW UP OUR BRAINS?
NO.
I DON'T KNOW.
SO MUCH OF WHAT RECONNECT HAS TOLD US IS BULLSHIT.
THEY DON'T WANT US TALKING TO OUR PAST SELVES BECAUSE THEY'RE SCARED OF WHAT THE FUTURE VERSIONS -- WHAT I -- MIGHT HAVE TO SAY.
THEY WANT US TO STAY IN THE DARK.
AND THIS WORK ≈COUGH≈...
WE'RE NOT ≈COUGH≈ WE'RE NOT SAVING ANYBODY. THIS WHOLE THING IS A FARCE.
A FARCE? WHAT DO YOU--
THEY'RE ≈COUGH≈ KILLING THEM.
KILLING WHO?

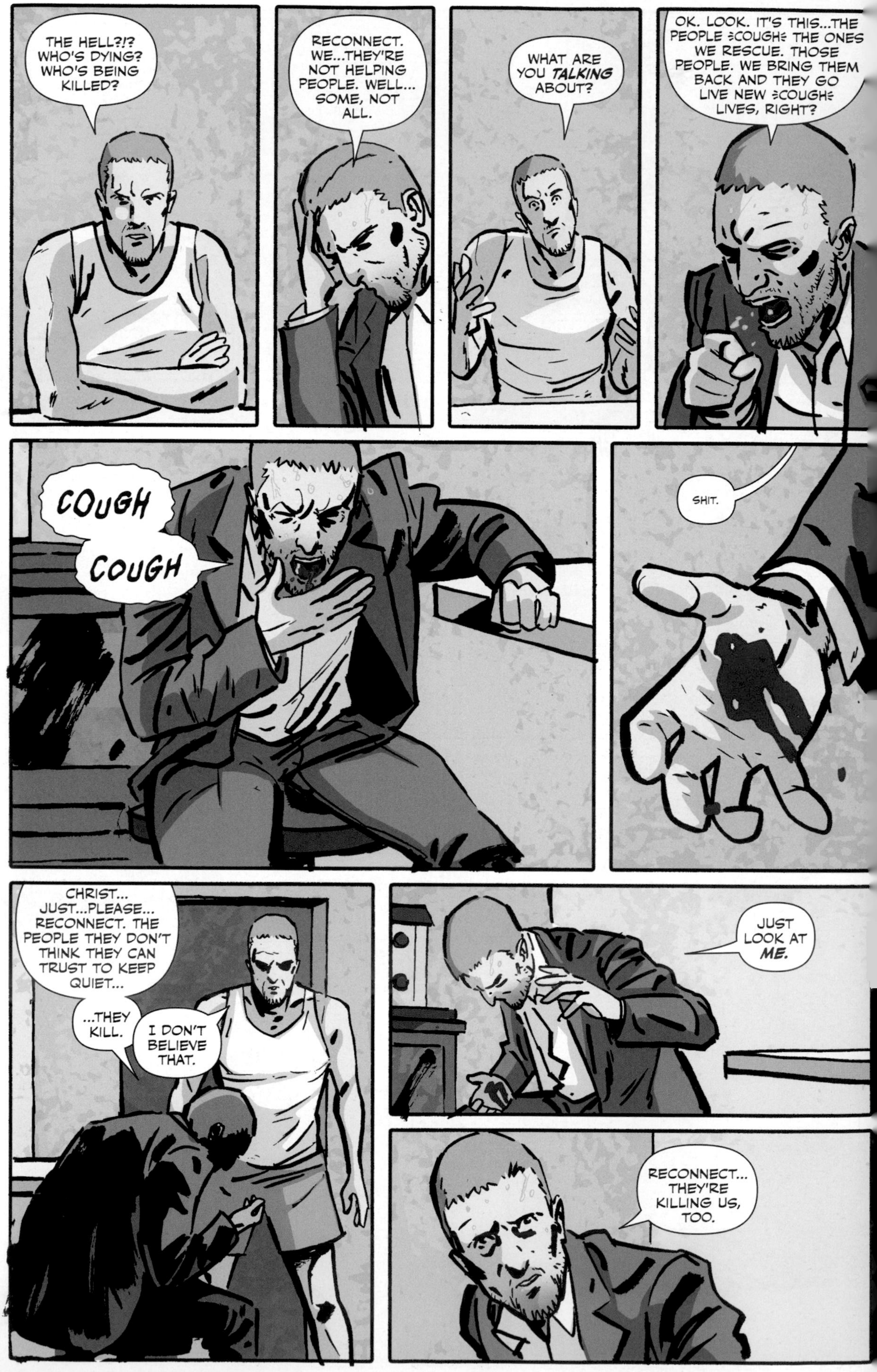
THE HELL?!? WHO'S DYING? WHO'S BEING KILLED?
RECONNECT. WE...THEY'RE NOT HELPING PEOPLE. WELL... SOME, NOT ALL.
WHAT ARE YOU *TALKING* ABOUT?
OK. LOOK. IT'S THIS...THE PEOPLE =COUGH= THE ONES WE RESCUE. THOSE PEOPLE. WE BRING THEM BACK AND THEY GO LIVE NEW =COUGH= LIVES, RIGHT?
COUGH
COUGH
SHIT.
CHRIST... JUST...PLEASE... RECONNECT. THE PEOPLE THEY DON'T THINK THEY CAN TRUST TO KEEP QUIET...
...THEY KILL.
I DON'T BELIEVE THAT.
JUST LOOK AT *ME.*
RECONNECT... THEY'RE KILLING US, TOO.

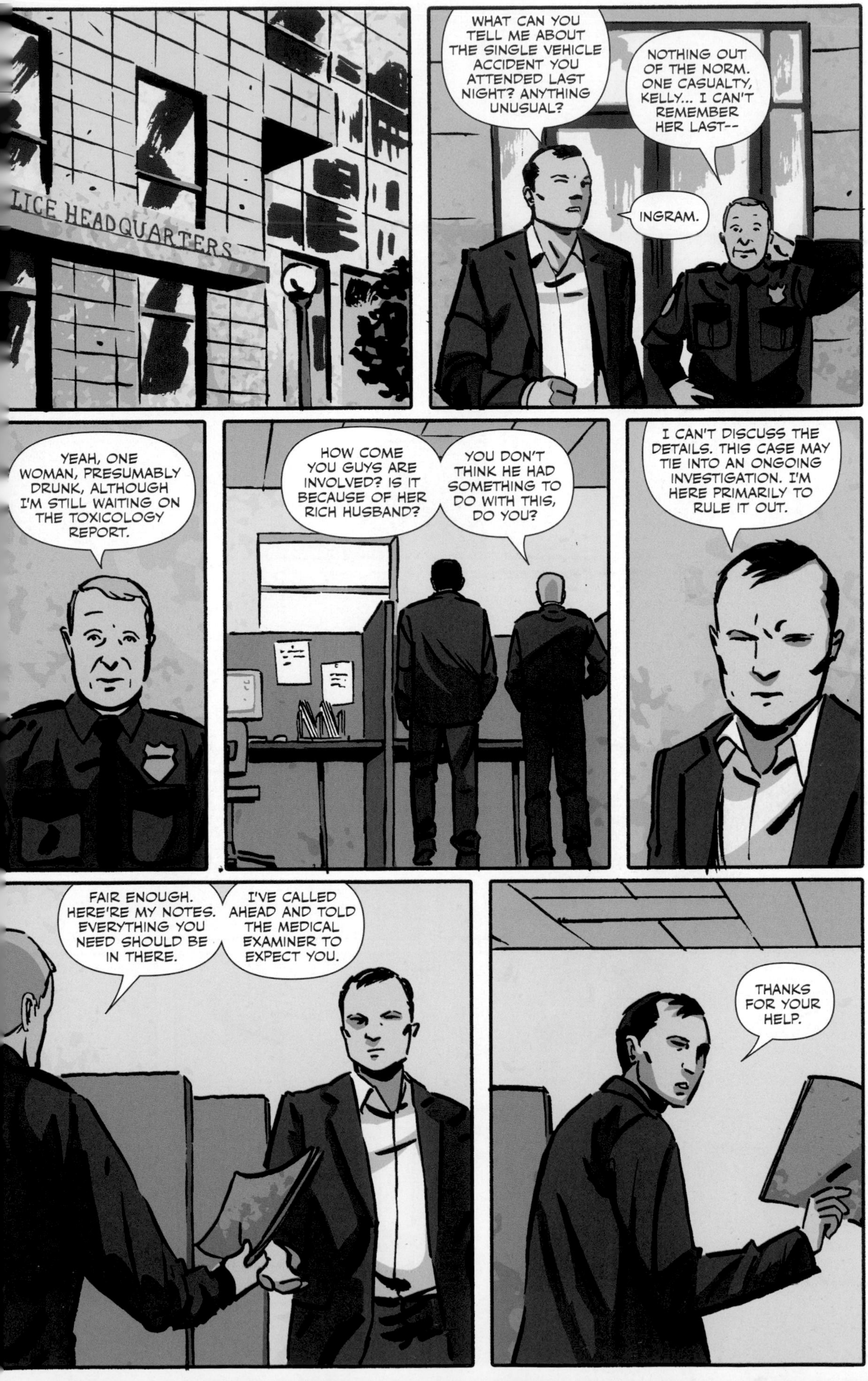
LICE HEADQUARTERS
WHAT CAN YOU TELL ME ABOUT THE SINGLE VEHICLE ACCIDENT YOU ATTENDED LAST NIGHT? ANYTHING UNUSUAL?
NOTHING OUT OF THE NORM. ONE CASUALTY, KELLY... I CAN'T REMEMBER HER LAST--
INGRAM.
YEAH, ONE WOMAN, PRESUMABLY DRUNK, ALTHOUGH I'M STILL WAITING ON THE TOXICOLOGY REPORT.
HOW COME YOU GUYS ARE INVOLVED? IS IT BECAUSE OF HER RICH HUSBAND?
YOU DON'T THINK HE HAD SOMETHING TO DO WITH THIS, DO YOU?
I CAN'T DISCUSS THE DETAILS. THIS CASE MAY TIE INTO AN ONGOING INVESTIGATION. I'M HERE PRIMARILY TO RULE IT OUT.
FAIR ENOUGH. HERE'RE MY NOTES. EVERYTHING YOU NEED SHOULD BE IN THERE.
I'VE CALLED AHEAD AND TOLD THE MEDICAL EXAMINER TO EXPECT YOU.
THANKS FOR YOUR HELP.

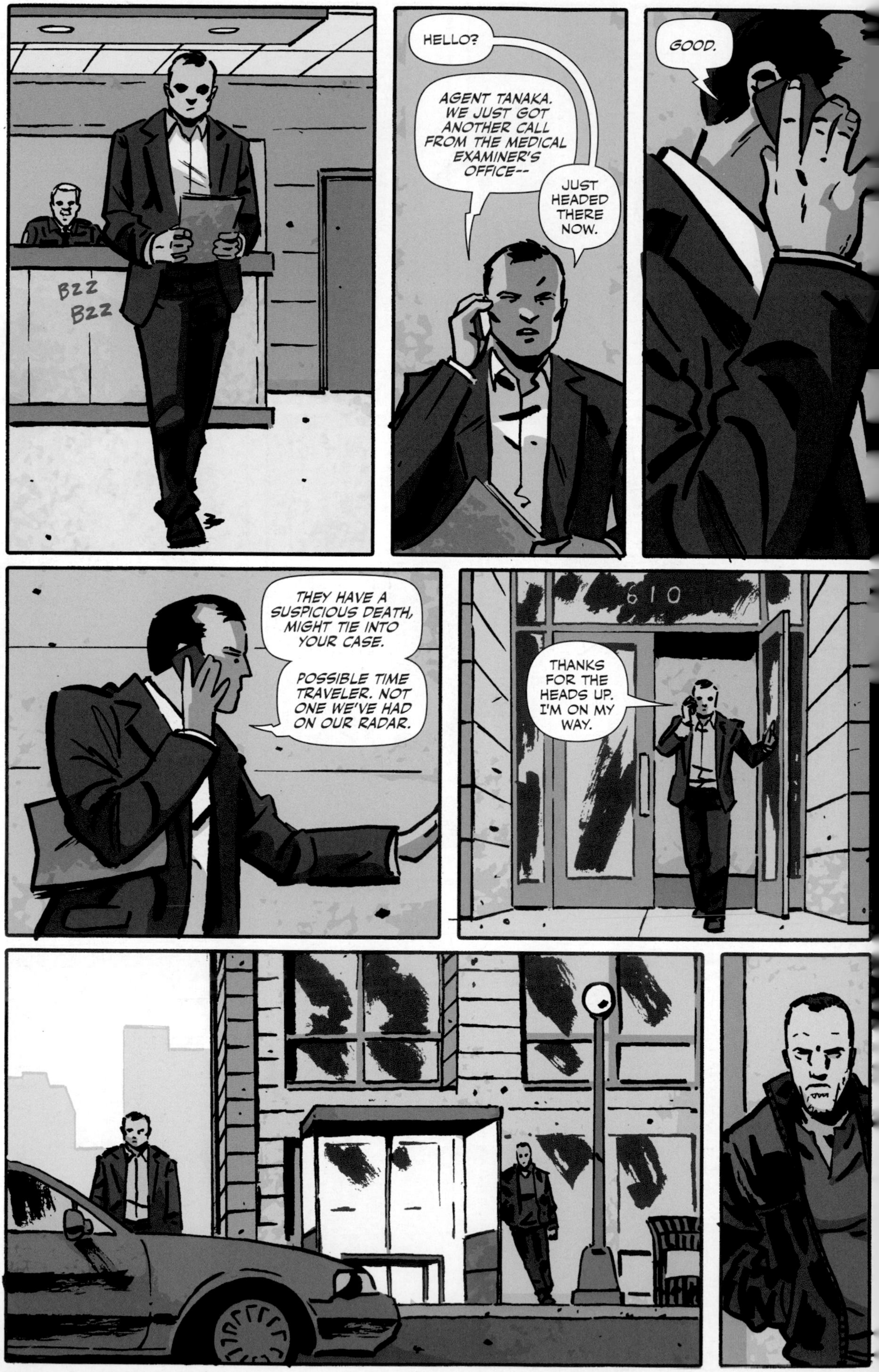
BZZ
BZZ
HELLO?
AGENT TANAKA. WE JUST GOT ANOTHER CALL FROM THE MEDICAL EXAMINER'S OFFICE--
JUST HEADED THERE NOW.
GOOD.
THEY HAVE A SUSPICIOUS DEATH, MIGHT TIE INTO YOUR CASE.
POSSIBLE TIME TRAVELER. NOT ONE WE'VE HAD ON OUR RADAR.
610
THANKS FOR THE HEADS UP. I'M ON MY WAY.

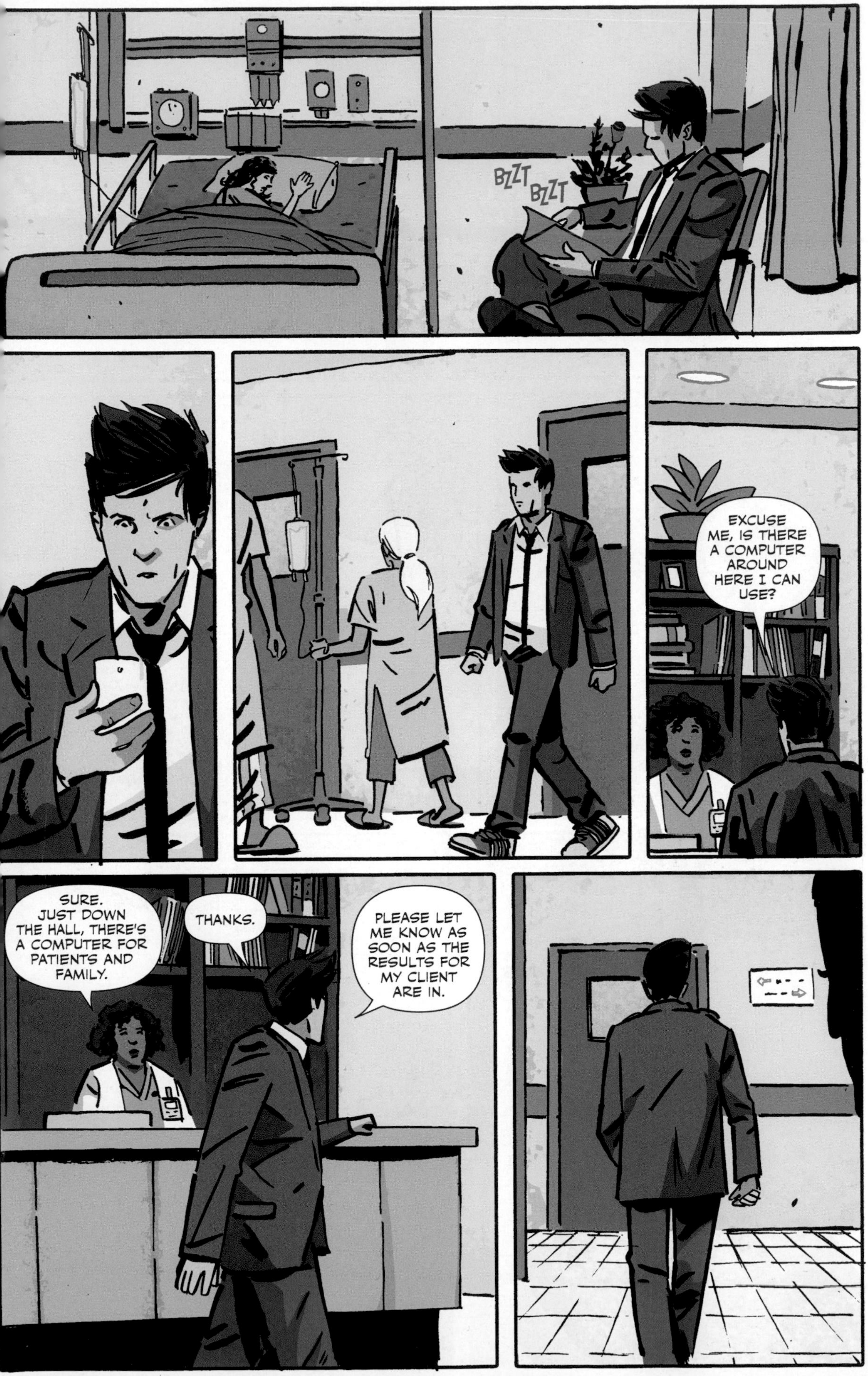
BZZT
BZZT
EXCUSE ME, IS THERE A COMPUTER AROUND HERE I CAN USE?
SURE. JUST DOWN THE HALL, THERE'S A COMPUTER FOR PATIENTS AND FAMILY.
THANKS.
PLEASE LET ME KNOW AS SOON AS THE RESULTS FOR MY CLIENT ARE IN.

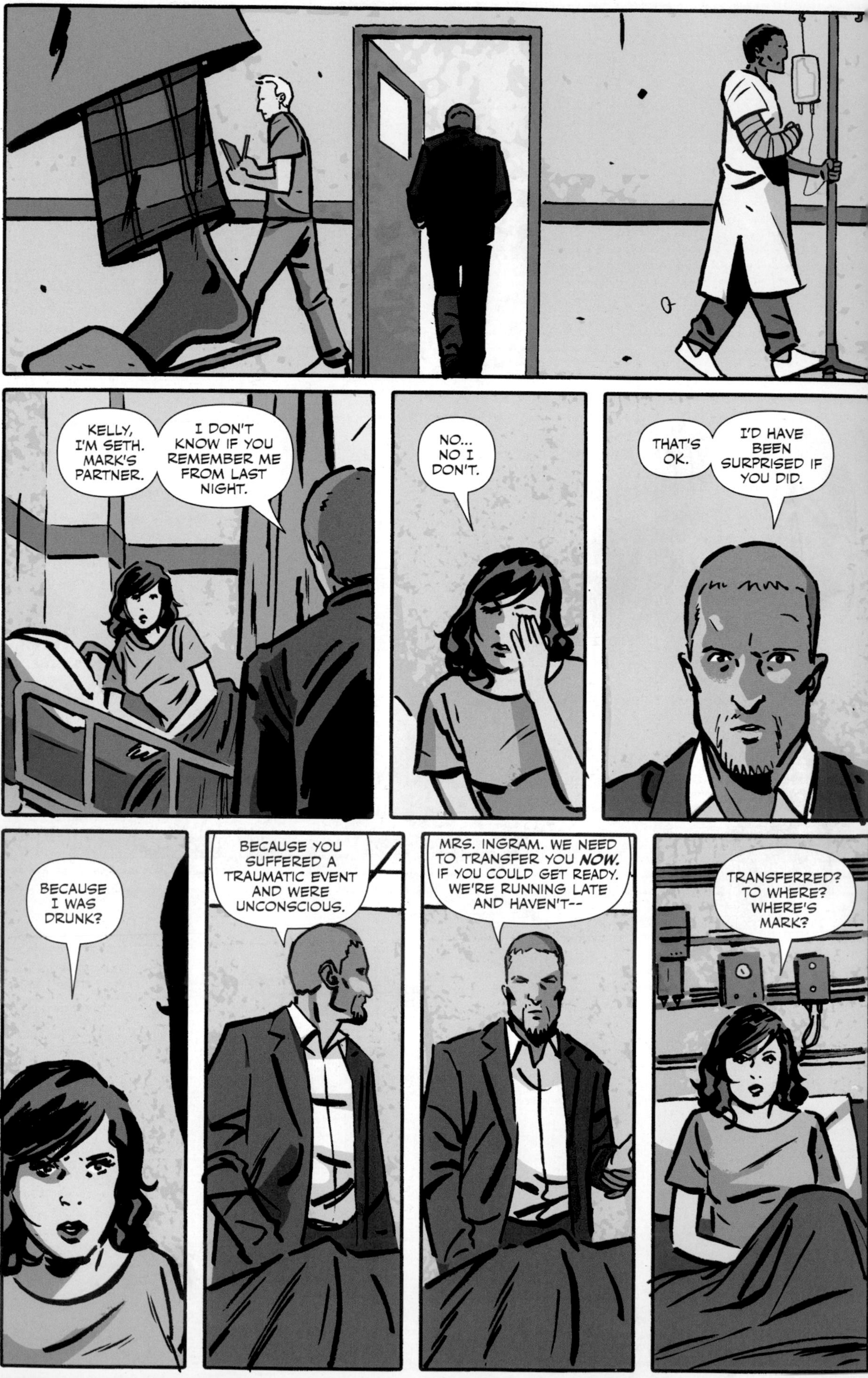
KELLY, I'M SETH. MARK'S PARTNER.
I DON'T KNOW IF YOU REMEMBER ME FROM LAST NIGHT.
NO... NO I DON'T.
THAT'S OK.
I'D HAVE BEEN SURPRISED IF YOU DID.
BECAUSE I WAS DRUNK?
BECAUSE YOU SUFFERED A TRAUMATIC EVENT AND WERE UNCONSCIOUS.
MRS. INGRAM. WE NEED TO TRANSFER YOU NOW. IF YOU COULD GET READY. WE'RE RUNNING LATE AND HAVEN'T--
TRANSFERRED? TO WHERE? WHERE'S MARK?

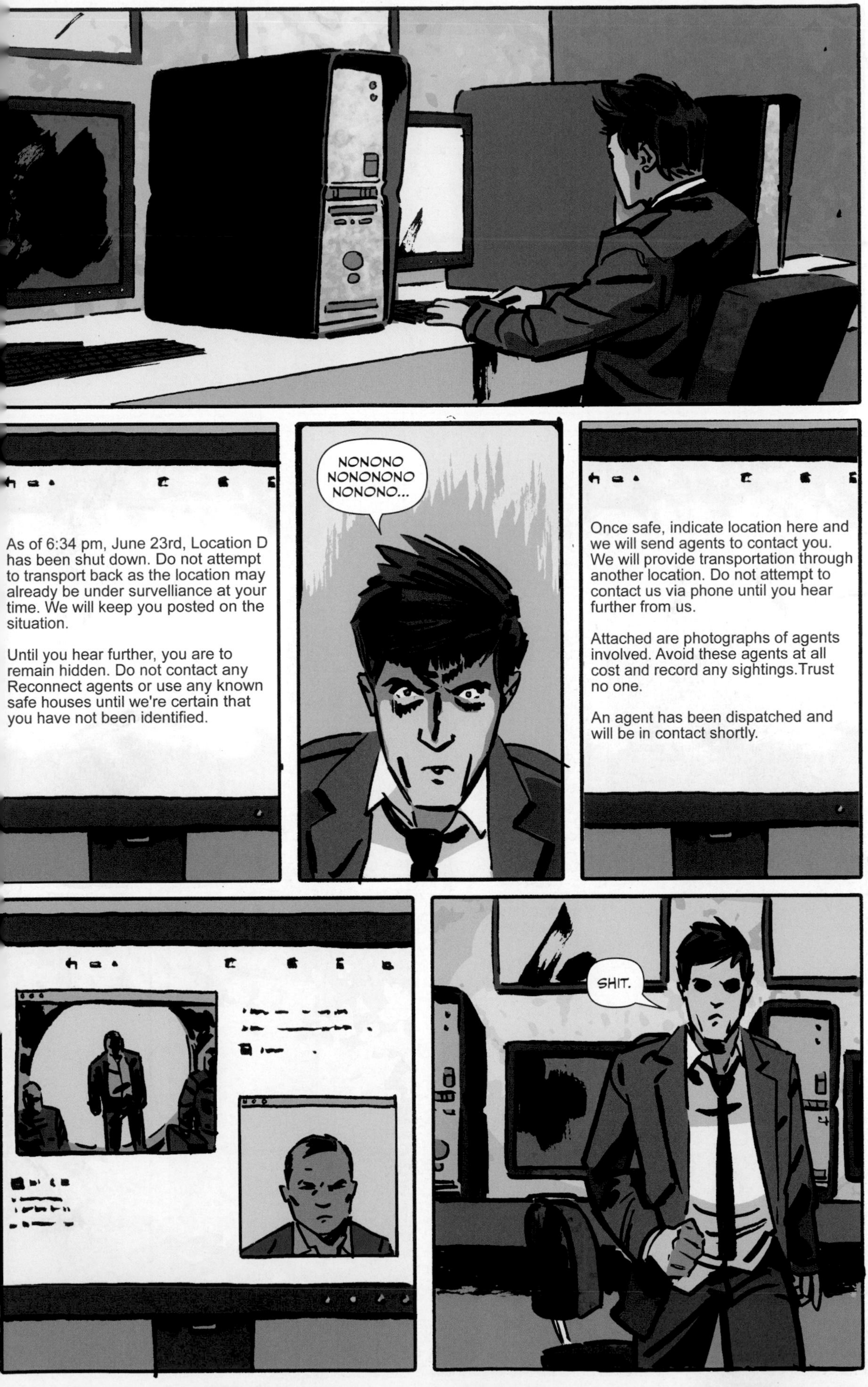
As of 6:34 pm, June 23rd, Location D has been shut down. Do not attempt to transport back as the location may already be under survelliance at your time. We will keep you posted on the situation.
Until you hear further, you are to remain hidden. Do not contact any Reconnect agents or use any known safe houses until we're certain that you have not been identified.
NONONO NONONONO NONONO...
Once safe, indicate location here and we will send agents to contact you. We will provide transportation through another location. Do not attempt to contact us via phone until you hear further from us.
Attached are photographs of agents involved. Avoid these agents at all cost and record any sightings.Trust no one.
An agent has been dispatched and will be in contact shortly.
SHIT.

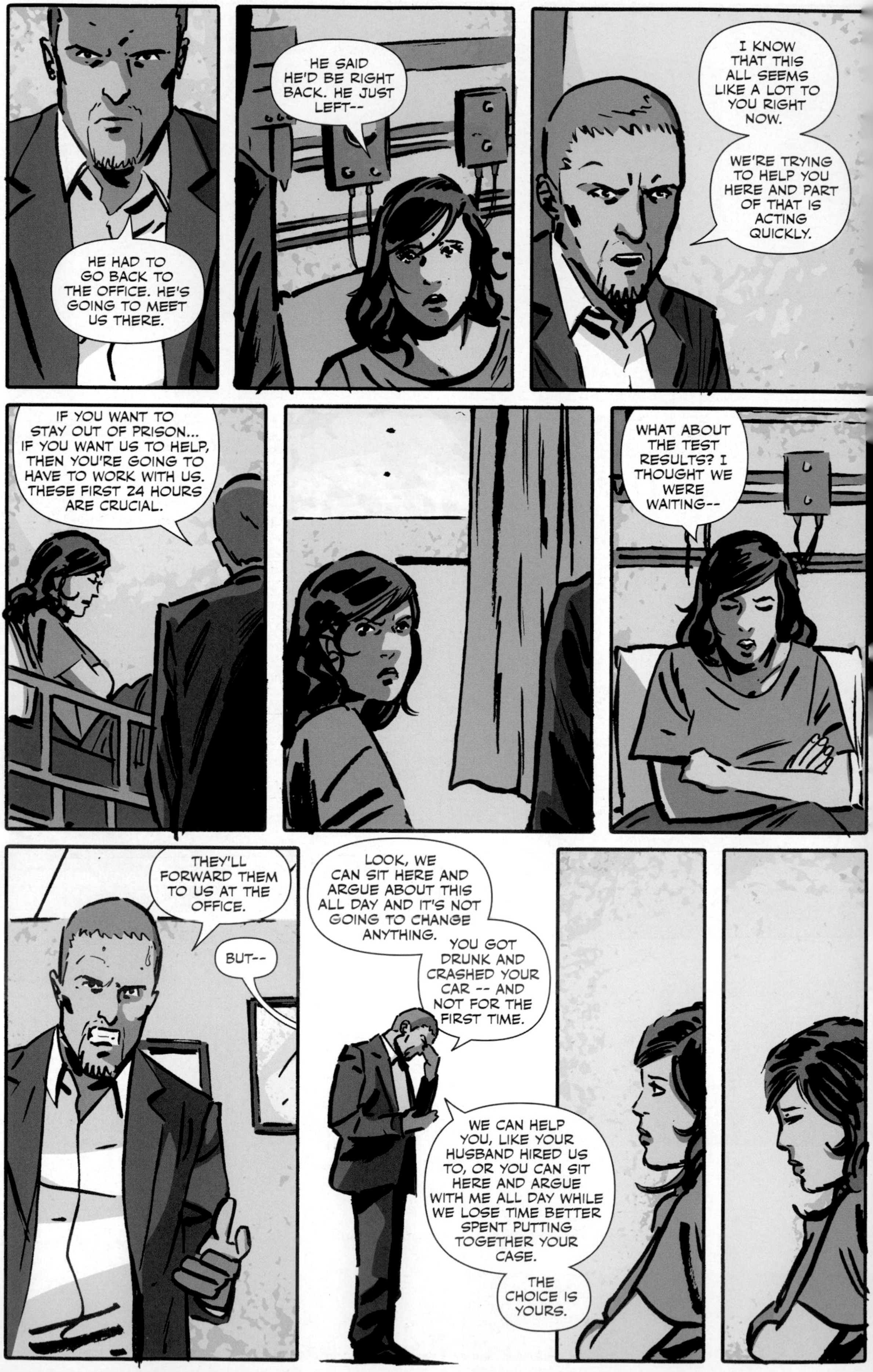
HE HAD TO GO BACK TO THE OFFICE. HE'S GOING TO MEET US THERE.
HE SAID HE'D BE RIGHT BACK. HE JUST LEFT--
I KNOW THAT THIS ALL SEEMS LIKE A LOT TO YOU RIGHT NOW.
WE'RE TRYING TO HELP YOU HERE AND PART OF THAT IS ACTING QUICKLY.
IF YOU WANT TO STAY OUT OF PRISON... IF YOU WANT US TO HELP, THEN YOU'RE GOING TO HAVE TO WORK WITH US. THESE FIRST 24 HOURS ARE CRUCIAL.
WHAT ABOUT THE TEST RESULTS? I THOUGHT WE WERE WAITING--
THEY'LL FORWARD THEM TO US AT THE OFFICE.
BUT--
LOOK, WE CAN SIT HERE AND ARGUE ABOUT THIS ALL DAY AND IT'S NOT GOING TO CHANGE ANYTHING.
YOU GOT DRUNK AND CRASHED YOUR CAR -- AND NOT FOR THE FIRST TIME.
WE CAN HELP YOU, LIKE YOUR HUSBAND HIRED US TO, OR YOU CAN SIT HERE AND ARGUE WITH ME ALL DAY WHILE WE LOSE TIME BETTER SPENT PUTTING TOGETHER YOUR CASE.
THE CHOICE IS YOURS.

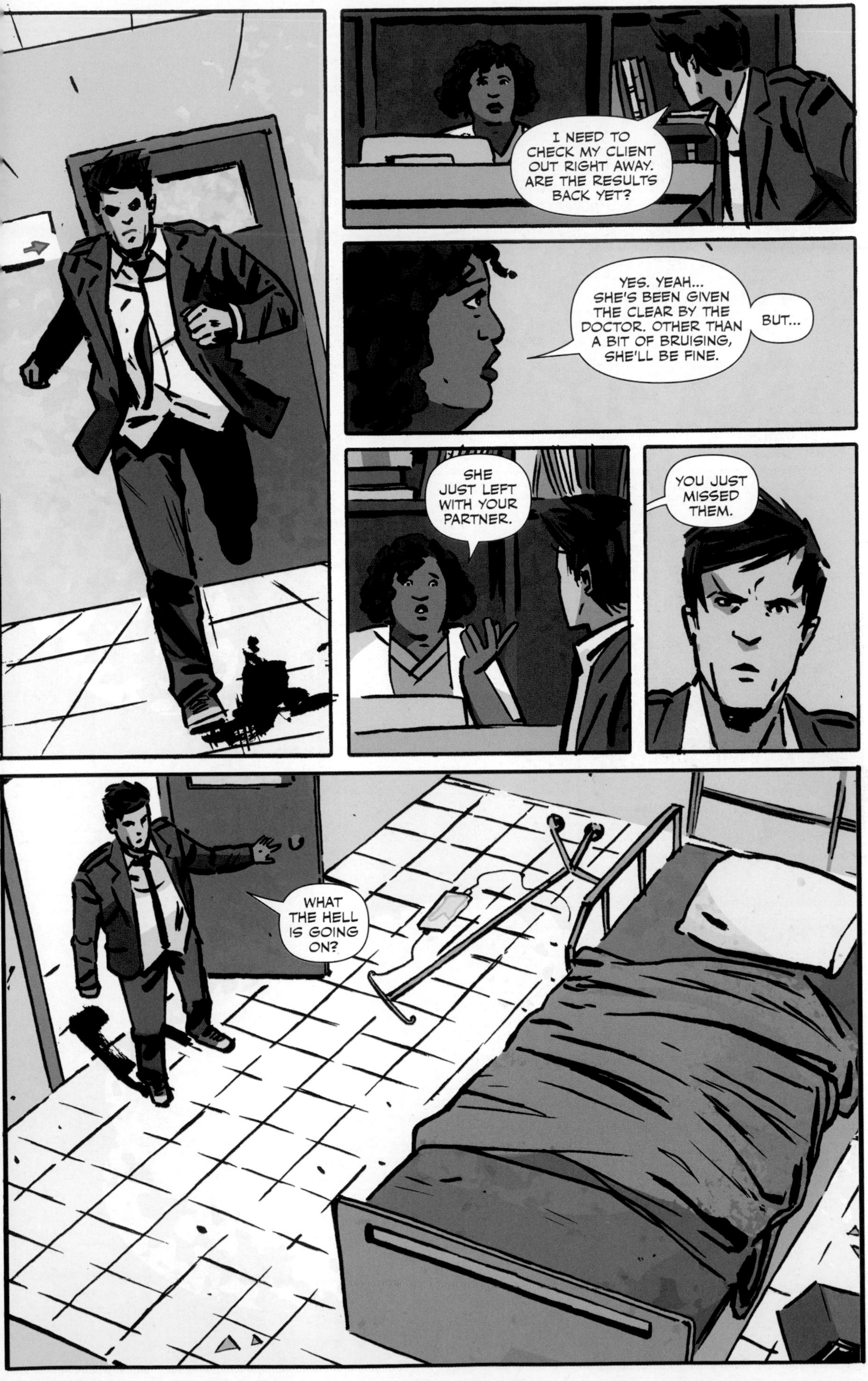
I NEED TO CHECK MY CLIENT OUT RIGHT AWAY. ARE THE RESULTS BACK YET?
YES. YEAH... SHE'S BEEN GIVEN THE CLEAR BY THE DOCTOR. OTHER THAN A BIT OF BRUISING, SHE'LL BE FINE.
BUT...
SHE JUST LEFT WITH YOUR PARTNER.
YOU JUST MISSED THEM.
WHAT THE HELL IS GOING ON?

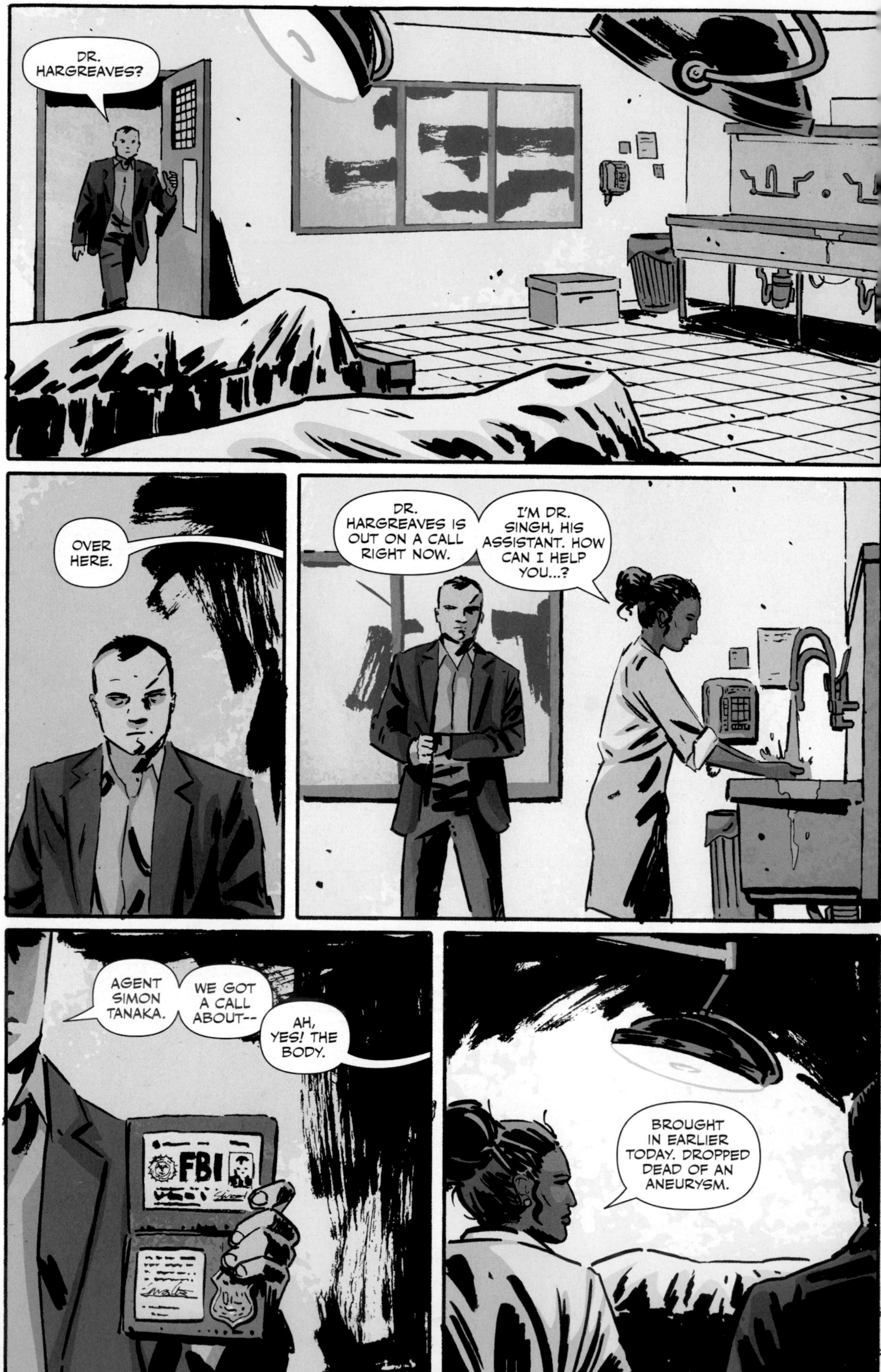
DR. HARGREAVES?
OVER HERE.
DR. HARGREAVES IS OUT ON A CALL RIGHT NOW.
I'M DR. SINGH, HIS ASSISTANT. HOW CAN I HELP YOU...?
AGENT SIMON TANAKA.
WE GOT A CALL ABOUT--
AH, YES! THE BODY.
FBI
BROUGHT IN EARLIER TODAY. DROPPED DEAD OF AN ANEURYSM.

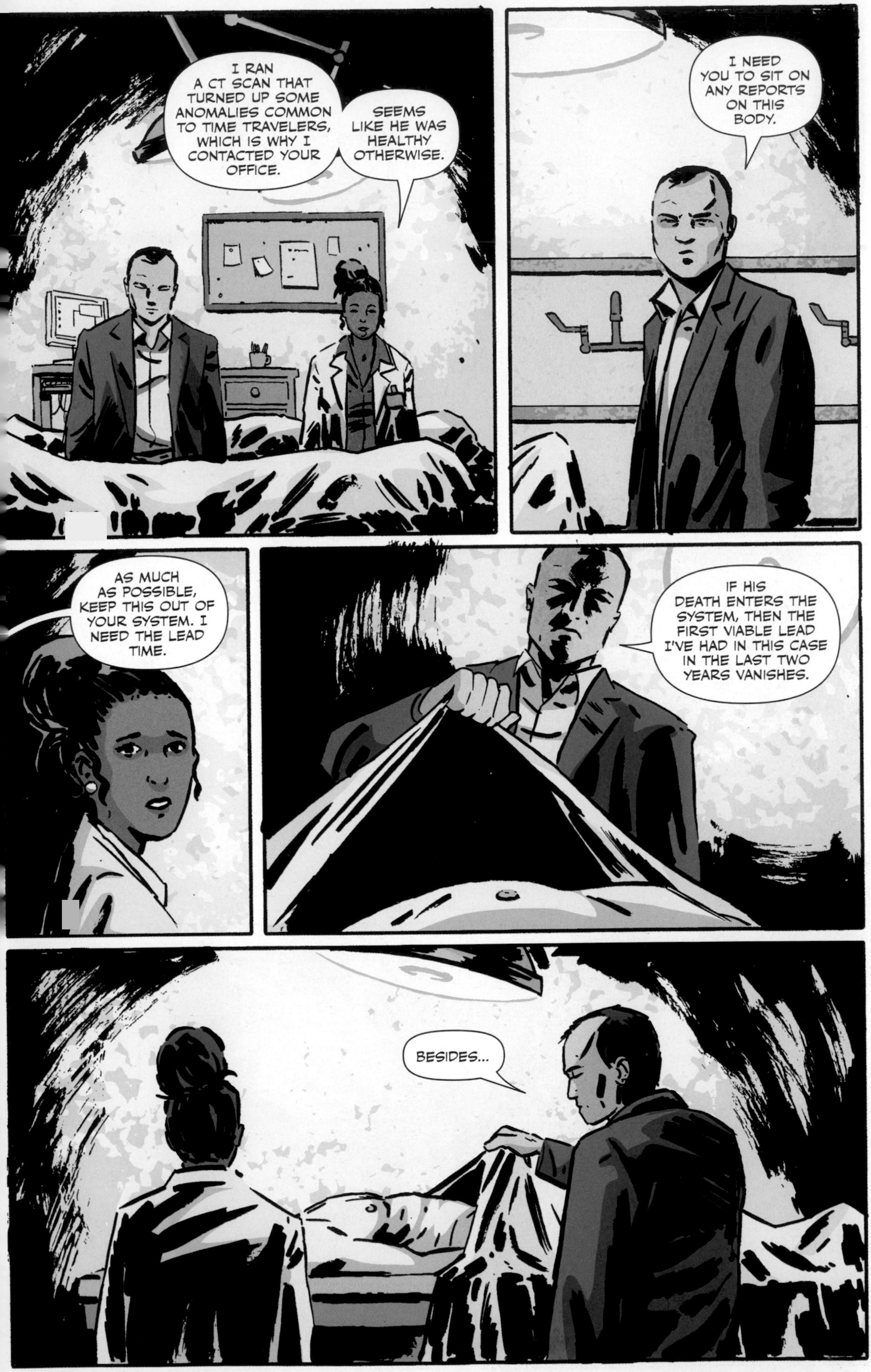
I RAN A CT SCAN THAT TURNED UP SOME ANOMALIES COMMON TO TIME TRAVELERS, WHICH IS WHY I CONTACTED YOUR OFFICE.
SEEMS LIKE HE WAS HEALTHY OTHERWISE.
I NEED YOU TO SIT ON ANY REPORTS ON THIS BODY.
AS MUCH AS POSSIBLE, KEEP THIS OUT OF YOUR SYSTEM. I NEED THE LEAD TIME.
IF HIS DEATH ENTERS THE SYSTEM, THEN THE FIRST VIABLE LEAD I'VE HAD IN THIS CASE IN THE LAST TWO YEARS VANISHES.
BESIDES...

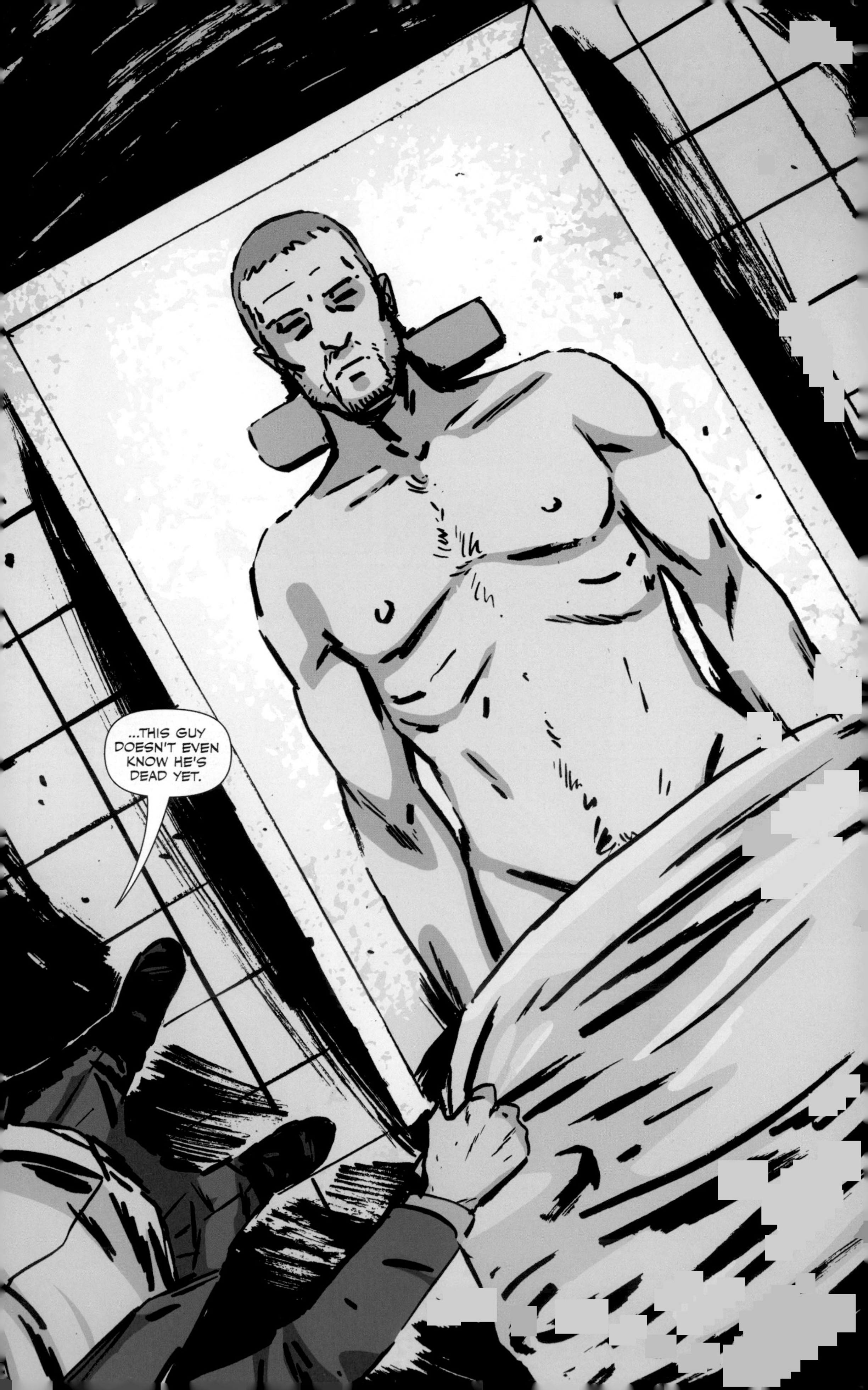
...THIS GUY DOESN'T EVEN KNOW HE'S DEAD YET.

CHAPTER THREE

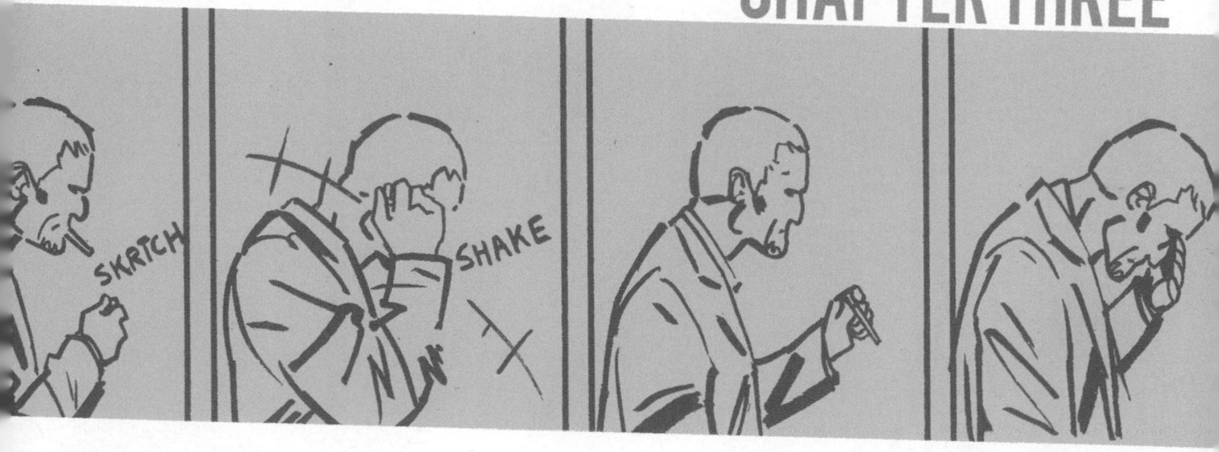
SKRTCH
SHAKE

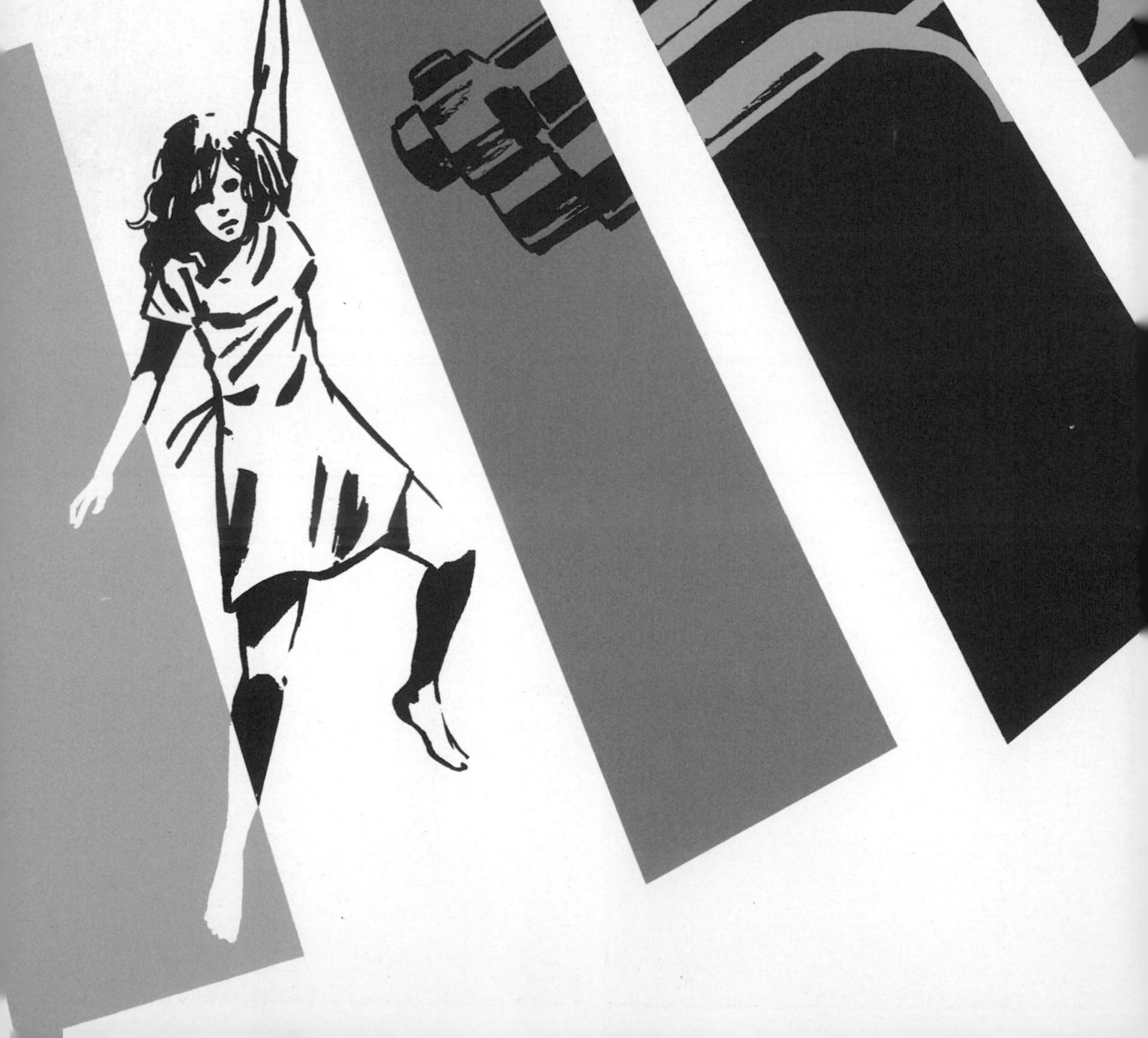

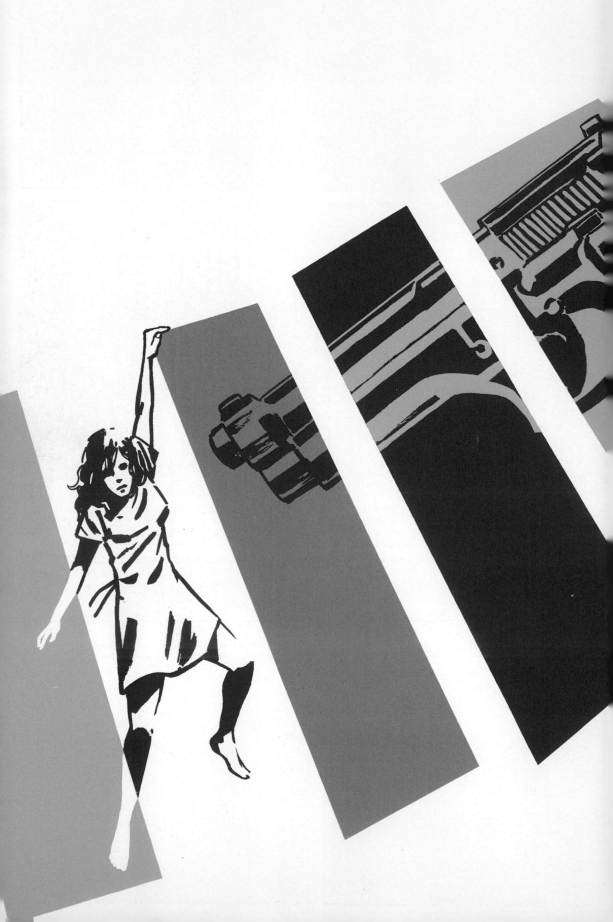

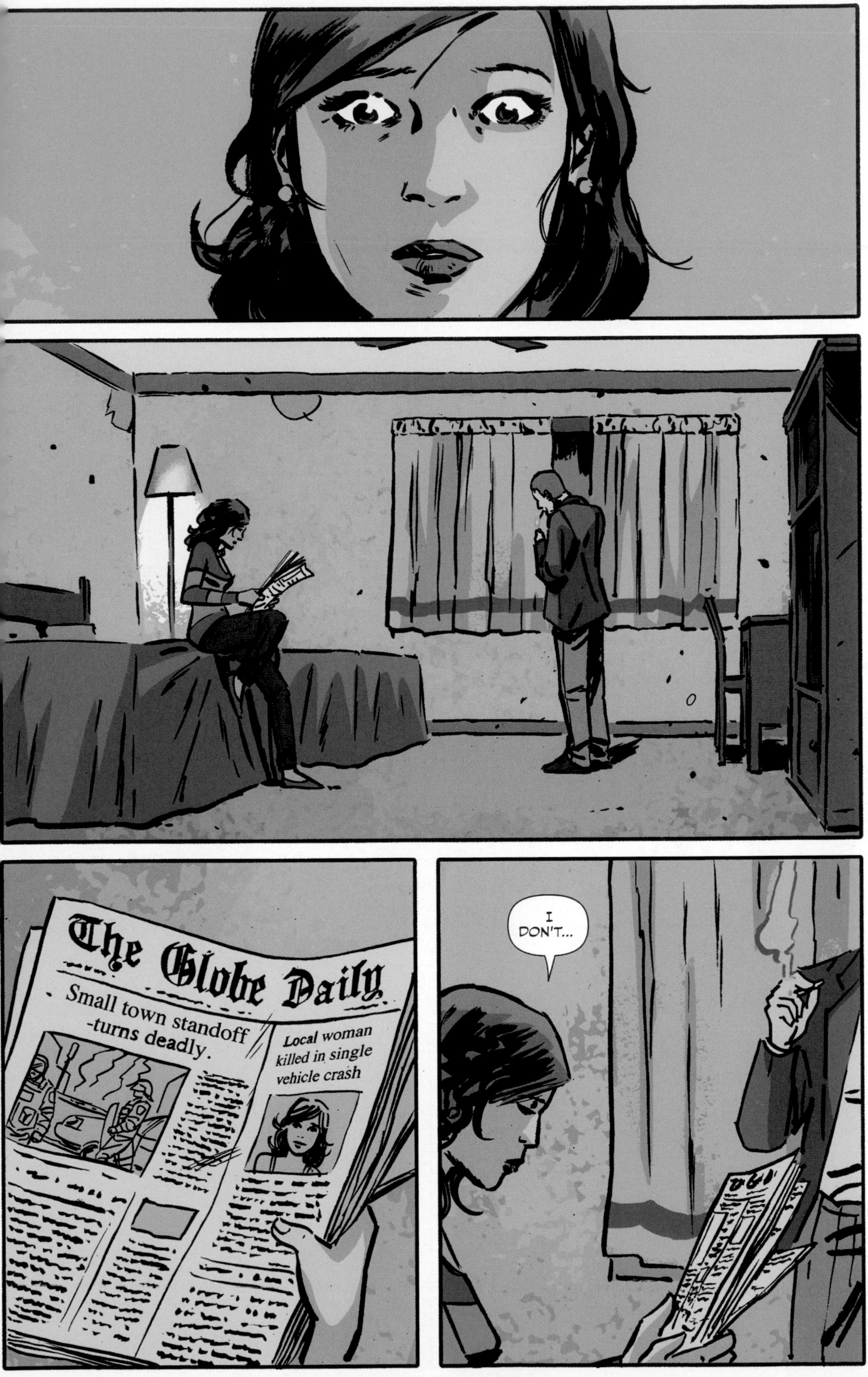
The Globe Daily
Small town standoff
-turns deadly.
Local woman
killed in single
vehicle crash
I DON'T...

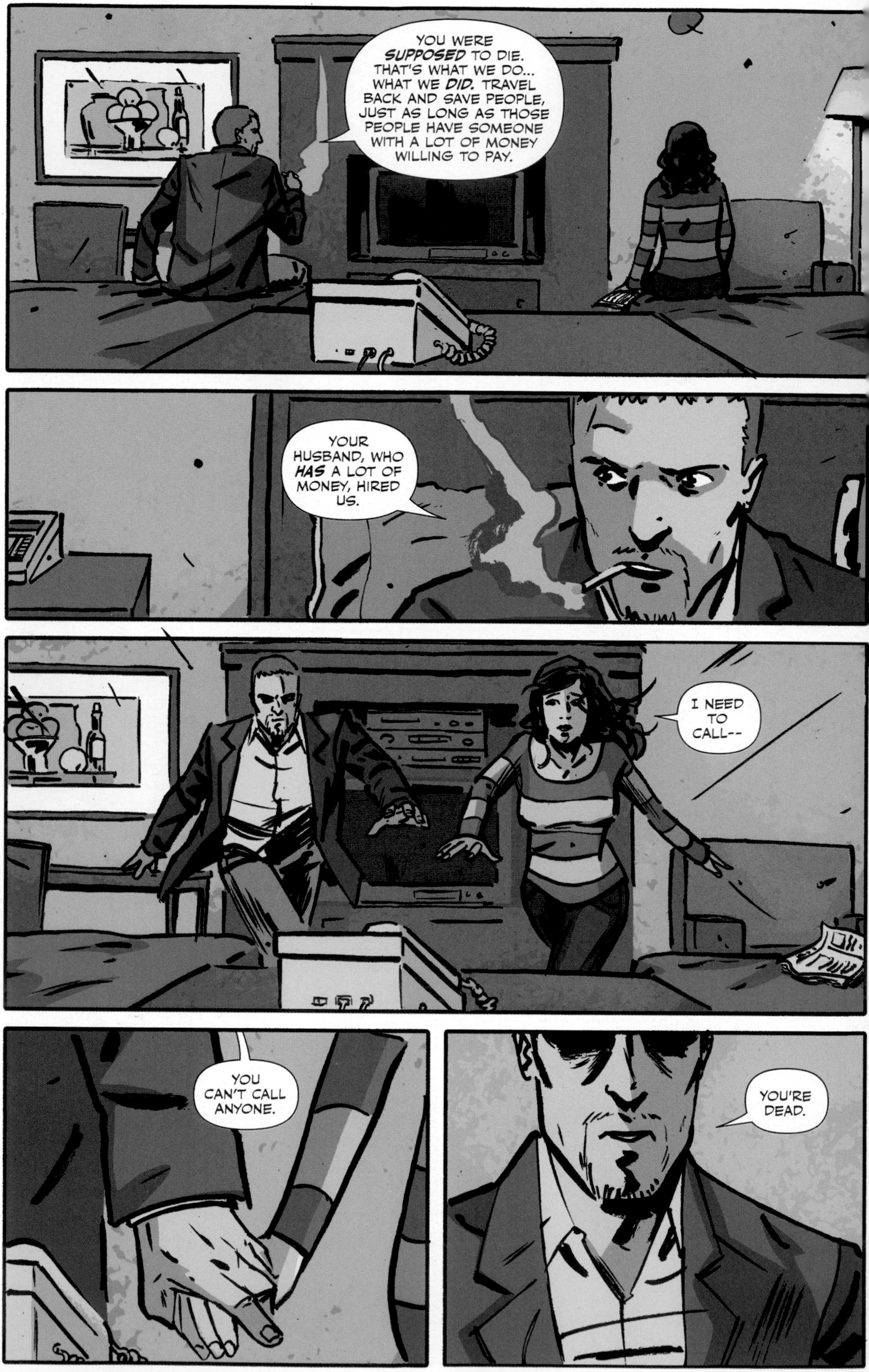
YOU WERE *SUPPOSED* TO DIE. THAT'S WHAT WE DO... WHAT WE *DID.* TRAVEL BACK AND SAVE PEOPLE, JUST AS LONG AS THOSE PEOPLE HAVE SOMEONE WITH A LOT OF MONEY WILLING TO PAY.
YOUR HUSBAND, WHO *HAS* A LOT OF MONEY, HIRED US.
I NEED TO CALL--
YOU CAN'T CALL ANYONE.
YOU'RE DEAD.

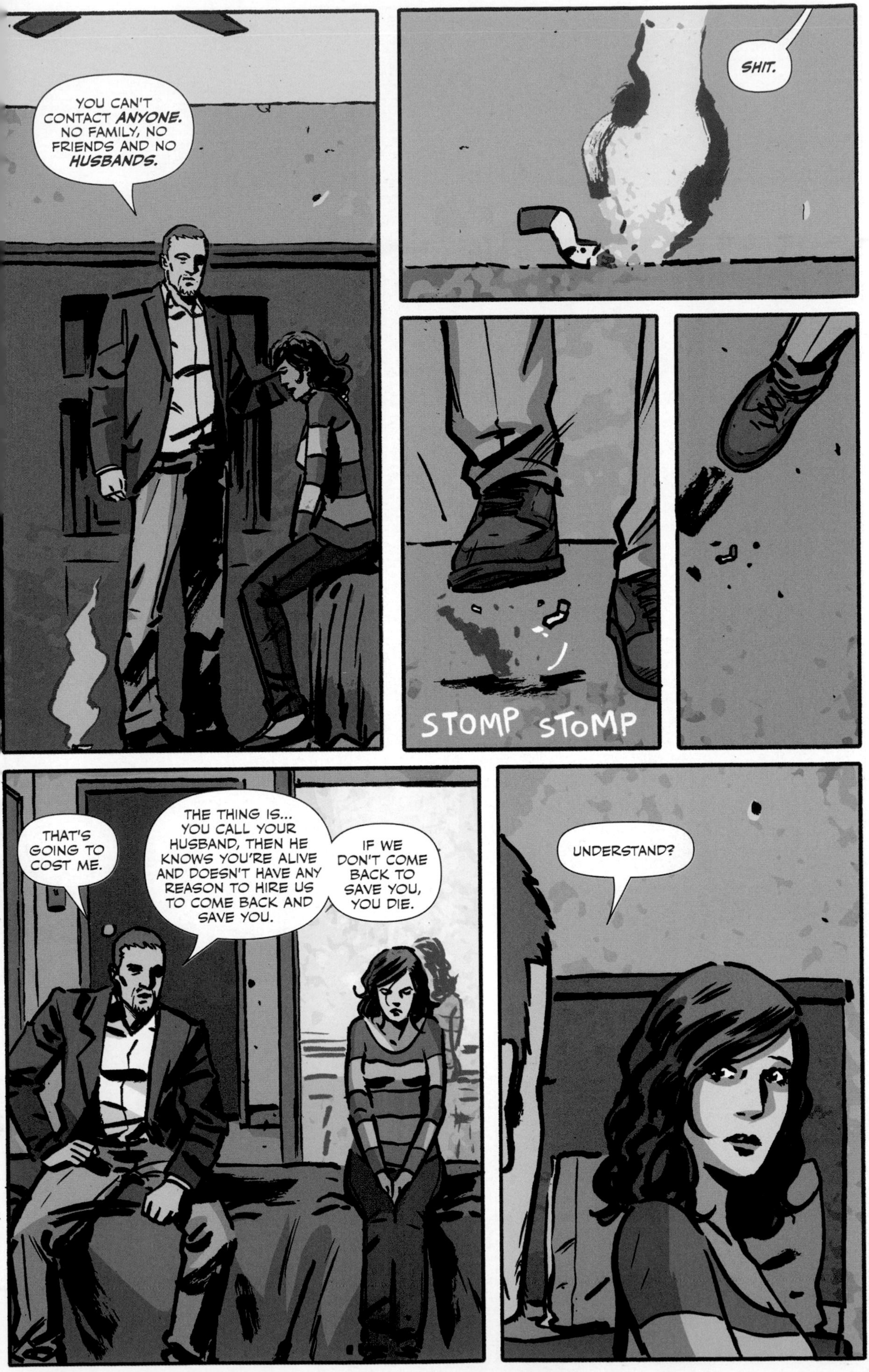
YOU CAN'T CONTACT ANYONE. NO FAMILY, NO FRIENDS AND NO HUSBANDS.
SHIT.
STOMP STOMP
THAT'S GOING TO COST ME.
THE THING IS... YOU CALL YOUR HUSBAND, THEN HE KNOWS YOU'RE ALIVE AND DOESN'T HAVE ANY REASON TO HIRE US TO COME BACK AND SAVE YOU.
IF WE DON'T COME BACK TO SAVE YOU, YOU DIE.
UNDERSTAND?

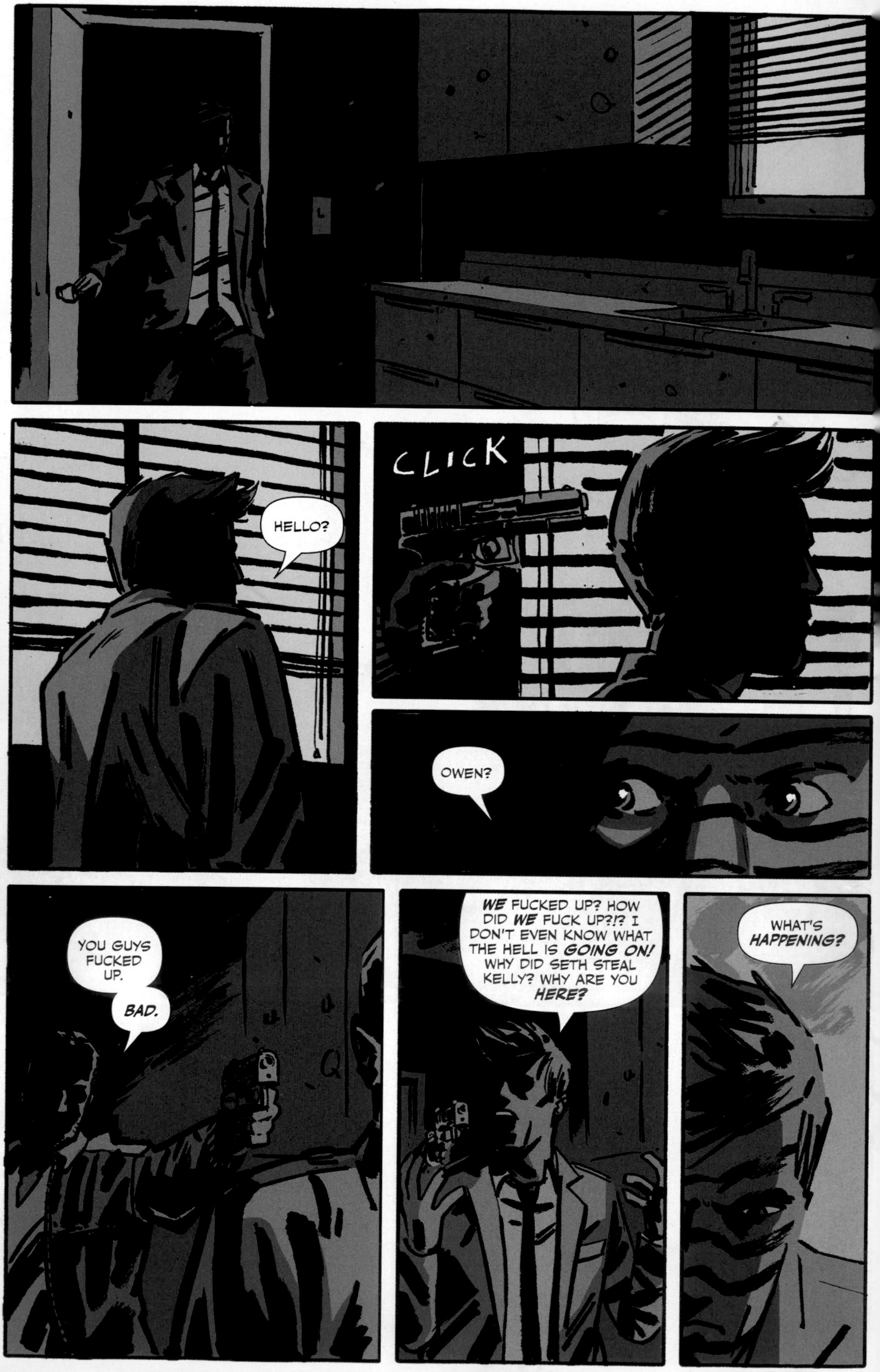
HELLO?
CLICK
OWEN?
YOU GUYS FUCKED UP.
BAD.
WE FUCKED UP? HOW DID WE FUCK UP?!? I DON'T EVEN KNOW WHAT THE HELL IS GOING ON! WHY DID SETH STEAL KELLY? WHY ARE YOU HERE?
WHAT'S HAPPENING?

SETH SOLD US OUT.

I DON'T BELIEVE YOU.

I DON'T GIVE A SHIT IF YOU BELIEVE ME.

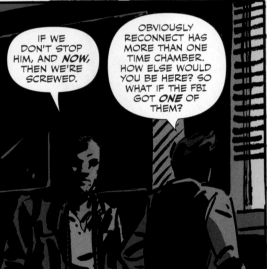

THE FBI SHUT DOWN ONE OF OUR MACHINES. MY MAN ON THE INSIDE TELLS ME IT WAS SETH THAT WAS FEEDING THEM INFO.

IF WE DON'T STOP HIM, AND *NOW,* THEN WE'RE SCREWED.

OBVIOUSLY RECONNECT HAS MORE THAN ONE TIME CHAMBER. HOW ELSE WOULD YOU BE HERE? SO WHAT IF THE FBI GOT *ONE* OF THEM?

THE "SO WHAT" IS THAT THEY KNOW *EVERYTHING* ABOUT RECONNECT. ABOUT ME. ABOUT TERRANCE. AND *YOU.*

I DON'T GIVE TWO SQUIRTS ABOUT LOSING ONE TIME MACHINE. WHAT I *DO* CARE ABOUT IS NOT GOING TO JAIL FOR THE REST OF MY GODDAMNED LIFE.

THEY SHUT DOWN RECONNECT AND WE *ALL* GO TO JAIL. THEN THE FBI TAKES EVERYONE YOU'VE RESCUED AND TOSSES THEM IN JAIL TOO.

OR *WORSE.*

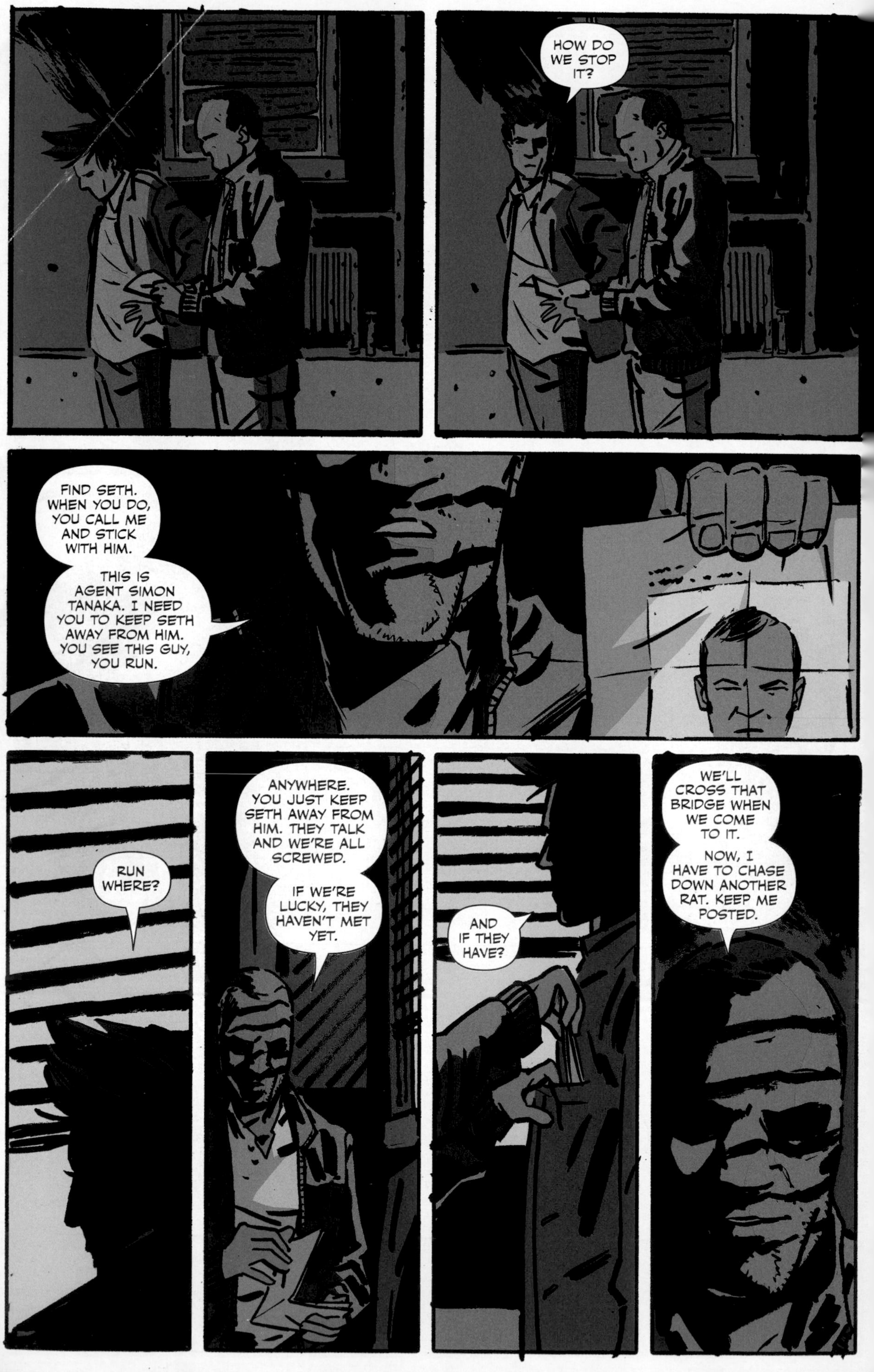
HOW DO WE STOP IT?
FIND SETH. WHEN YOU DO, YOU CALL ME AND STICK WITH HIM.
THIS IS AGENT SIMON TANAKA. I NEED YOU TO KEEP SETH AWAY FROM HIM. YOU SEE THIS GUY, YOU RUN.
RUN WHERE?
ANYWHERE. YOU JUST KEEP SETH AWAY FROM HIM. THEY TALK AND WE'RE ALL SCREWED.
IF WE'RE LUCKY, THEY HAVEN'T MET YET.
AND IF THEY HAVE?
WE'LL CROSS THAT BRIDGE WHEN WE COME TO IT.
NOW, I HAVE TO CHASE DOWN ANOTHER RAT. KEEP ME POSTED.

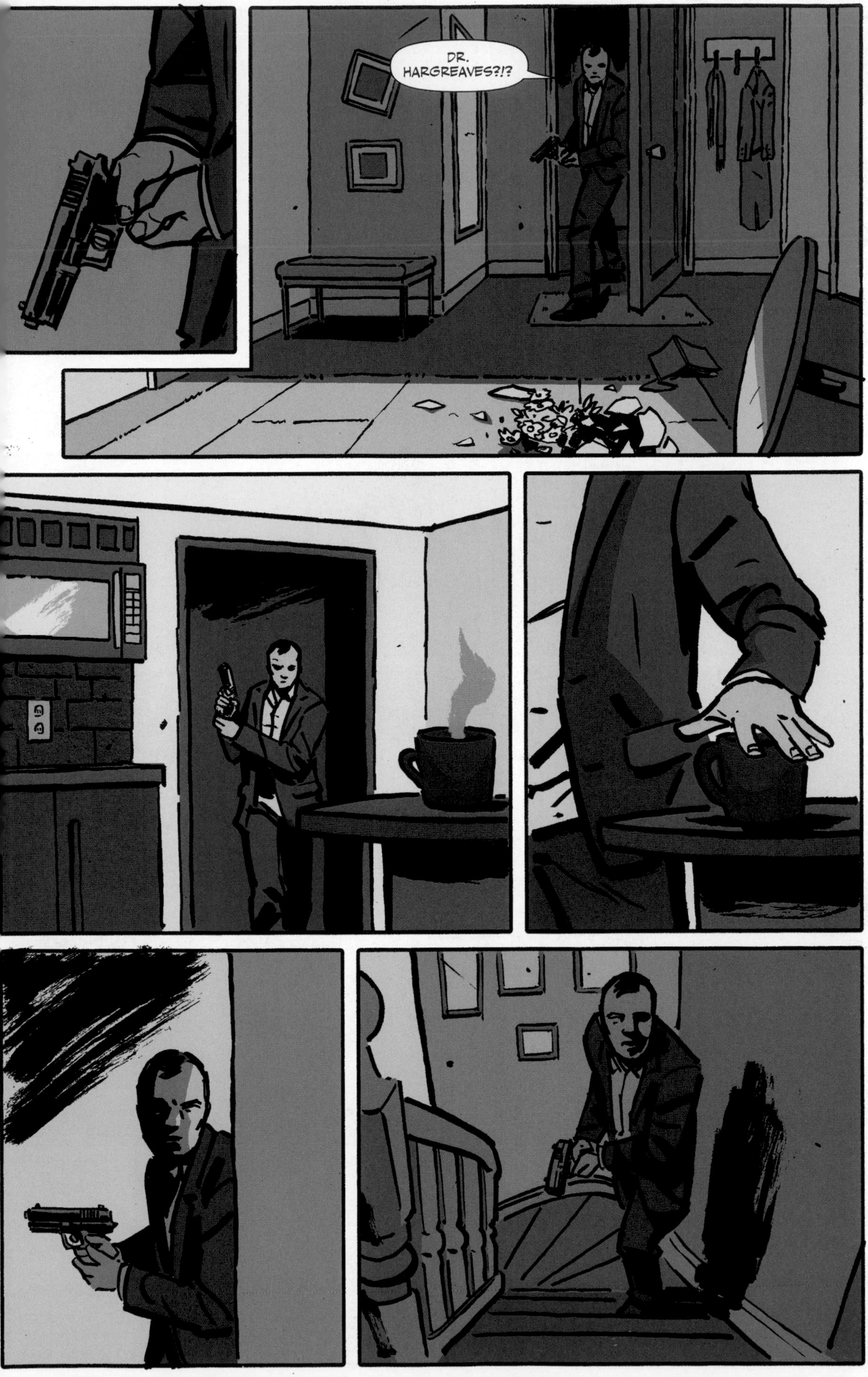
DR. HARGREAVES?!?

Recent Calls

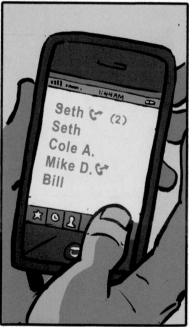

Seth (2)
Seth
Cole A.
Mike D.
Bill

HARGREAVES. YOU STUPID, BEAUTIFUL BASTARD.

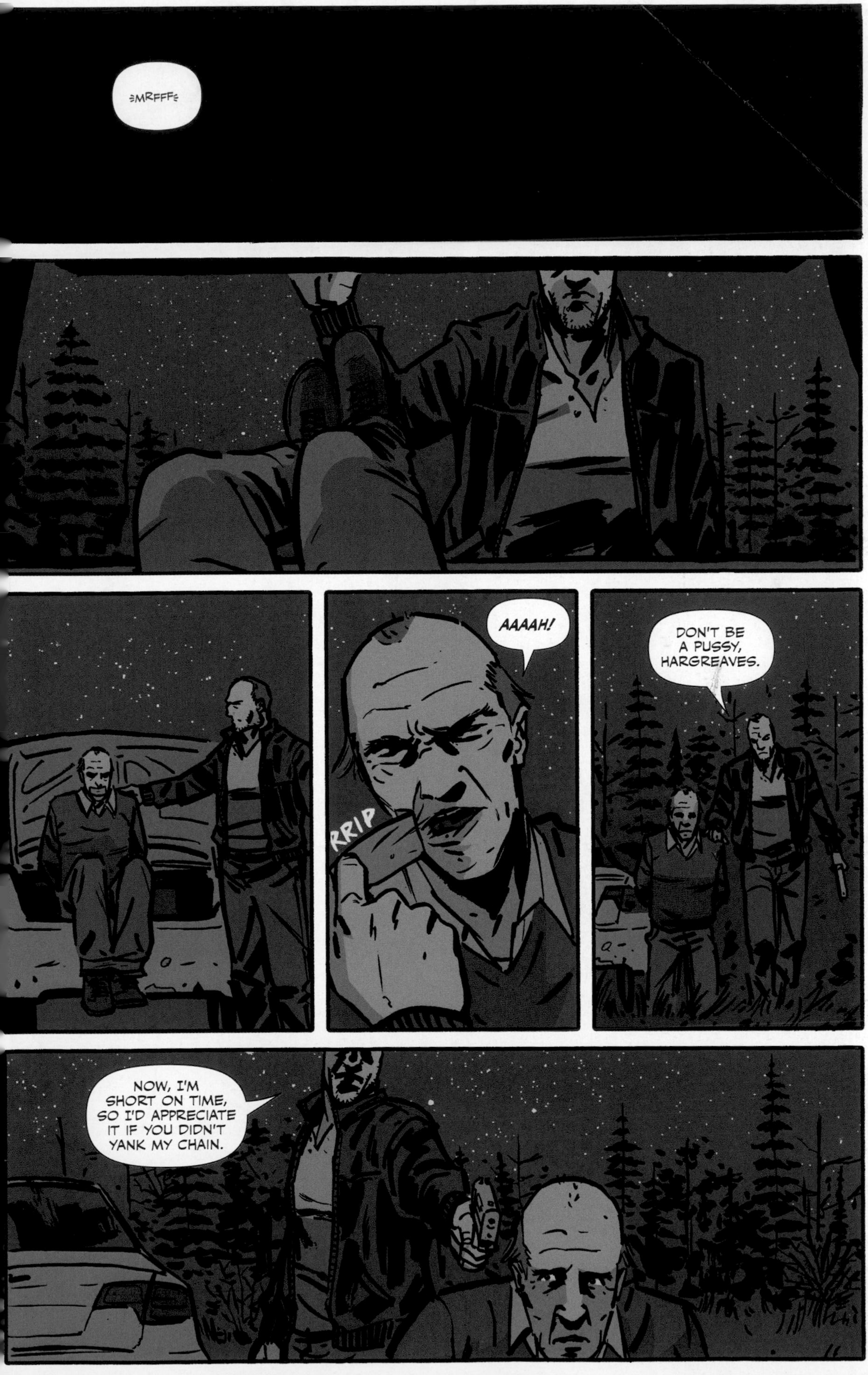
MRFFF
AAAAH!
RRIP
DON'T BE A PUSSY, HARGREAVES.
NOW, I'M SHORT ON TIME, SO I'D APPRECIATE IT IF YOU DIDN'T YANK MY CHAIN.

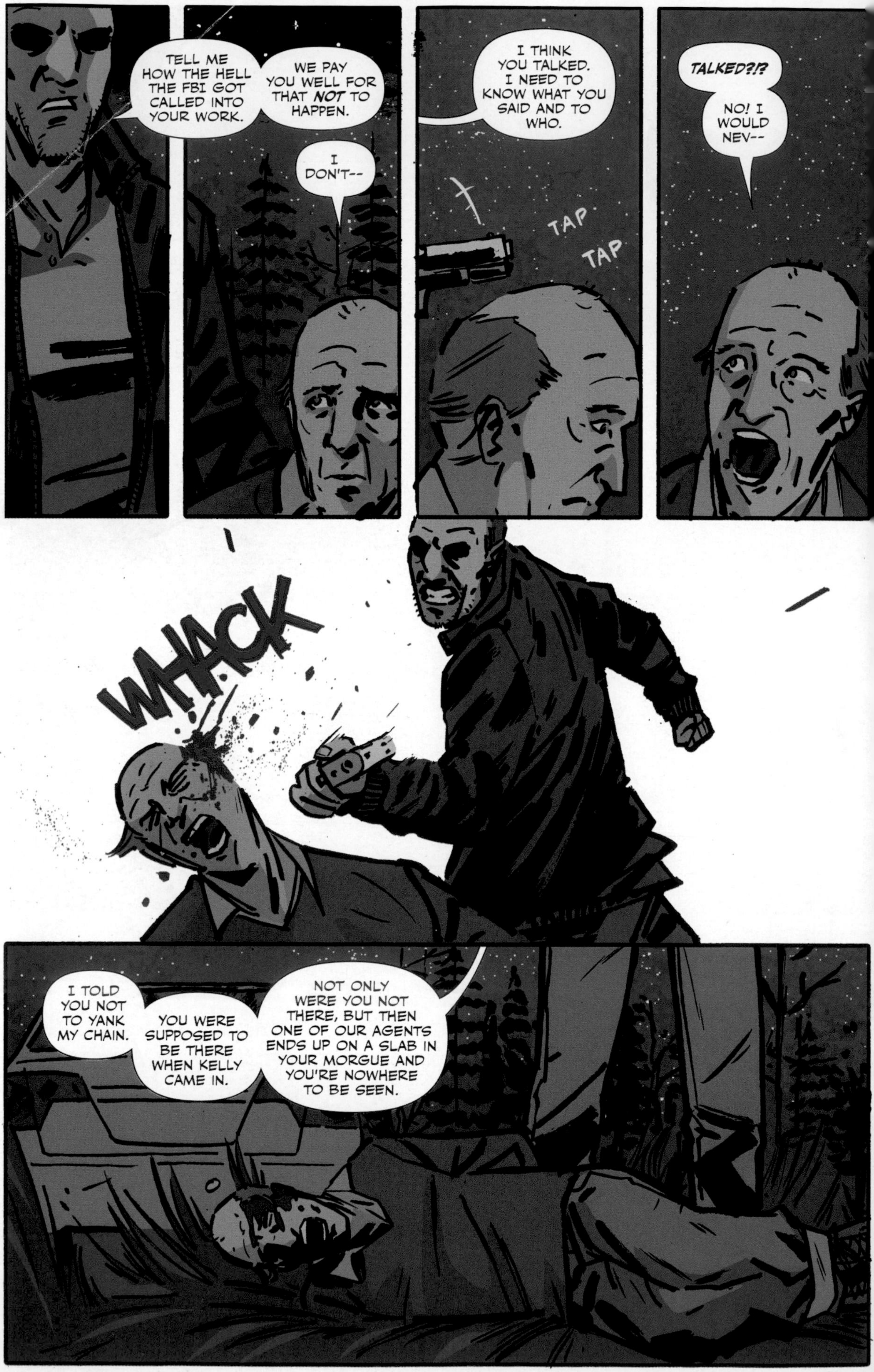
TELL ME HOW THE HELL THE FBI GOT CALLED INTO YOUR WORK.
WE PAY YOU WELL FOR THAT NOT TO HAPPEN.
I DON'T--
I THINK YOU TALKED. I NEED TO KNOW WHAT YOU SAID AND TO WHO.
TAP
TAP
TALKED?!?
NO! I WOULD NEV--
WHACK
I TOLD YOU NOT TO YANK MY CHAIN.
YOU WERE SUPPOSED TO BE THERE WHEN KELLY CAME IN.
NOT ONLY WERE YOU NOT THERE, BUT THEN ONE OF OUR AGENTS ENDS UP ON A SLAB IN YOUR MORGUE AND YOU'RE NOWHERE TO BE SEEN.

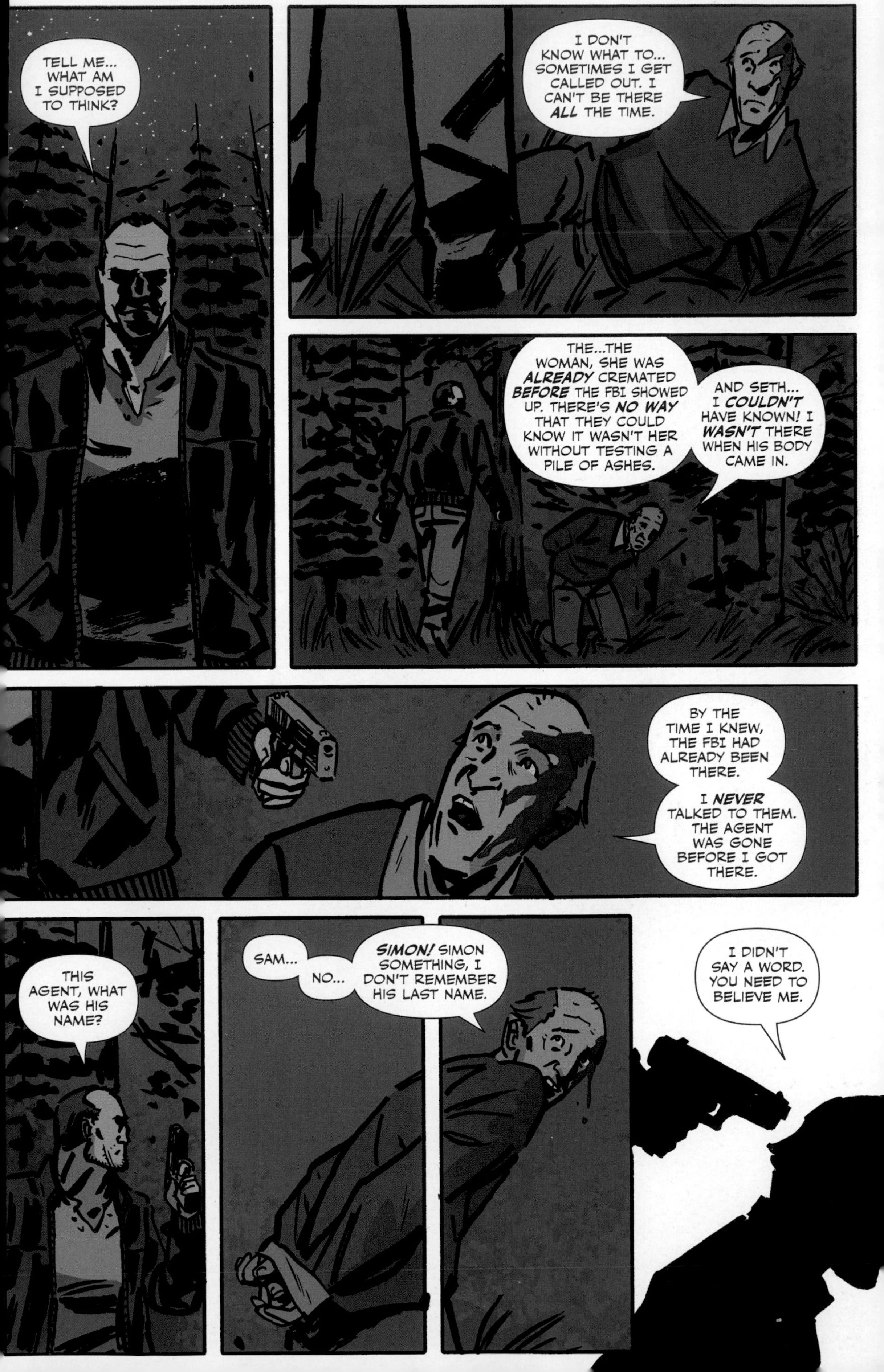
TELL ME... WHAT AM I SUPPOSED TO THINK?
I DON'T KNOW WHAT TO... SOMETIMES I GET CALLED OUT. I CAN'T BE THERE ALL THE TIME.
THE...THE WOMAN, SHE WAS ALREADY CREMATED BEFORE THE FBI SHOWED UP. THERE'S NO WAY THAT THEY COULD KNOW IT WASN'T HER WITHOUT TESTING A PILE OF ASHES.
AND SETH... I COULDN'T HAVE KNOWN! I WASN'T THERE WHEN HIS BODY CAME IN.
BY THE TIME I KNEW, THE FBI HAD ALREADY BEEN THERE.
I NEVER TALKED TO THEM. THE AGENT WAS GONE BEFORE I GOT THERE.
THIS AGENT, WHAT WAS HIS NAME?
SAM...
NO...
SIMON! SIMON SOMETHING, I DON'T REMEMBER HIS LAST NAME.
I DIDN'T SAY A WORD. YOU NEED TO BELIEVE ME.

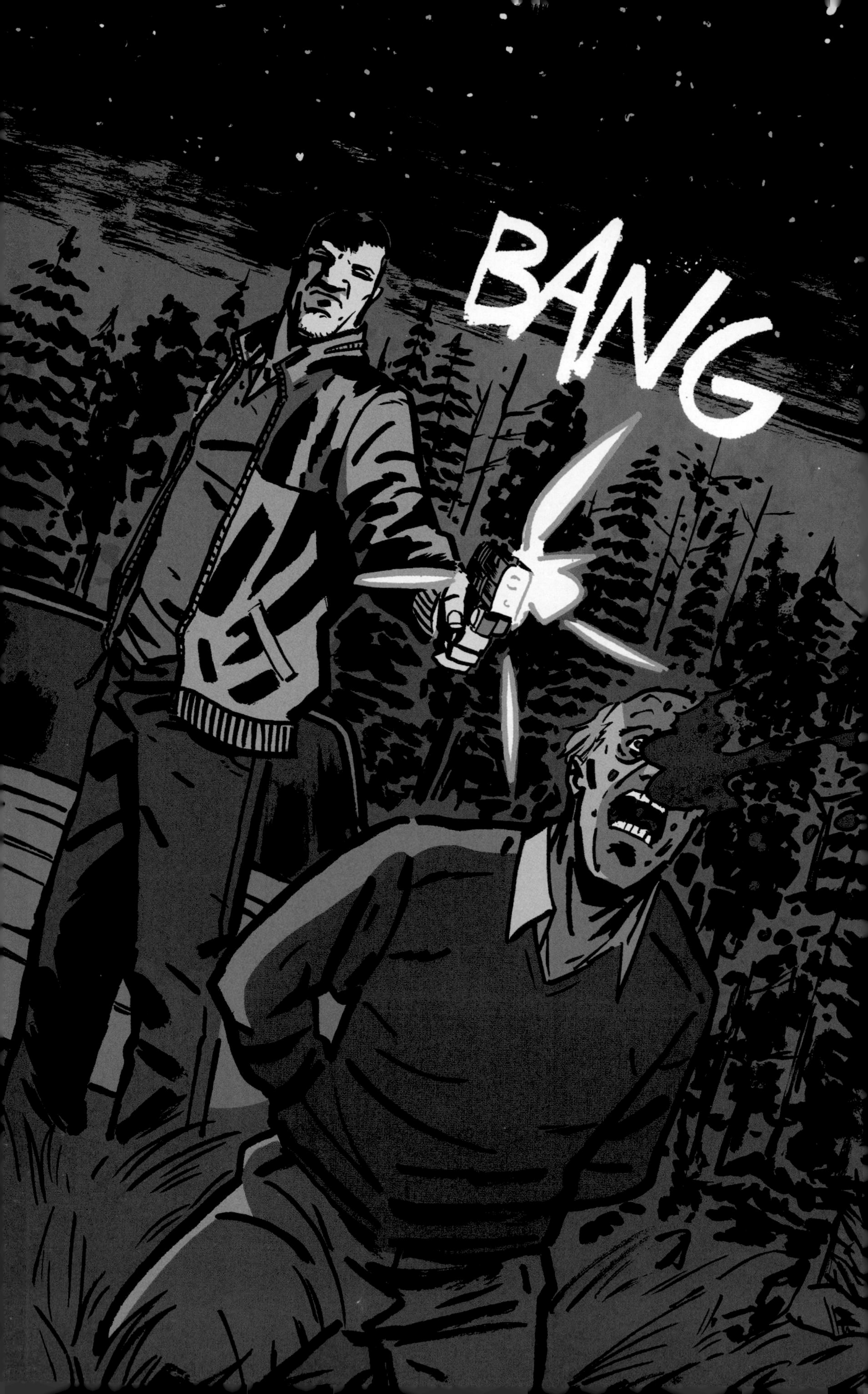
BANG

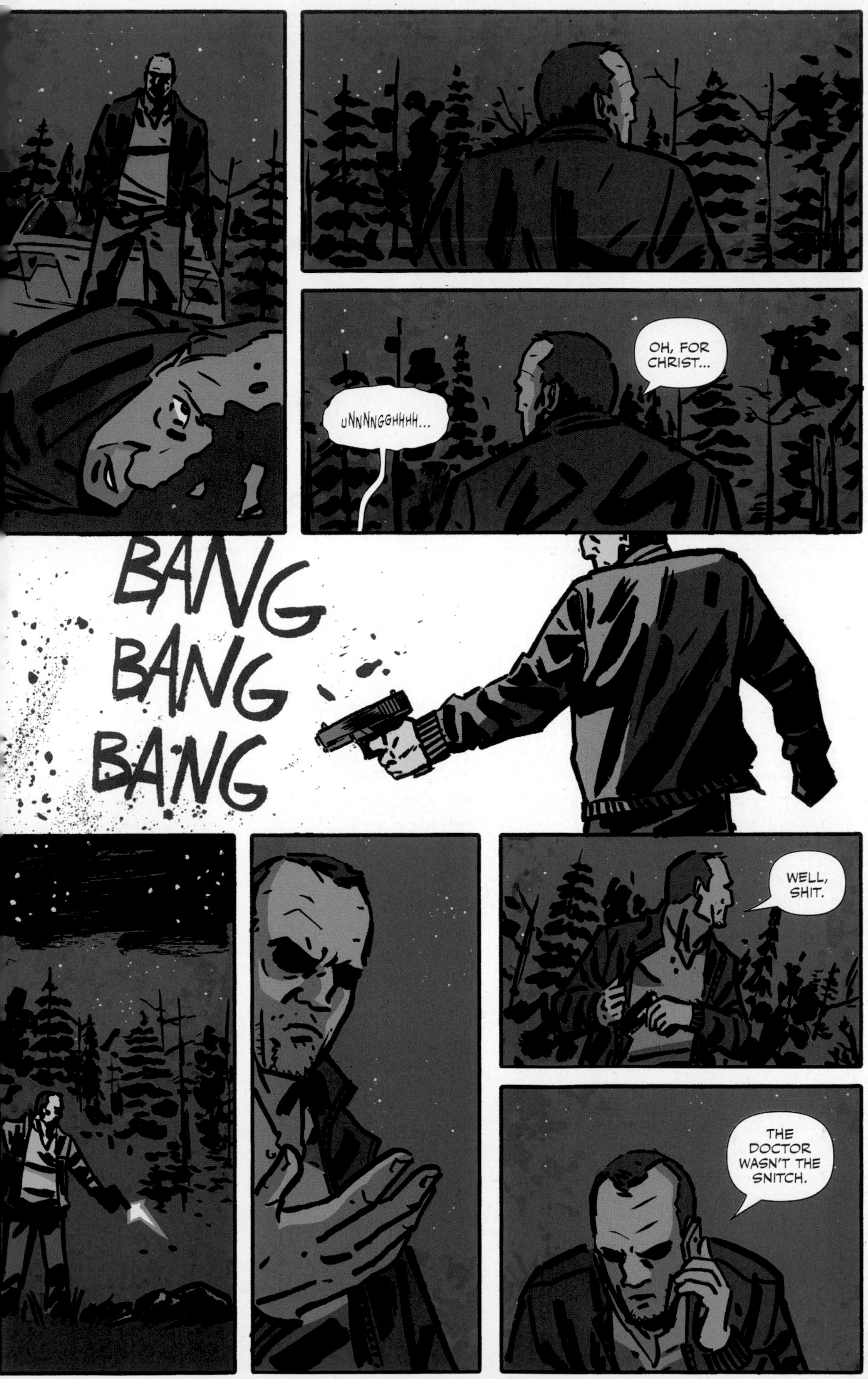
OH, FOR CHRIST...
UNNNNGGHHHH...
BANG
BANG
BANG
WELL, SHIT.
THE DOCTOR WASN'T THE SNITCH.

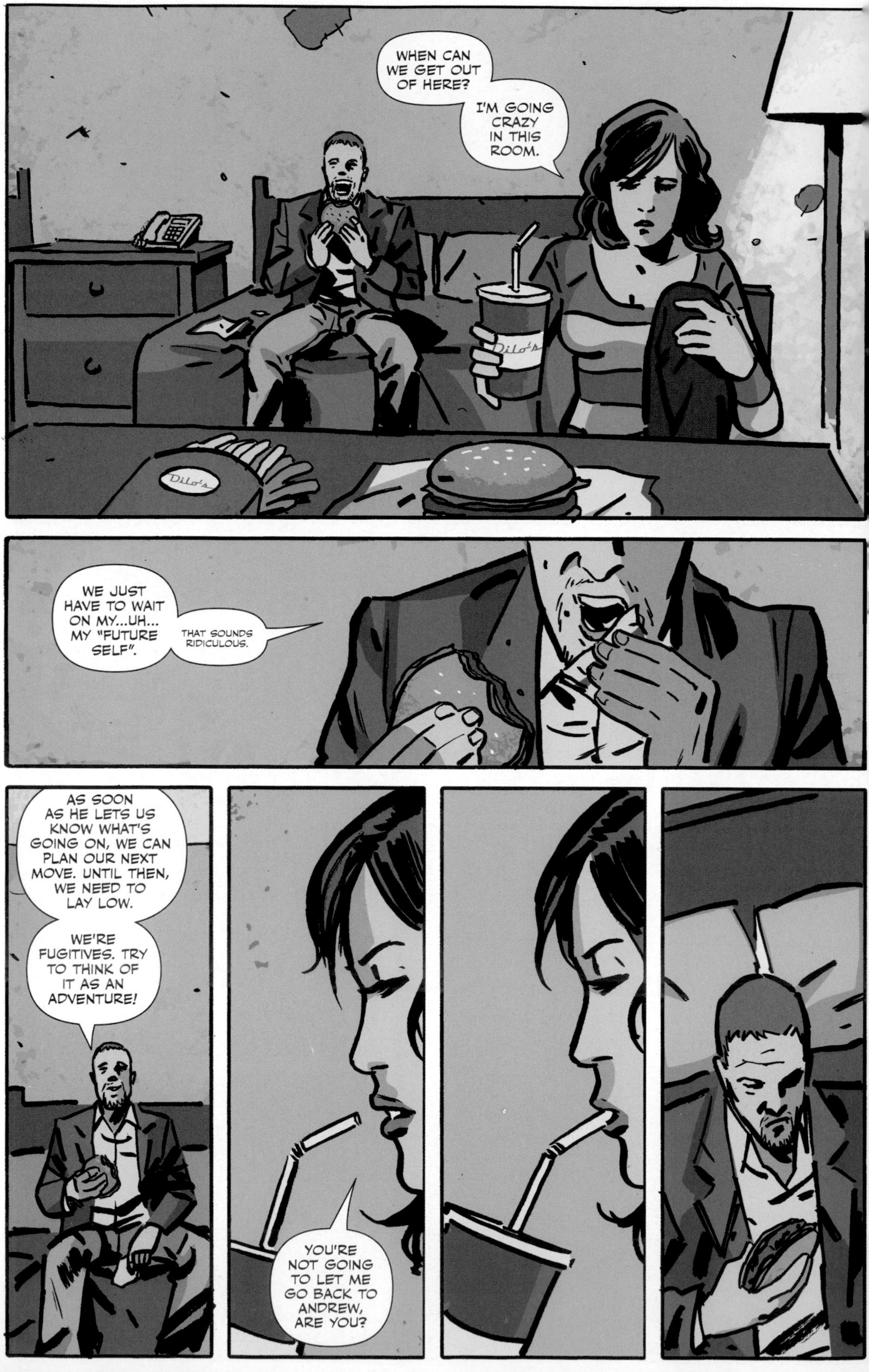

WHEN CAN WE GET OUT OF HERE?
I'M GOING CRAZY IN THIS ROOM.
Dilo's
Dilo's
WE JUST HAVE TO WAIT ON MY...UH... MY "FUTURE SELF".
THAT SOUNDS RIDICULOUS.
AS SOON AS HE LETS US KNOW WHAT'S GOING ON, WE CAN PLAN OUR NEXT MOVE. UNTIL THEN, WE NEED TO LAY LOW.
WE'RE FUGITIVES. TRY TO THINK OF IT AS AN ADVENTURE!
YOU'RE NOT GOING TO LET ME GO BACK TO ANDREW, ARE YOU?

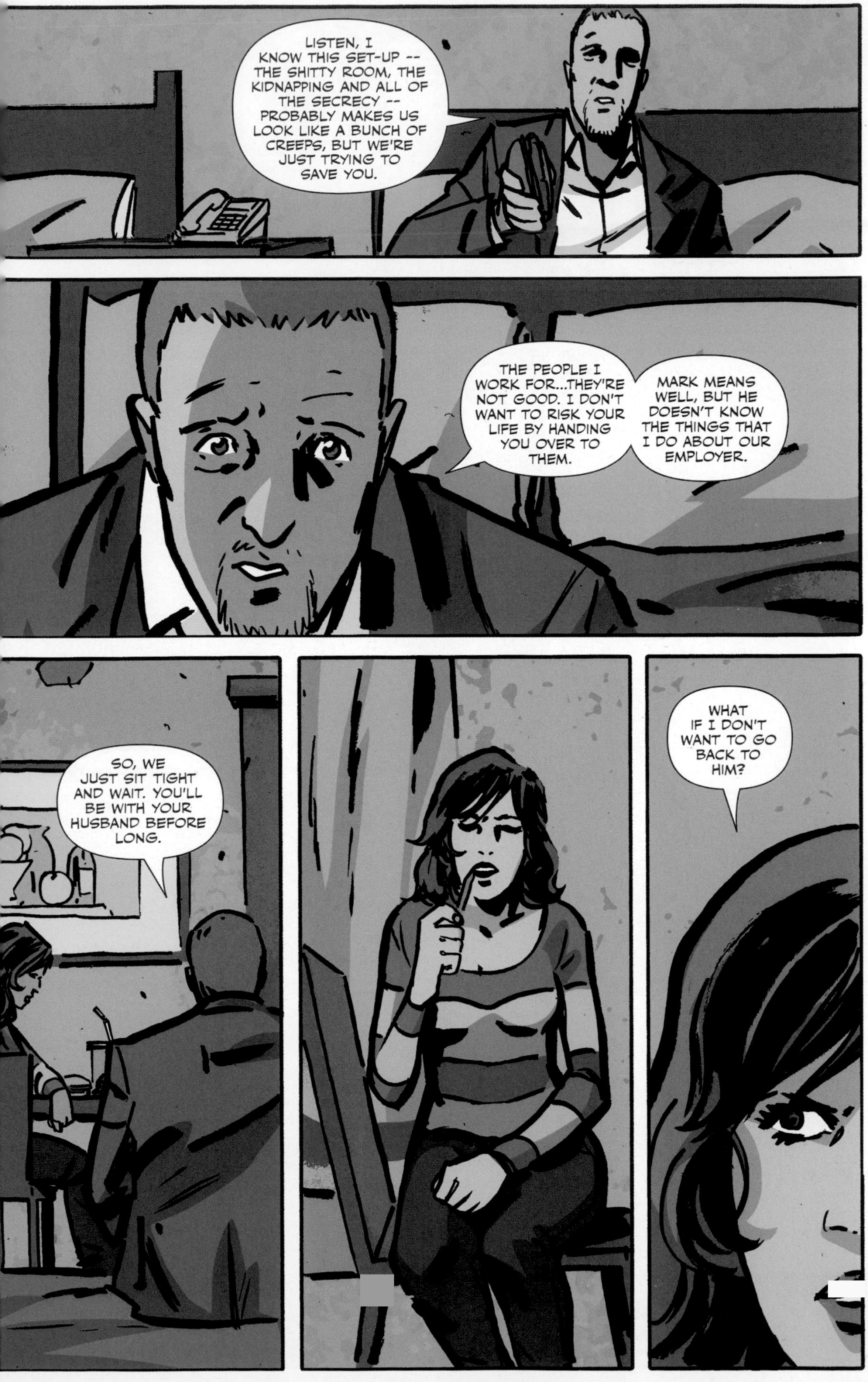
LISTEN, I KNOW THIS SET-UP -- THE SHITTY ROOM, THE KIDNAPPING AND ALL OF THE SECRECY -- PROBABLY MAKES US LOOK LIKE A BUNCH OF CREEPS, BUT WE'RE JUST TRYING TO SAVE YOU.
THE PEOPLE I WORK FOR...THEY'RE NOT GOOD. I DON'T WANT TO RISK YOUR LIFE BY HANDING YOU OVER TO THEM.
MARK MEANS WELL, BUT HE DOESN'T KNOW THE THINGS THAT I DO ABOUT OUR EMPLOYER.
SO, WE JUST SIT TIGHT AND WAIT. YOU'LL BE WITH YOUR HUSBAND BEFORE LONG.
WHAT IF I DON'T WANT TO GO BACK TO HIM?

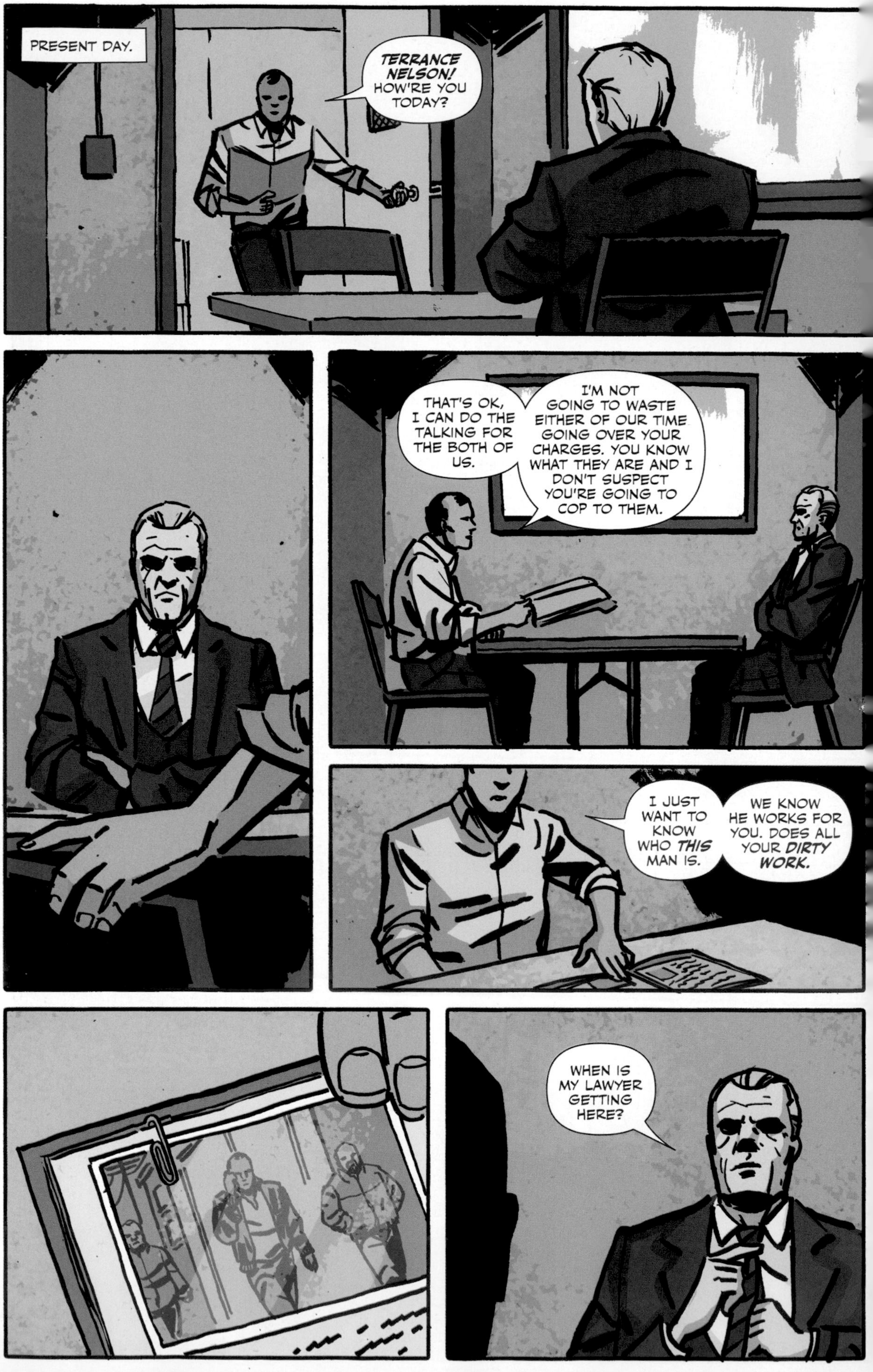
PRESENT DAY.
TERRANCE NELSON! HOW'RE YOU TODAY?
THAT'S OK, I CAN DO THE TALKING FOR THE BOTH OF US.
I'M NOT GOING TO WASTE EITHER OF OUR TIME GOING OVER YOUR CHARGES. YOU KNOW WHAT THEY ARE AND I DON'T SUSPECT YOU'RE GOING TO COP TO THEM.
I JUST WANT TO KNOW WHO *THIS* MAN IS.
WE KNOW HE WORKS FOR YOU. DOES ALL YOUR *DIRTY WORK.*
WHEN IS MY LAWYER GETTING HERE?

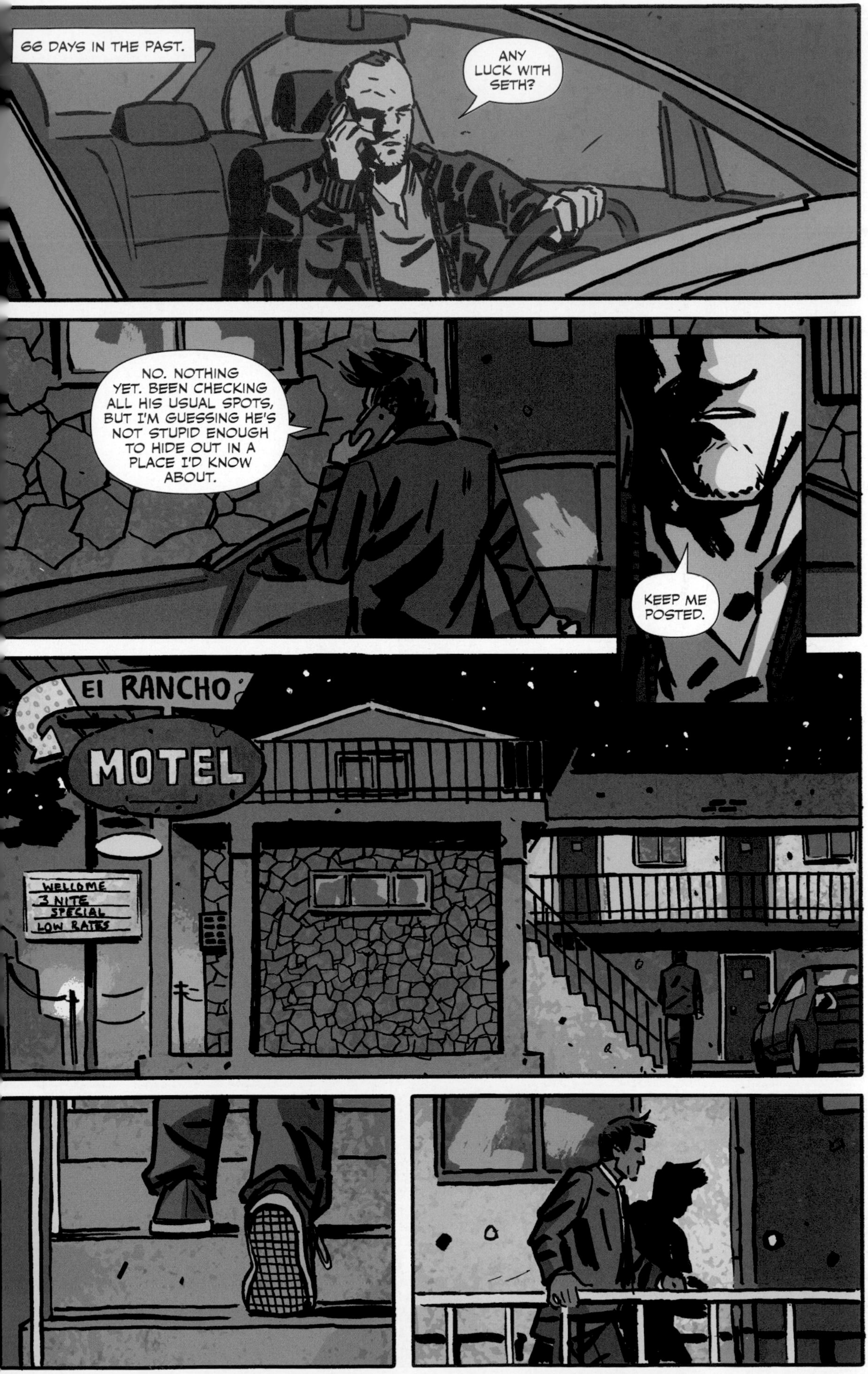
66 DAYS IN THE PAST.
ANY LUCK WITH SETH?
NO. NOTHING YET. BEEN CHECKING ALL HIS USUAL SPOTS, BUT I'M GUESSING HE'S NOT STUPID ENOUGH TO HIDE OUT IN A PLACE I'D KNOW ABOUT.
KEEP ME POSTED.
EI RANCHO
MOTEL
WELLOME
3 NITE
SPECIAL
LOW RATES

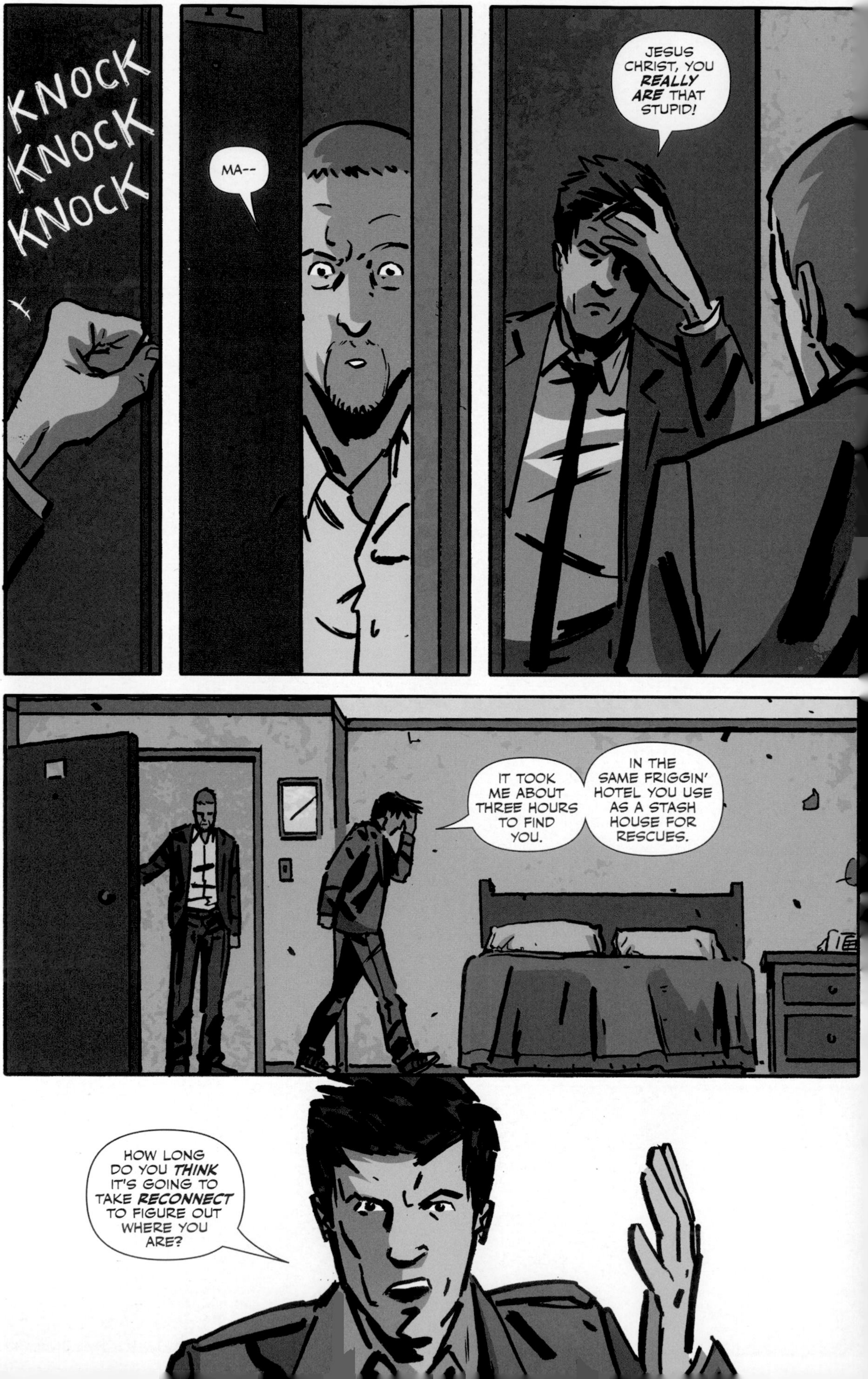
KNOCK KNOCK KNOCK
MA--
JESUS CHRIST, YOU REALLY ARE THAT STUPID!
IT TOOK ME ABOUT THREE HOURS TO FIND YOU.
IN THE SAME FRIGGIN' HOTEL YOU USE AS A STASH HOUSE FOR RESCUES.
HOW LONG DO YOU THINK IT'S GOING TO TAKE RECONNECT TO FIGURE OUT WHERE YOU ARE?

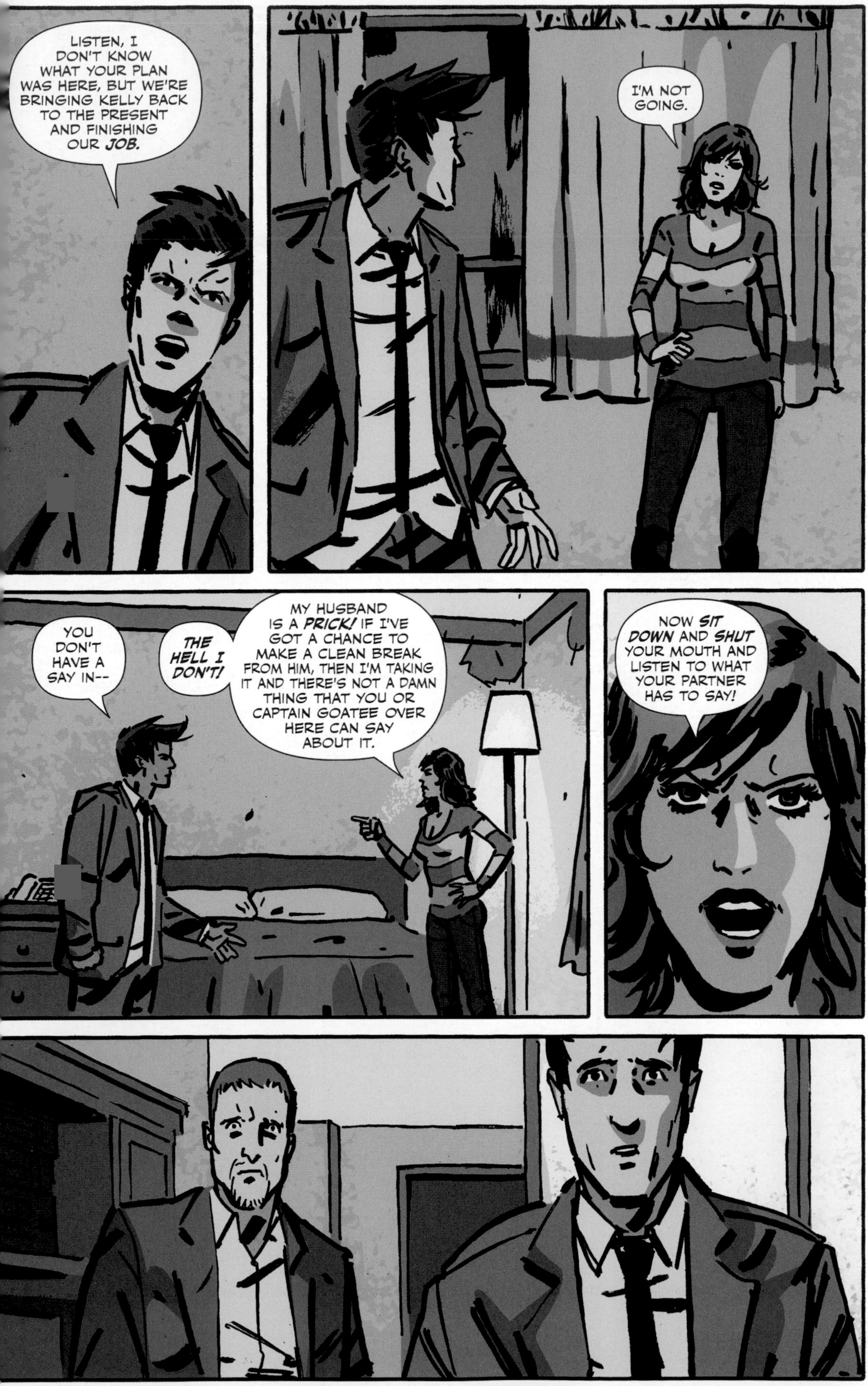
LISTEN, I DON'T KNOW WHAT YOUR PLAN WAS HERE, BUT WE'RE BRINGING KELLY BACK TO THE PRESENT AND FINISHING OUR JOB.
I'M NOT GOING.
YOU DON'T HAVE A SAY IN--
THE HELL I DON'T!
MY HUSBAND IS A PRICK! IF I'VE GOT A CHANCE TO MAKE A CLEAN BREAK FROM HIM, THEN I'M TAKING IT AND THERE'S NOT A DAMN THING THAT YOU OR CAPTAIN GOATEE OVER HERE CAN SAY ABOUT IT.
NOW SIT DOWN AND SHUT YOUR MOUTH AND LISTEN TO WHAT YOUR PARTNER HAS TO SAY!

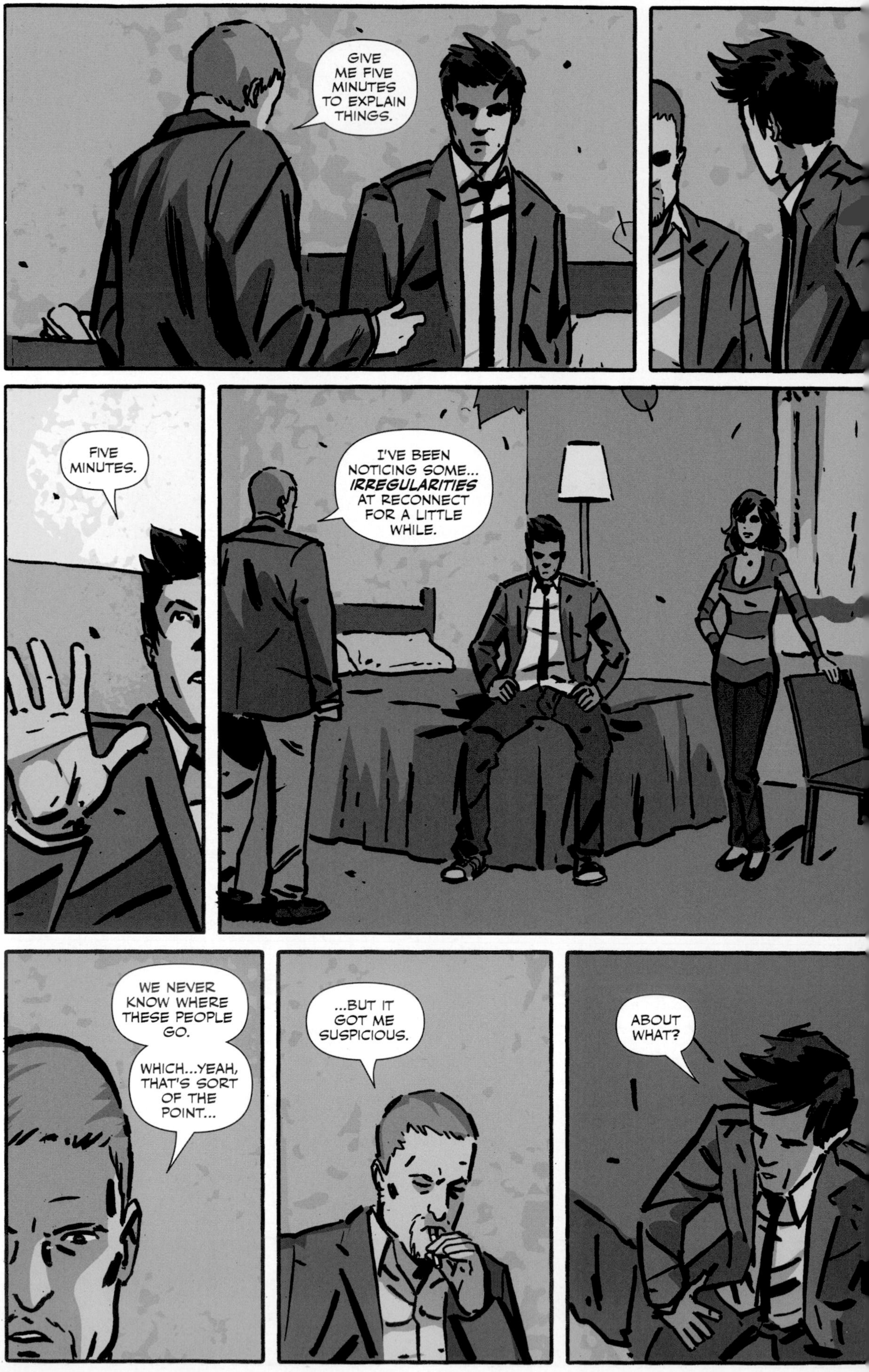
GIVE ME FIVE MINUTES TO EXPLAIN THINGS.
FIVE MINUTES.
I'VE BEEN NOTICING SOME... *IRREGULARITIES* AT RECONNECT FOR A LITTLE WHILE.
WE NEVER KNOW WHERE THESE PEOPLE GO.
WHICH...YEAH, THAT'S SORT OF THE POINT...
...BUT IT GOT ME SUSPICIOUS.
ABOUT WHAT?

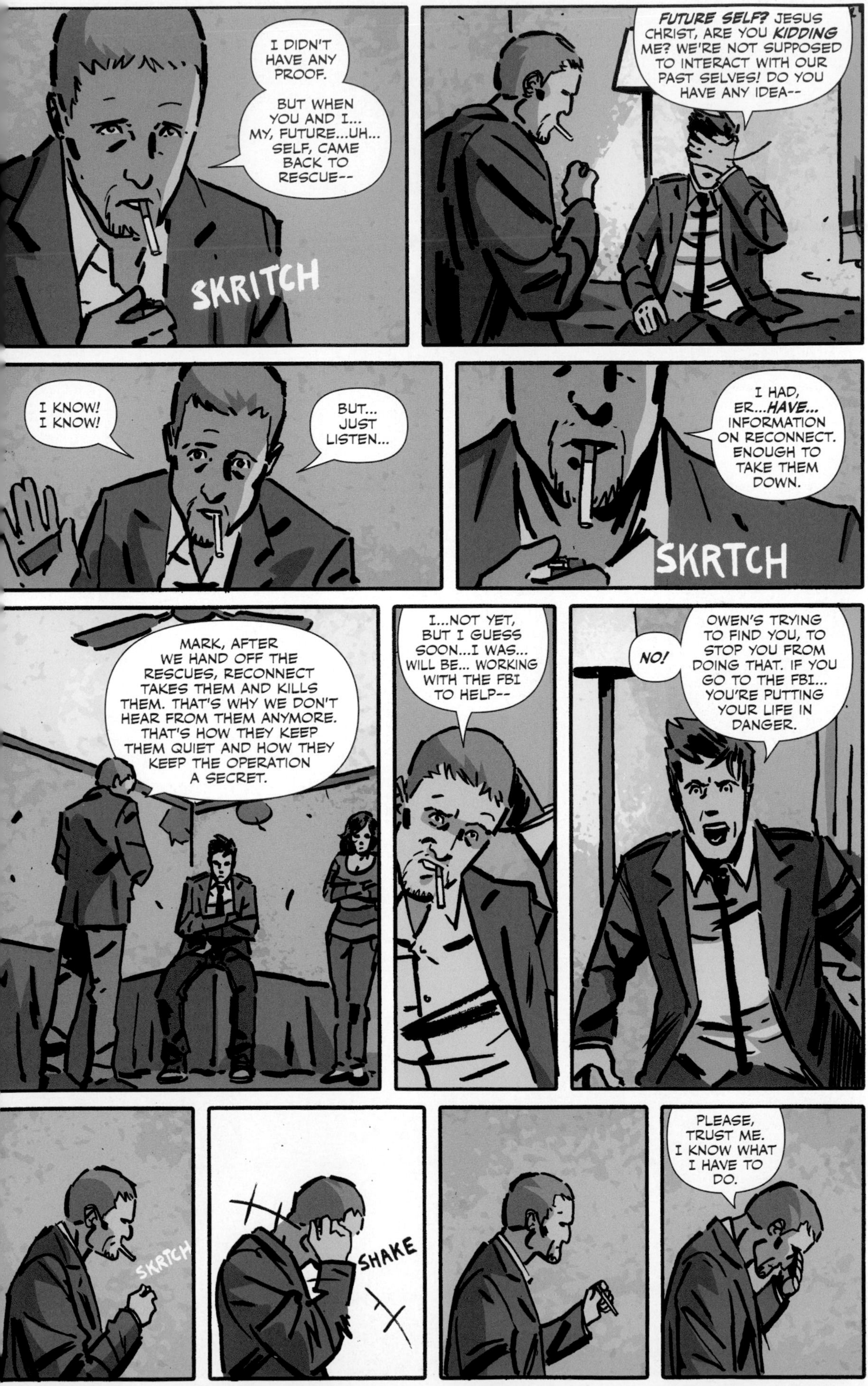
I DIDN'T HAVE ANY PROOF.
BUT WHEN YOU AND I... MY, FUTURE...UH... SELF, CAME BACK TO RESCUE--
SKRITCH
FUTURE SELF? JESUS CHRIST, ARE YOU KIDDING ME? WE'RE NOT SUPPOSED TO INTERACT WITH OUR PAST SELVES! DO YOU HAVE ANY IDEA--
I KNOW! I KNOW!
BUT... JUST LISTEN...
I HAD, ER...HAVE... INFORMATION ON RECONNECT. ENOUGH TO TAKE THEM DOWN.
SKRTCH
MARK, AFTER WE HAND OFF THE RESCUES, RECONNECT TAKES THEM AND KILLS THEM. THAT'S WHY WE DON'T HEAR FROM THEM ANYMORE. THAT'S HOW THEY KEEP THEM QUIET AND HOW THEY KEEP THE OPERATION A SECRET.
I...NOT YET, BUT I GUESS SOON...I WAS... WILL BE... WORKING WITH THE FBI TO HELP--
NO!
OWEN'S TRYING TO FIND YOU, TO STOP YOU FROM DOING THAT. IF YOU GO TO THE FBI... YOU'RE PUTTING YOUR LIFE IN DANGER.
SKRTCH
SHAKE
PLEASE, TRUST ME. I KNOW WHAT I HAVE TO DO.

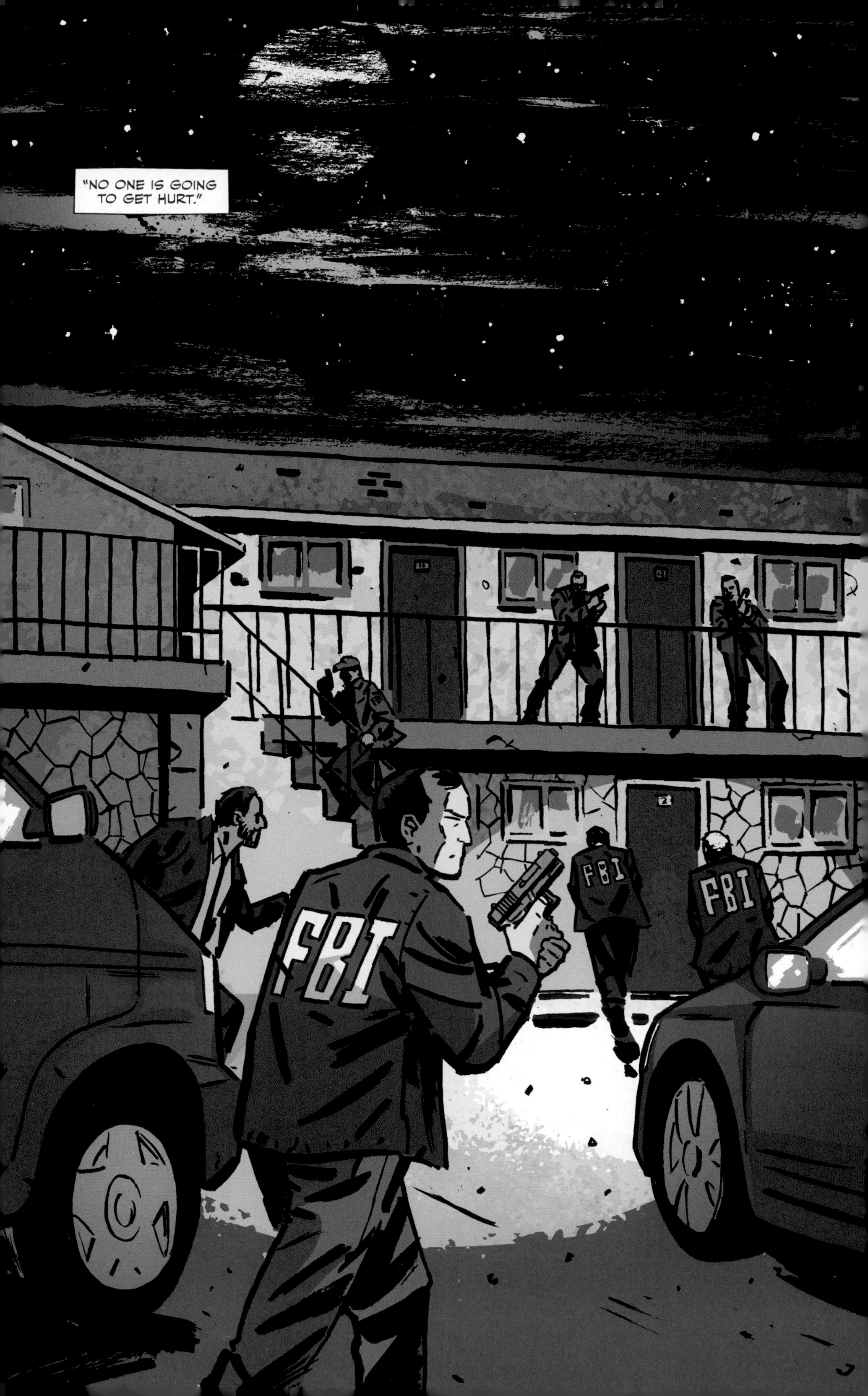
"NO ONE IS GOING TO GET HURT."
FBI
FBI
FBI
FBI
2

CHAPTER FOUR

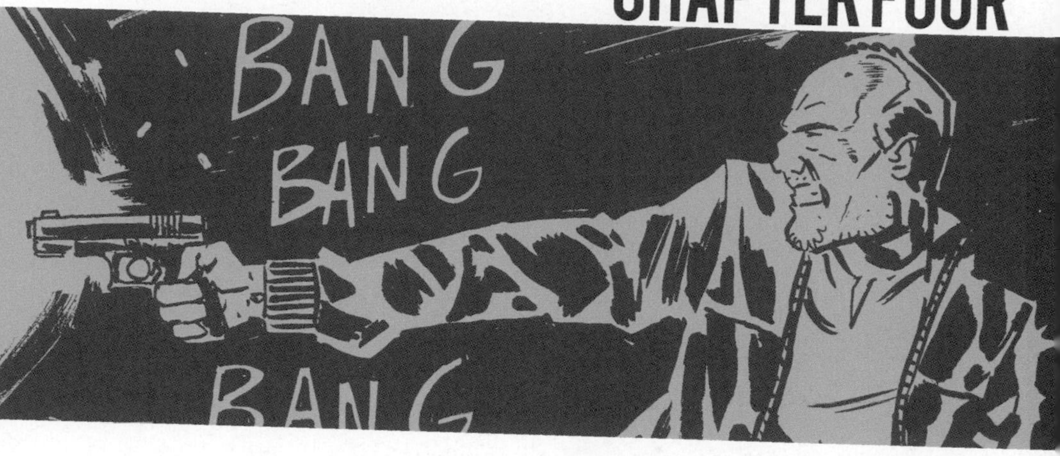
BANG
BANG
BANG

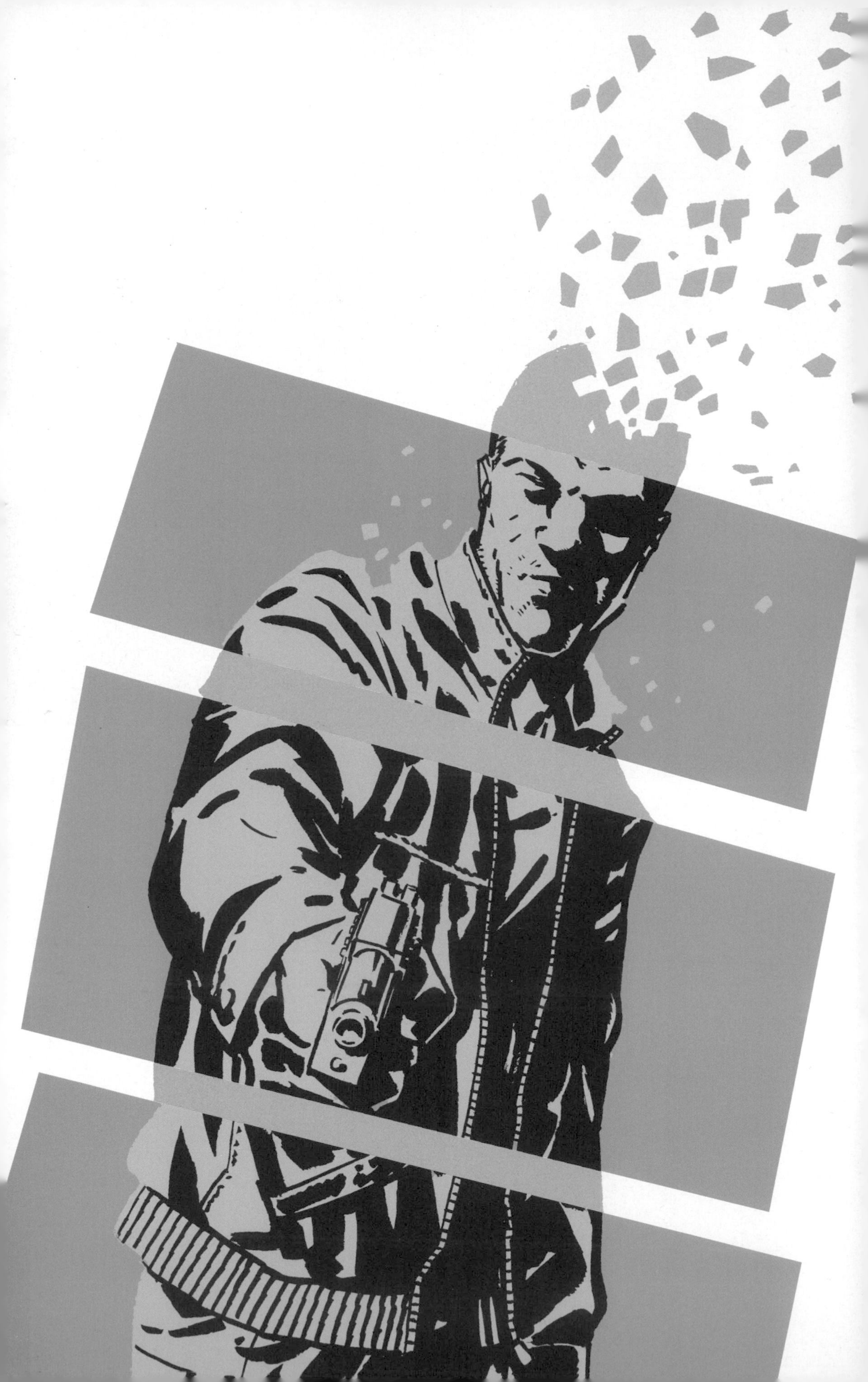

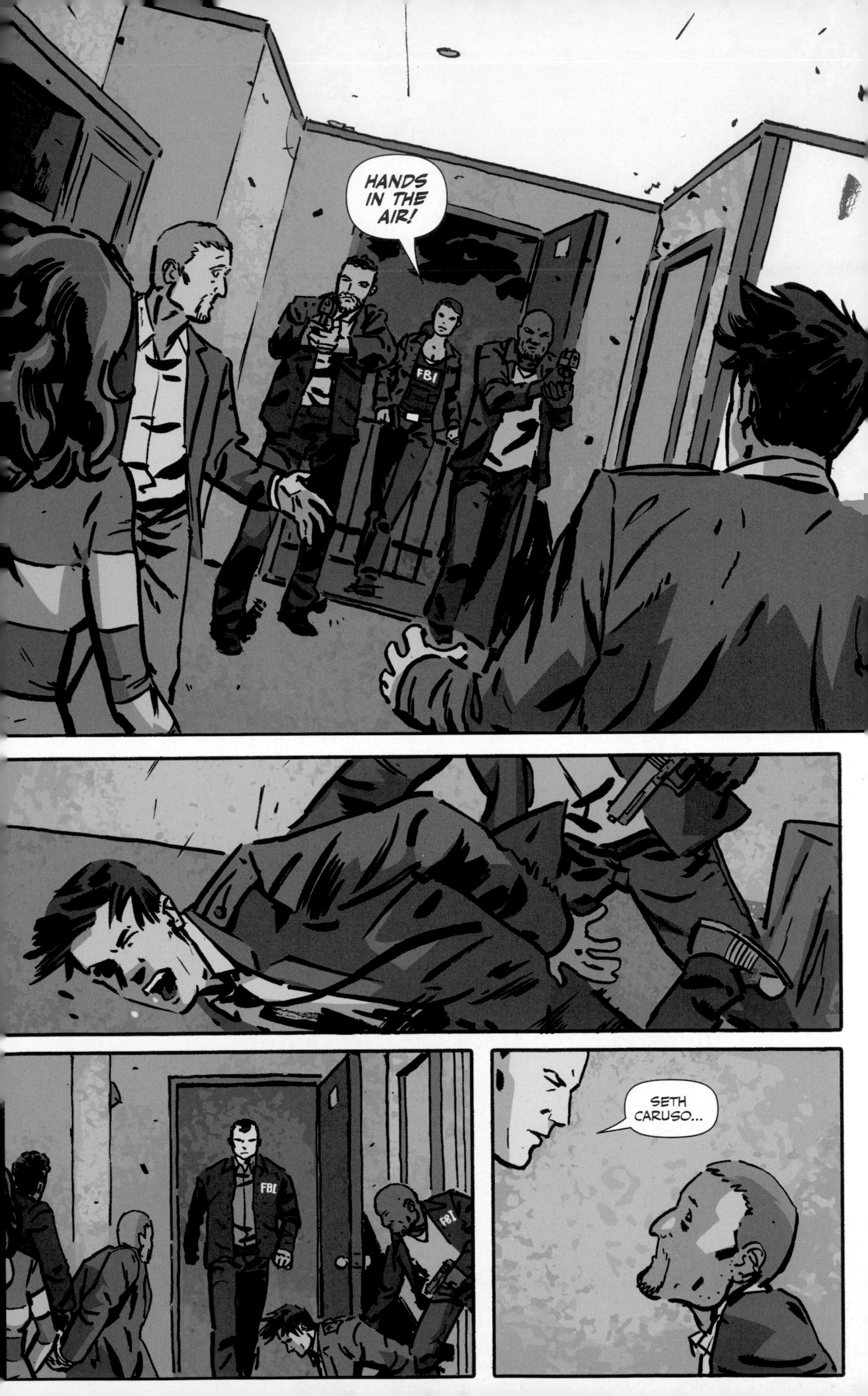
HANDS IN THE AIR!
FBI
FBI
FBI
SETH CARUSO...

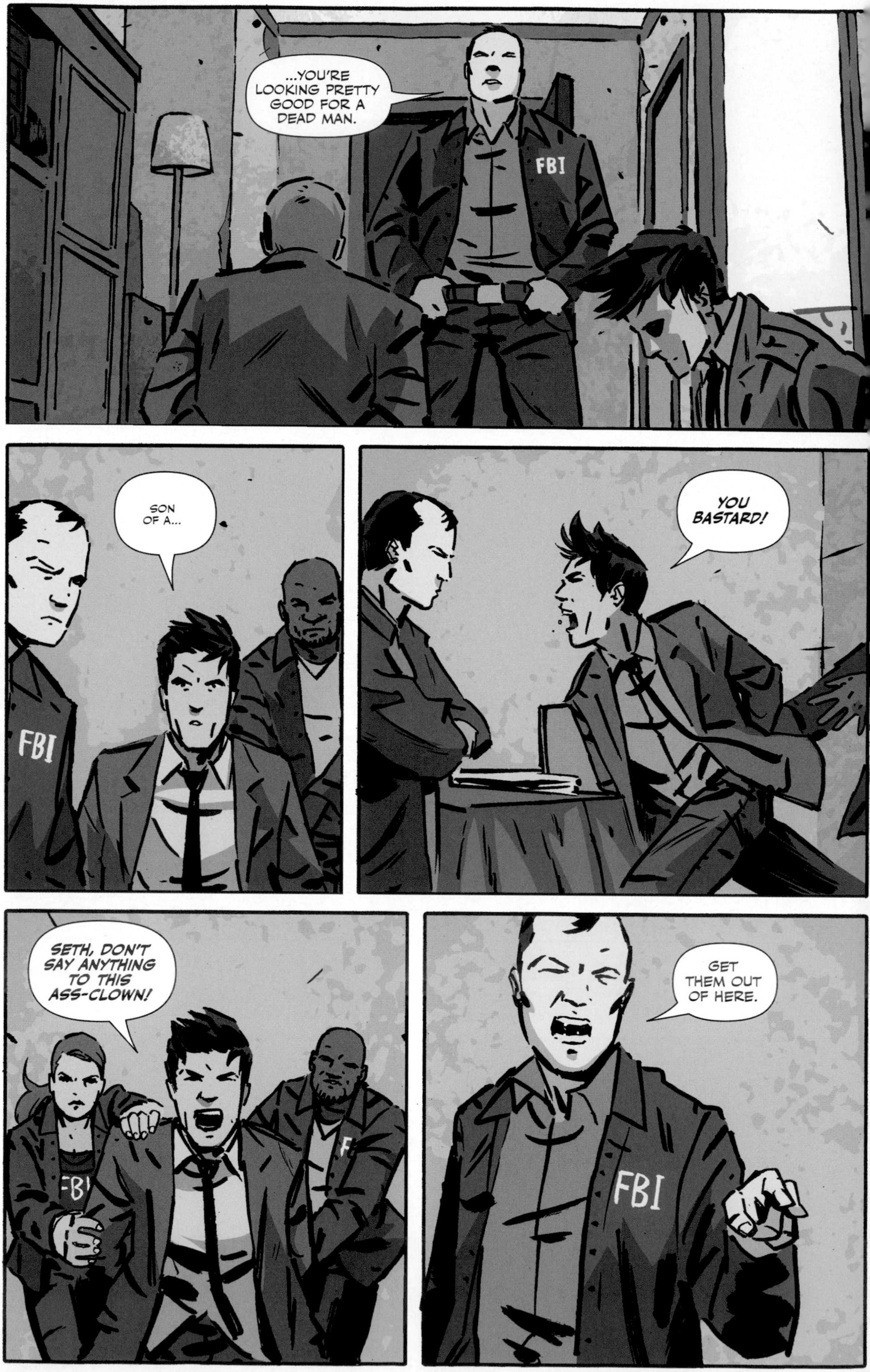
...YOU'RE LOOKING PRETTY GOOD FOR A DEAD MAN.
SON OF A...
YOU BASTARD!
SETH, DON'T SAY ANYTHING TO THIS ASS-CLOWN!
GET THEM OUT OF HERE.

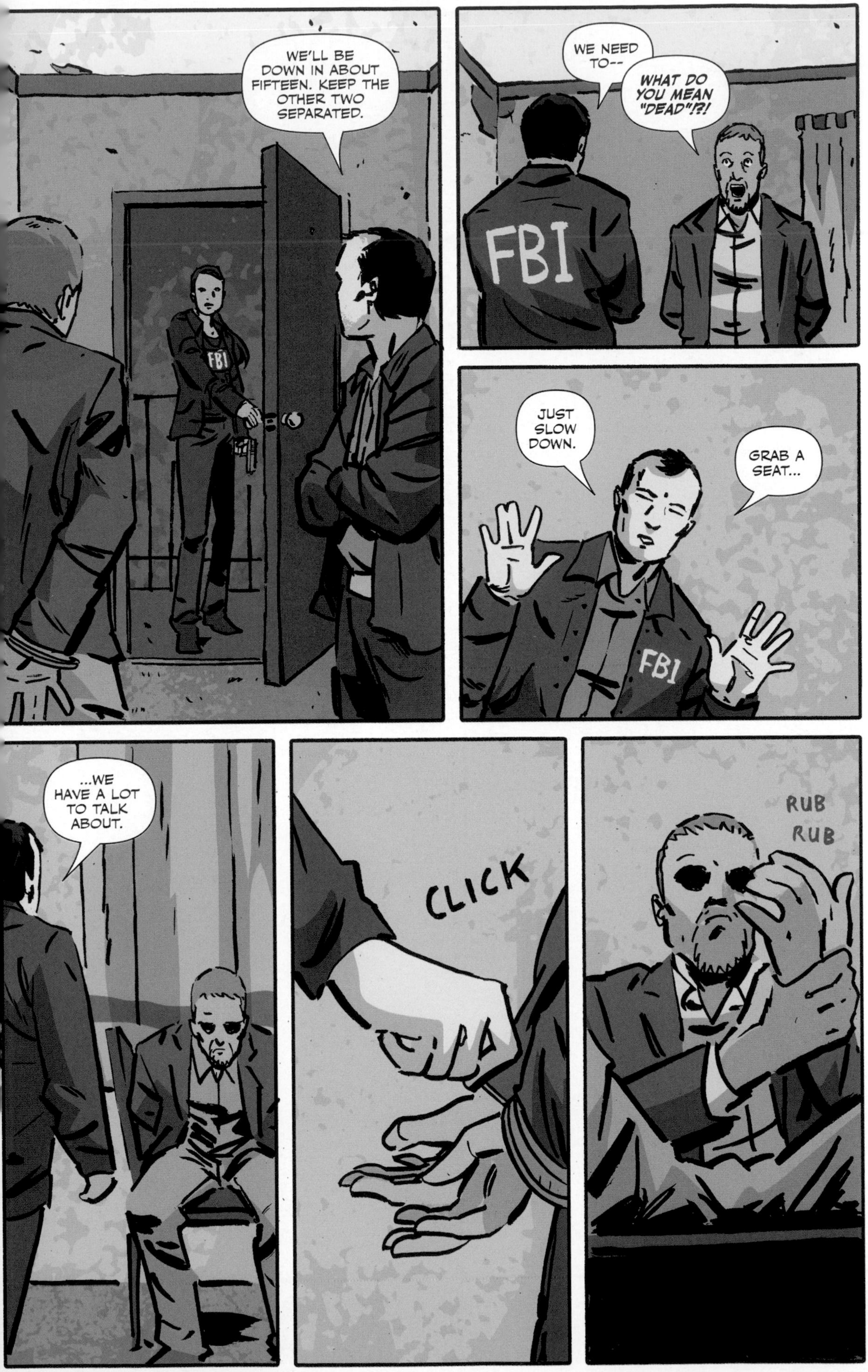
WE'LL BE DOWN IN ABOUT FIFTEEN. KEEP THE OTHER TWO SEPARATED.
WE NEED TO--
WHAT DO YOU MEAN "DEAD"!?!
FBI
JUST SLOW DOWN.
GRAB A SEAT...
FBI
...WE HAVE A LOT TO TALK ABOUT.
CLICK
RUB
RUB

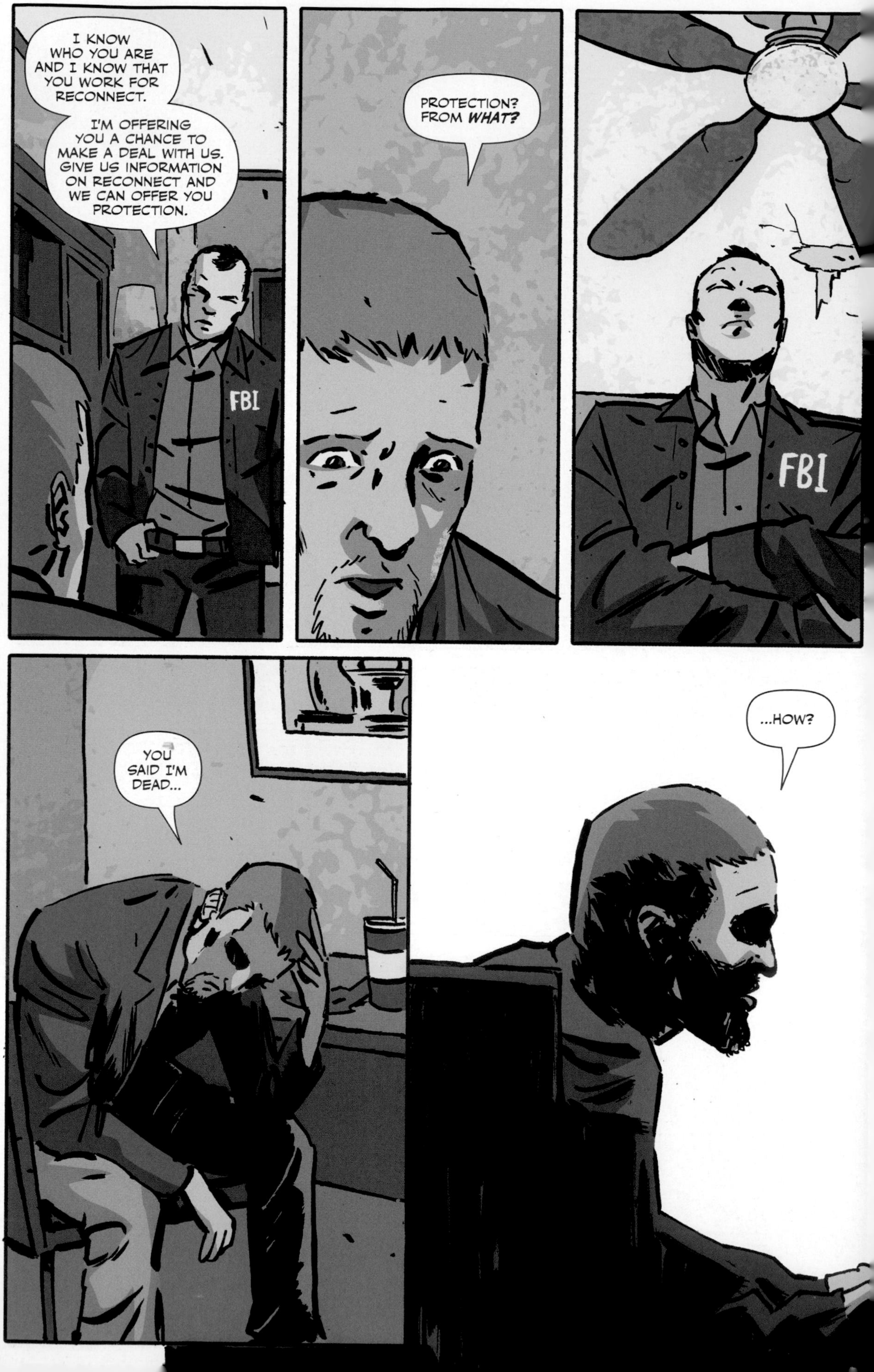
I KNOW WHO YOU ARE AND I KNOW THAT YOU WORK FOR RECONNECT.
I'M OFFERING YOU A CHANCE TO MAKE A DEAL WITH US. GIVE US INFORMATION ON RECONNECT AND WE CAN OFFER YOU PROTECTION.
FBI
PROTECTION? FROM *WHAT?*
FBI
YOU SAID I'M DEAD...
...HOW?

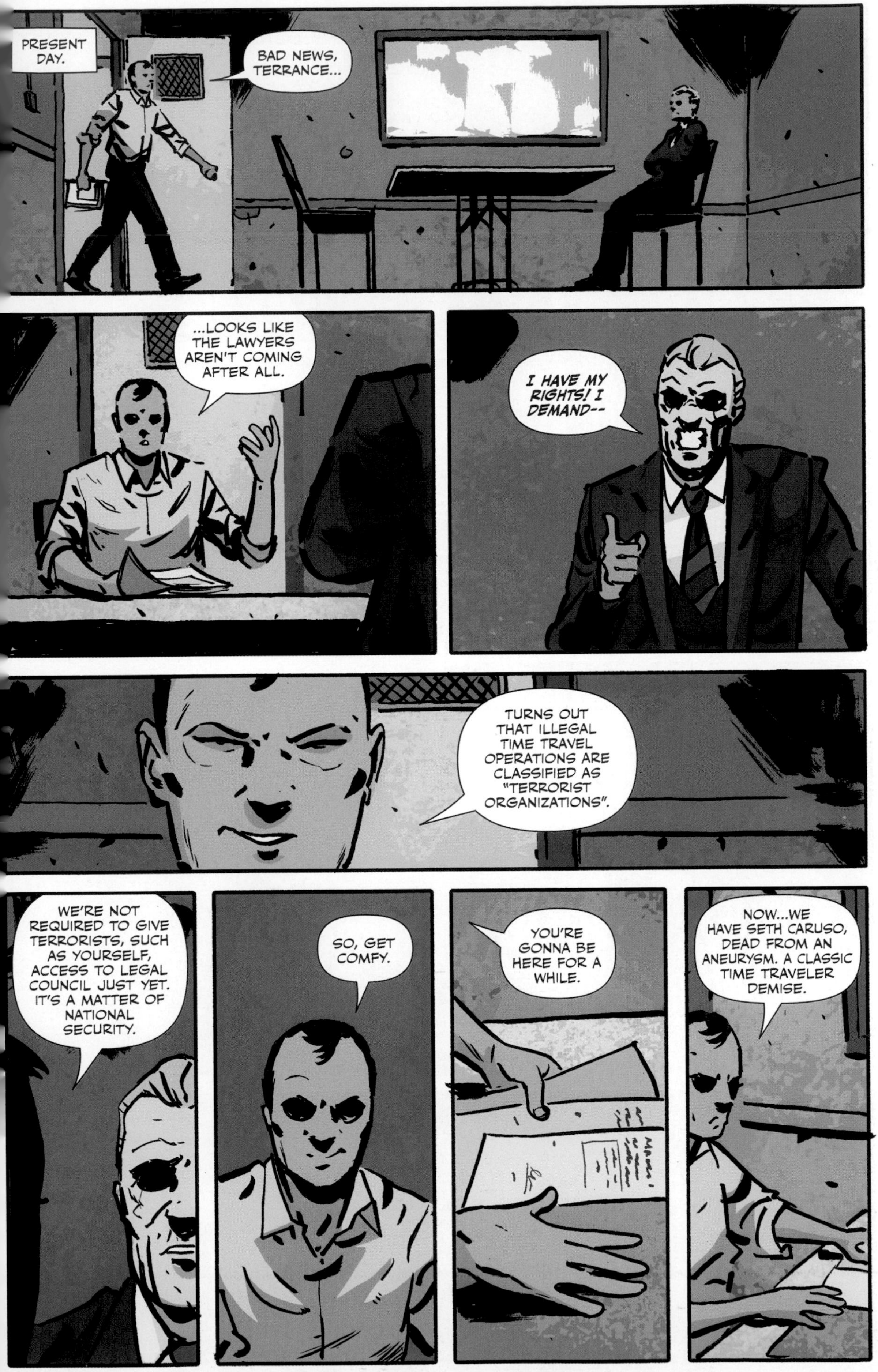
PRESENT DAY.
BAD NEWS, TERRANCE...
...LOOKS LIKE THE LAWYERS AREN'T COMING AFTER ALL.
I HAVE MY RIGHTS! I DEMAND--
TURNS OUT THAT ILLEGAL TIME TRAVEL OPERATIONS ARE CLASSIFIED AS "TERRORIST ORGANIZATIONS".
WE'RE NOT REQUIRED TO GIVE TERRORISTS, SUCH AS YOURSELF, ACCESS TO LEGAL COUNCIL JUST YET. IT'S A MATTER OF NATIONAL SECURITY.
SO, GET COMFY.
YOU'RE GONNA BE HERE FOR A WHILE.
NOW...WE HAVE SETH CARUSO, DEAD FROM AN ANEURYSM. A CLASSIC TIME TRAVELER DEMISE.

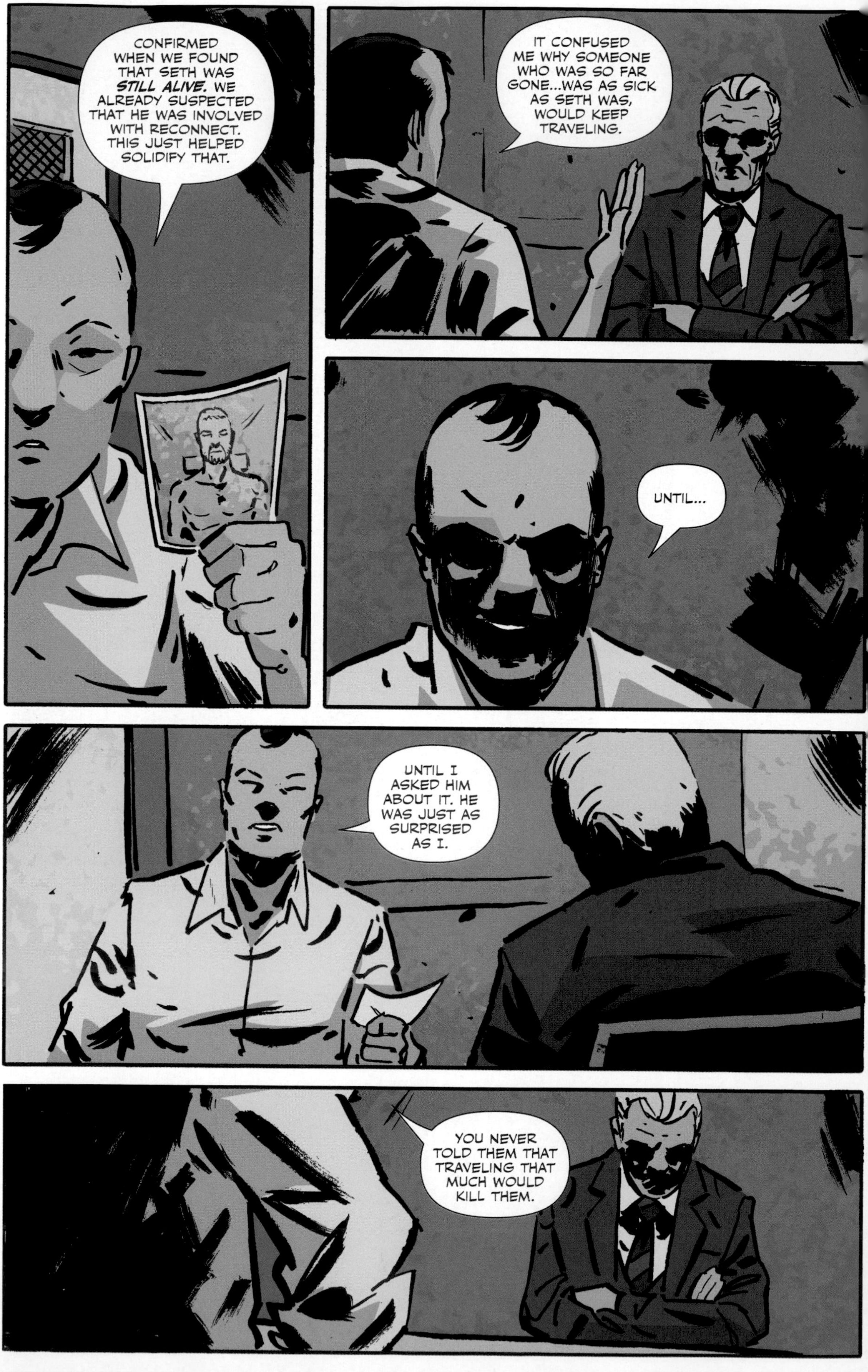
CONFIRMED WHEN WE FOUND THAT SETH WAS *STILL ALIVE.* WE ALREADY SUSPECTED THAT HE WAS INVOLVED WITH RECONNECT. THIS JUST HELPED SOLIDIFY THAT.
IT CONFUSED ME WHY SOMEONE WHO WAS SO FAR GONE...WAS AS SICK AS SETH WAS, WOULD KEEP TRAVELING.
UNTIL...
UNTIL I ASKED HIM ABOUT IT. HE WAS JUST AS SURPRISED AS I.
YOU NEVER TOLD THEM THAT TRAVELING THAT MUCH WOULD KILL THEM.

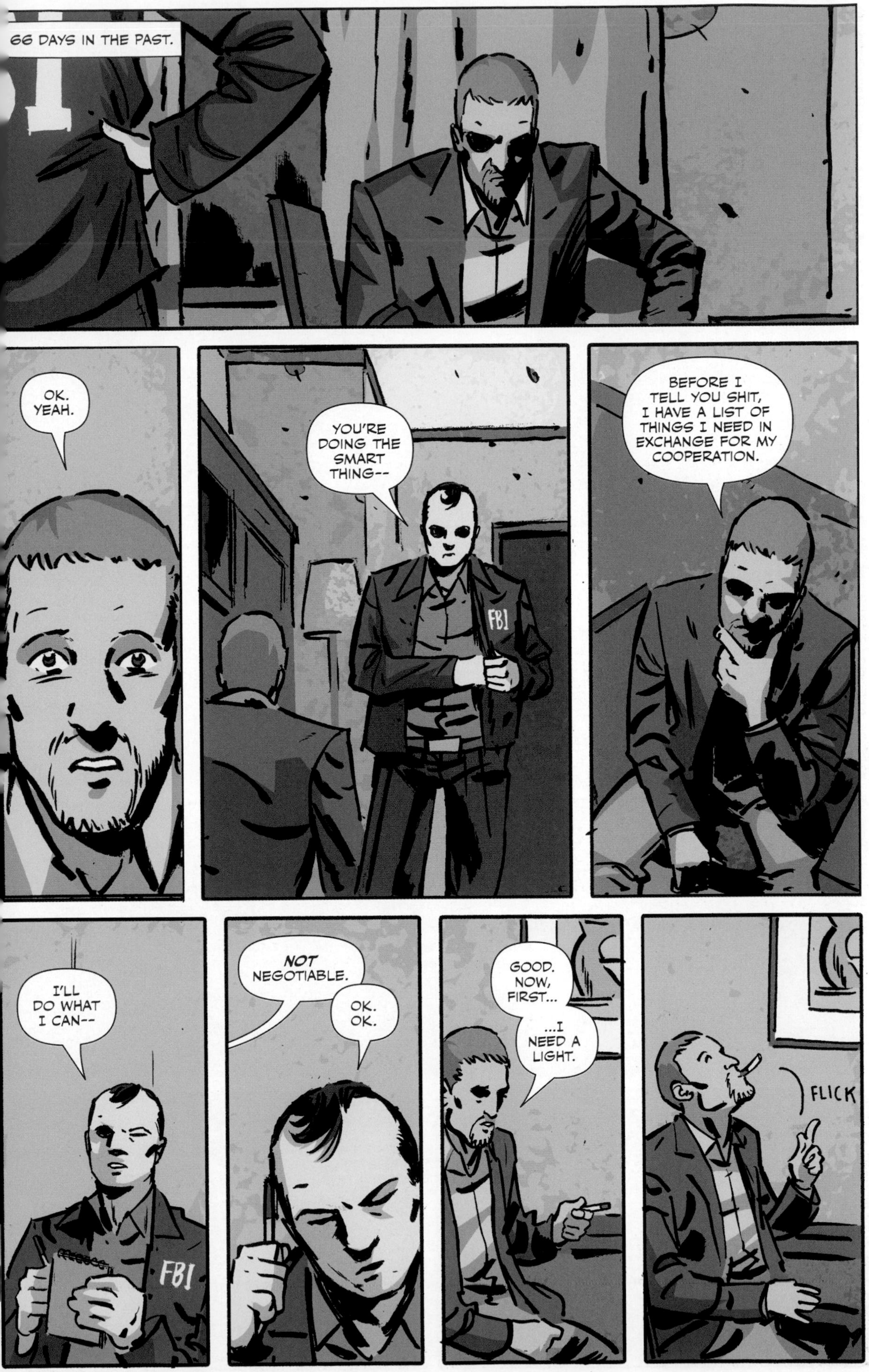
66 DAYS IN THE PAST.
OK. YEAH.
YOU'RE DOING THE SMART THING--
FBI
BEFORE I TELL YOU SHIT, I HAVE A LIST OF THINGS I NEED IN EXCHANGE FOR MY COOPERATION.
I'LL DO WHAT I CAN--
FBI
NOT NEGOTIABLE.
OK. OK.
GOOD. NOW, FIRST...
...I NEED A LIGHT.
FLICK

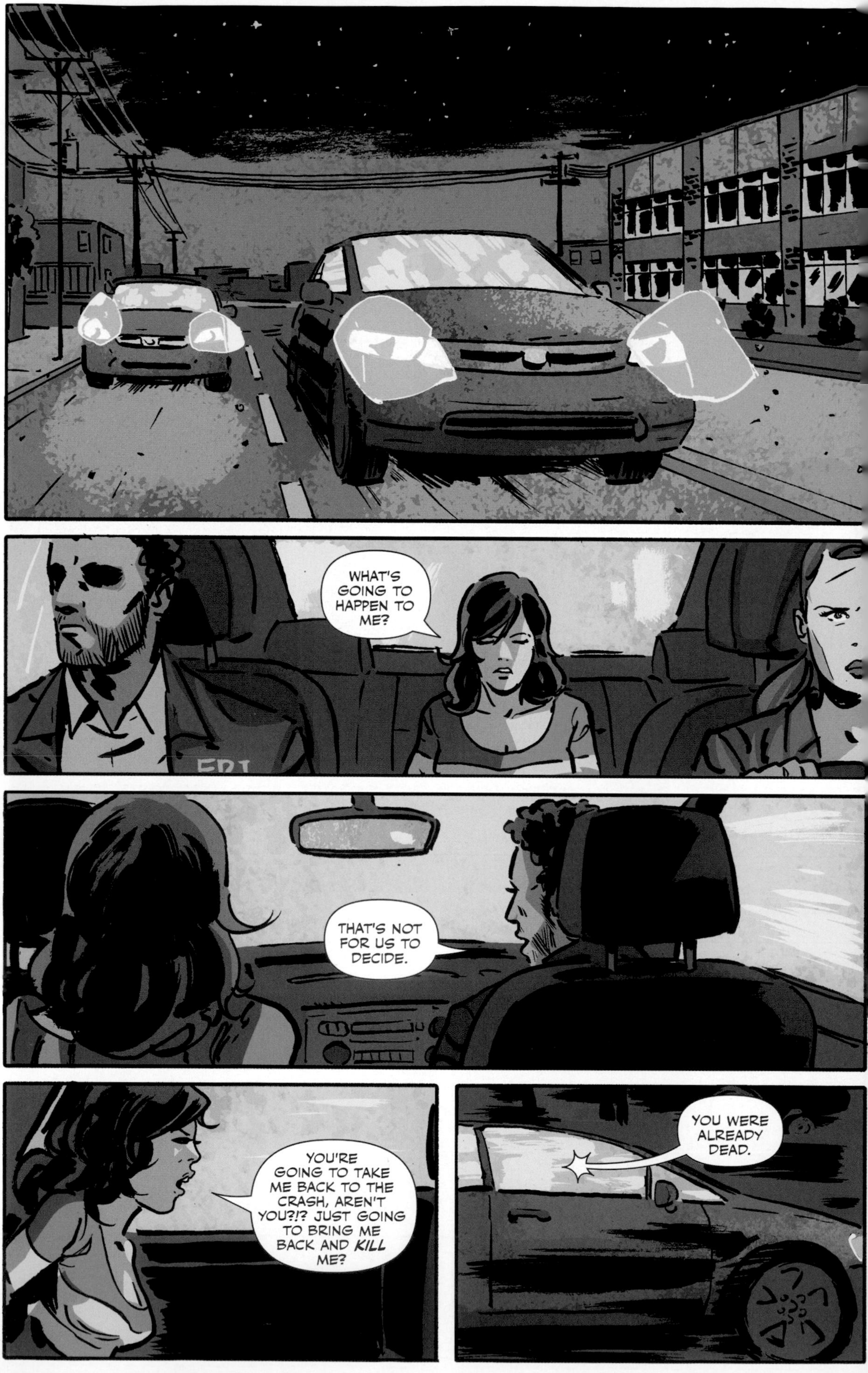
FBI
WHAT'S GOING TO HAPPEN TO ME?
THAT'S NOT FOR US TO DECIDE.
YOU'RE GOING TO TAKE ME BACK TO THE CRASH, AREN'T YOU?!? JUST GOING TO BRING ME BACK AND *KILL* ME?
YOU WERE ALREADY DEAD.

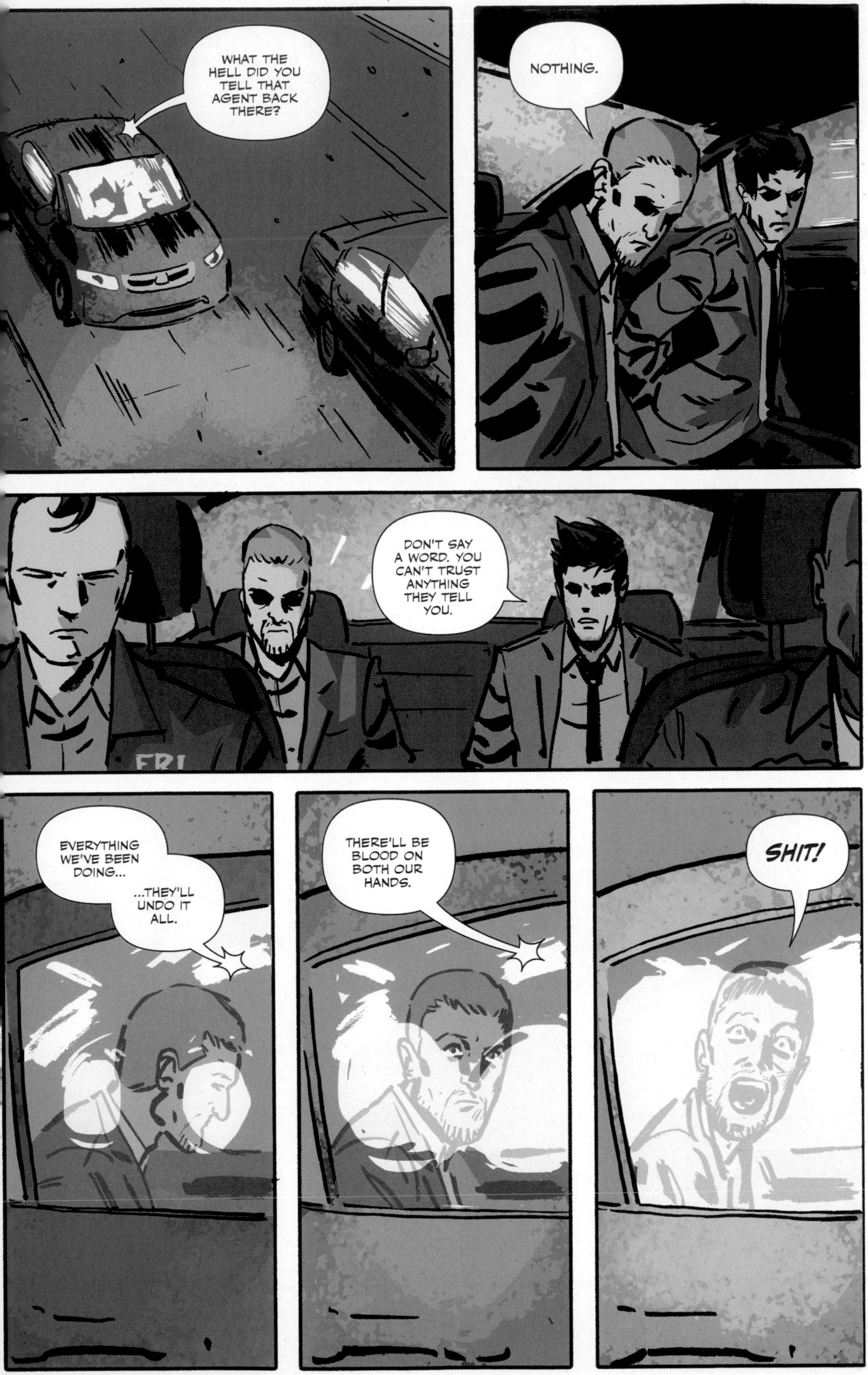
WHAT THE HELL DID YOU TELL THAT AGENT BACK THERE?
NOTHING.
DON'T SAY A WORD. YOU CAN'T TRUST ANYTHING THEY TELL YOU.
FBI
EVERYTHING WE'VE BEEN DOING...
...THEY'LL UNDO IT ALL.
THERE'LL BE BLOOD ON BOTH OUR HANDS.
SHIT!

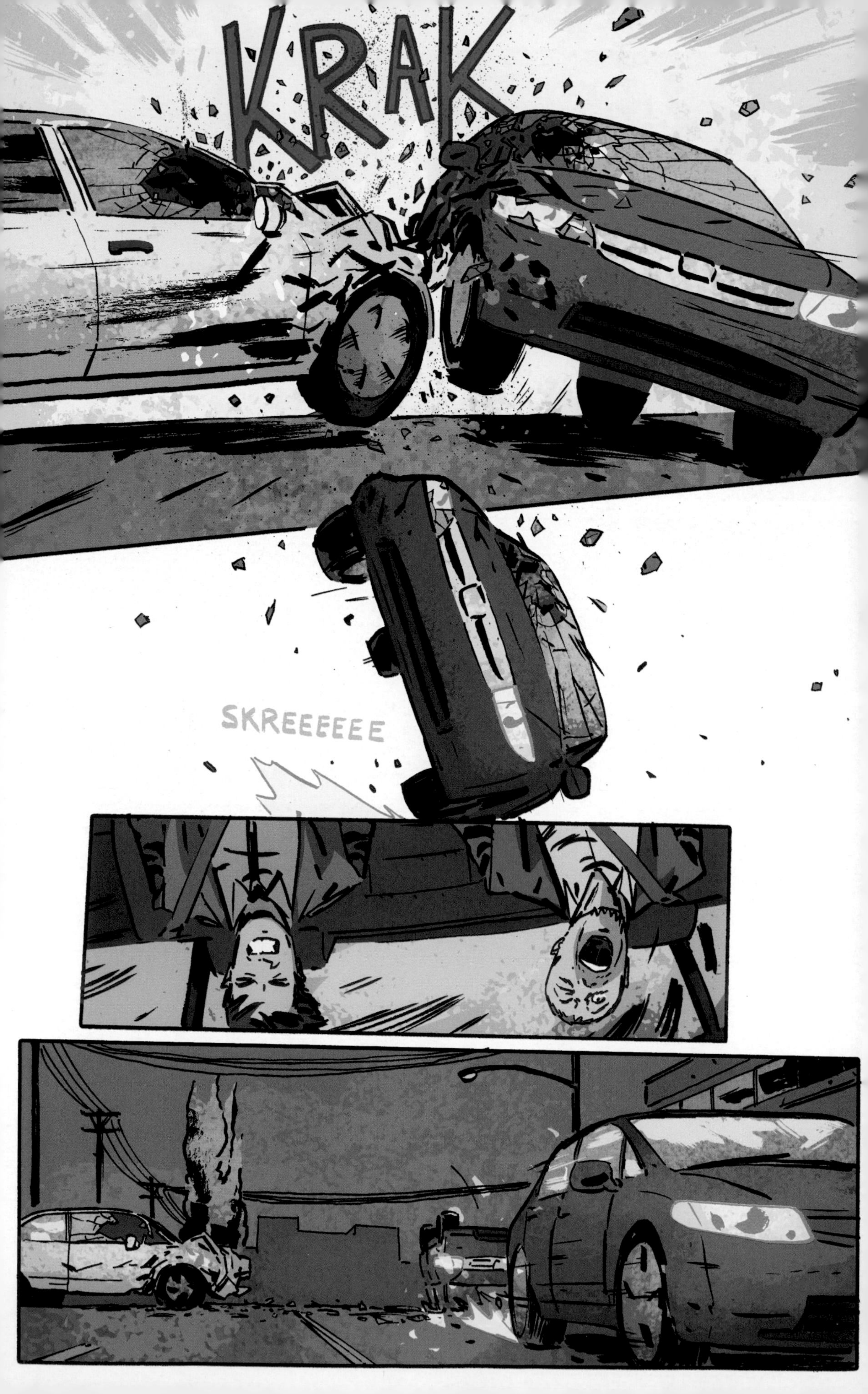
KRAK
SKREEEEEE

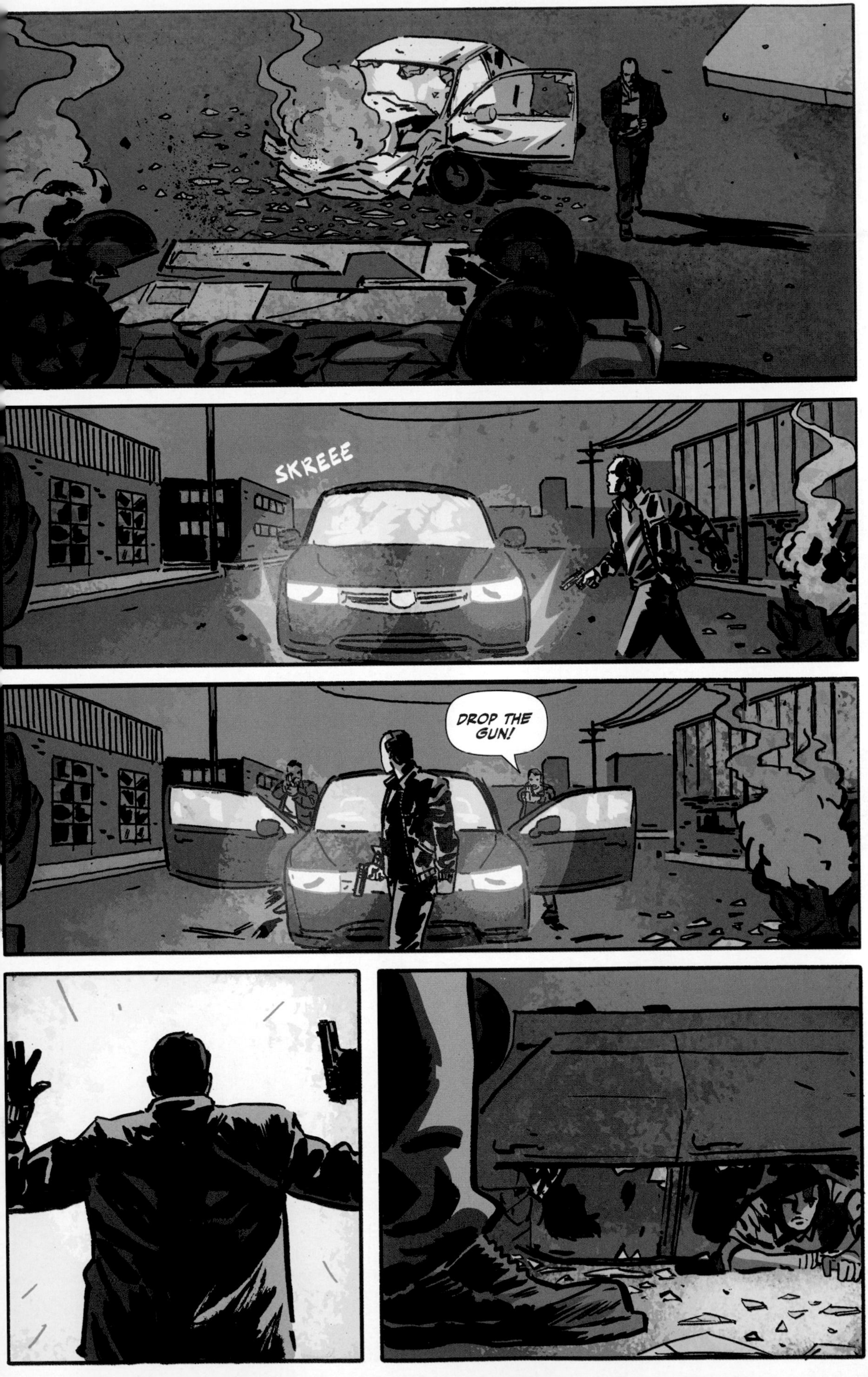
SKREEE
DROP THE GUN!

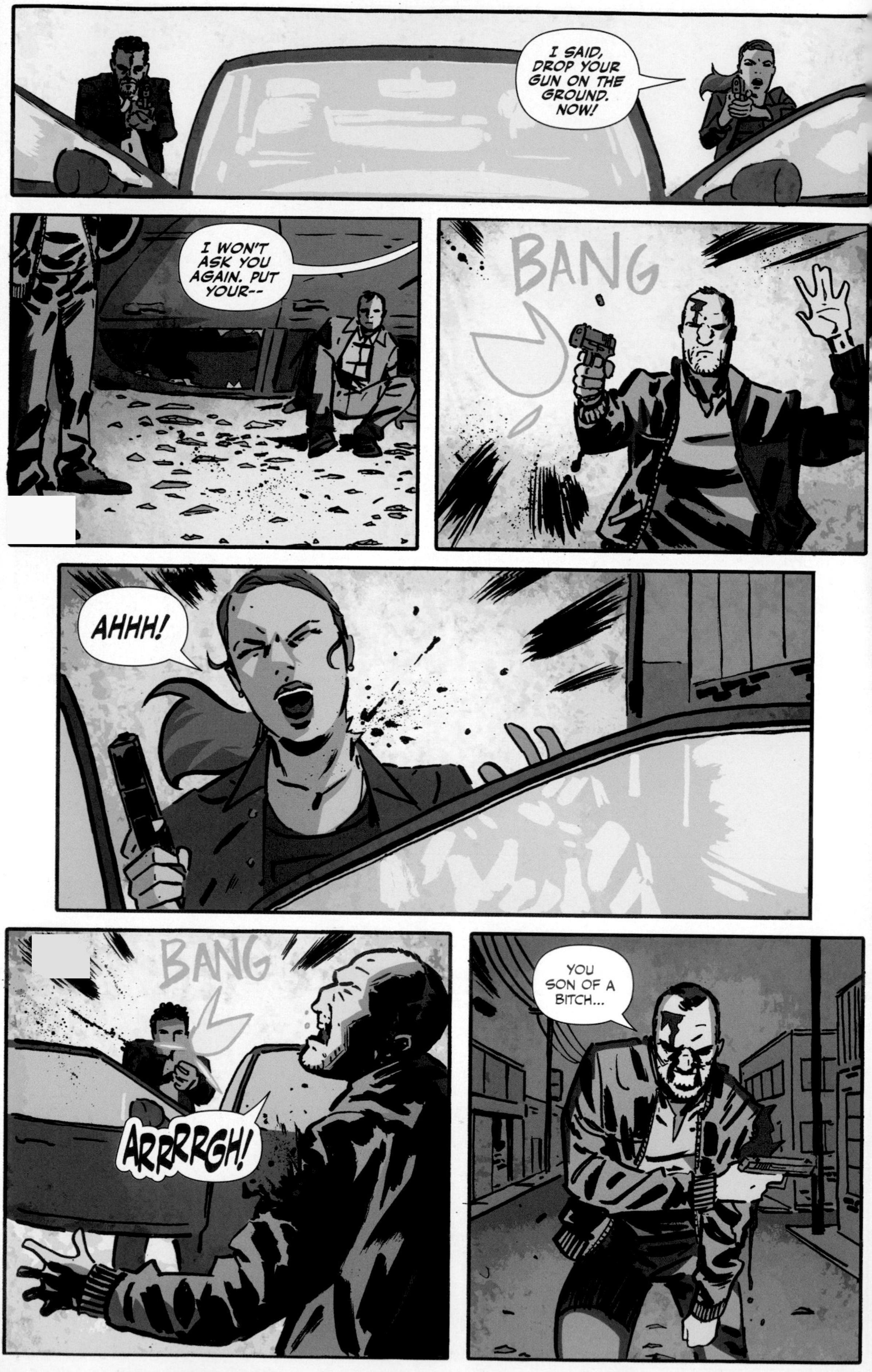
I SAID, DROP YOUR GUN ON THE GROUND. NOW!
I WON'T ASK YOU AGAIN. PUT YOUR--
BANG
AHHH!
BANG
ARRRRGH!
YOU SON OF A BITCH...

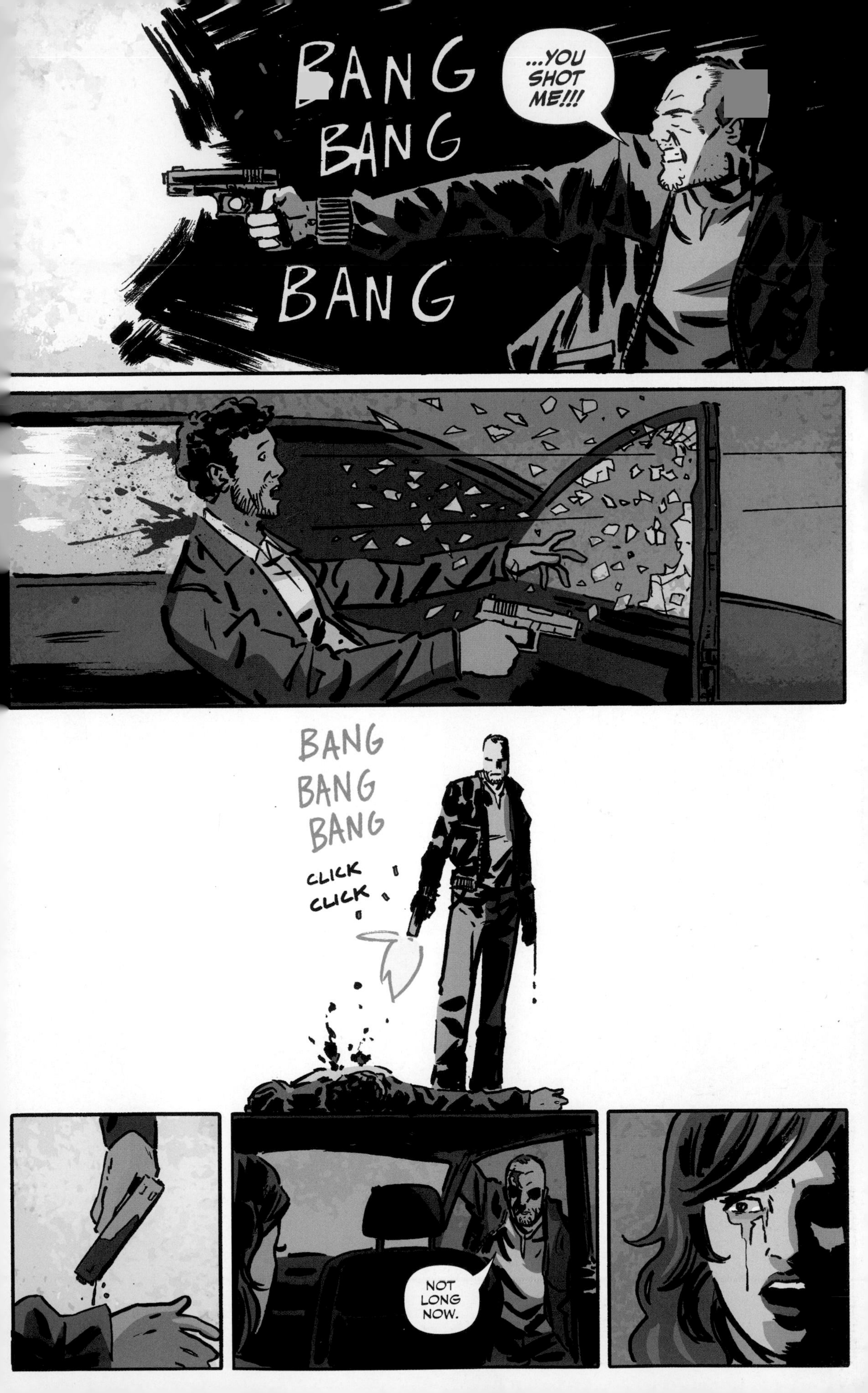
BANG
BANG
BANG
...YOU SHOT ME!!!
BANG
BANG
BANG
CLICK
CLICK
NOT LONG NOW.

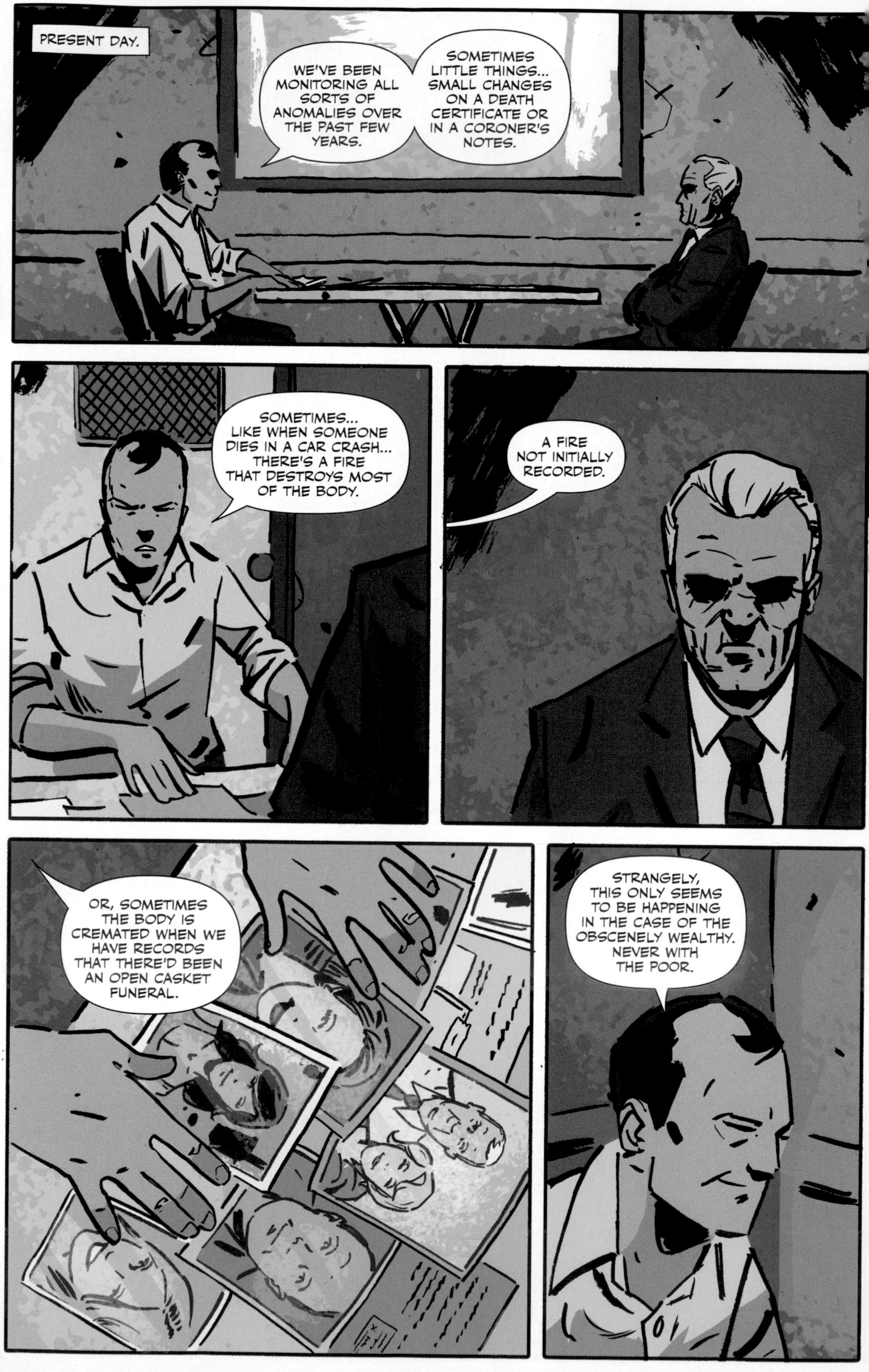
PRESENT DAY.
WE'VE BEEN MONITORING ALL SORTS OF ANOMALIES OVER THE PAST FEW YEARS.
SOMETIMES LITTLE THINGS... SMALL CHANGES ON A DEATH CERTIFICATE OR IN A CORONER'S NOTES.
SOMETIMES... LIKE WHEN SOMEONE DIES IN A CAR CRASH... THERE'S A FIRE THAT DESTROYS MOST OF THE BODY.
A FIRE NOT INITIALLY RECORDED.
OR, SOMETIMES THE BODY IS CREMATED WHEN WE HAVE RECORDS THAT THERE'D BEEN AN OPEN CASKET FUNERAL.
STRANGELY, THIS ONLY SEEMS TO BE HAPPENING IN THE CASE OF THE OBSCENELY WEALTHY. NEVER WITH THE POOR.

THIS IS MR. GARY FIELDS AND HIS DAUGHTER GRACE. SHORTLY AFTER WE HAVE HIM DYING IN A...

...A *FIRE?* HOW VERY INTERESTING, DON'T YOU THINK?

A COUPLE OF MONTHS AFTER HE DIES IN A FIRE, HIS DAUGHTER VANISHES.

BUT NOT BEFORE SHE CLEARED FIVE MILLION FROM HIS BANK ACCOUNT.

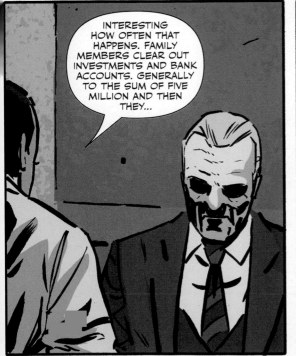

INTERESTING HOW OFTEN THAT HAPPENS. FAMILY MEMBERS CLEAR OUT INVESTMENTS AND BANK ACCOUNTS. GENERALLY TO THE SUM OF FIVE MILLION AND THEN THEY...

RIIIIP

...VANISH!

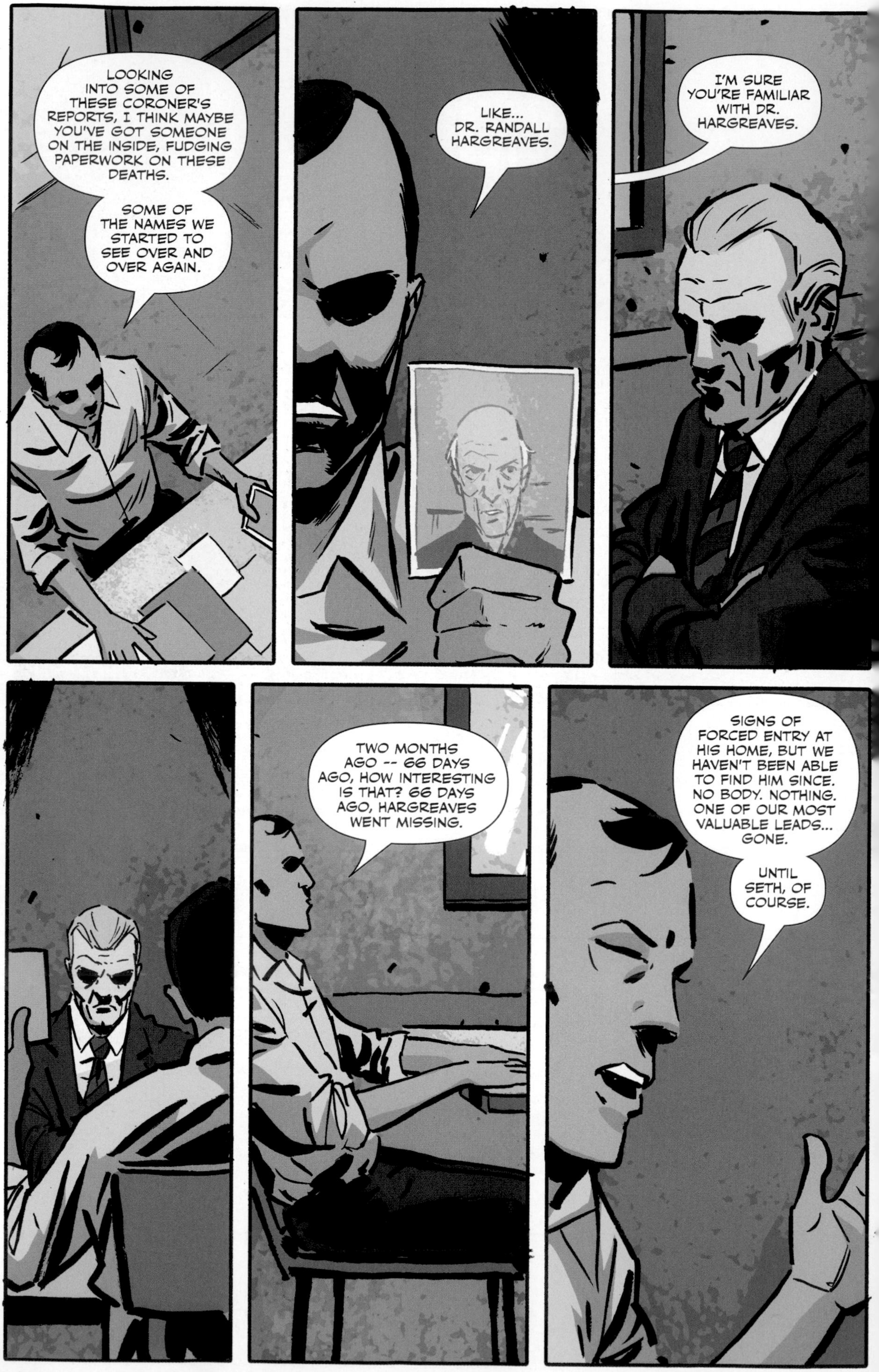
LOOKING INTO SOME OF THESE CORONER'S REPORTS, I THINK MAYBE YOU'VE GOT SOMEONE ON THE INSIDE, FUDGING PAPERWORK ON THESE DEATHS.
SOME OF THE NAMES WE STARTED TO SEE OVER AND OVER AGAIN.
LIKE... DR. RANDALL HARGREAVES.
I'M SURE YOU'RE FAMILIAR WITH DR. HARGREAVES.
TWO MONTHS AGO -- 66 DAYS AGO, HOW INTERESTING IS THAT? 66 DAYS AGO, HARGREAVES WENT MISSING.
SIGNS OF FORCED ENTRY AT HIS HOME, BUT WE HAVEN'T BEEN ABLE TO FIND HIM SINCE. NO BODY. NOTHING. ONE OF OUR MOST VALUABLE LEADS... GONE.
UNTIL SETH, OF COURSE.

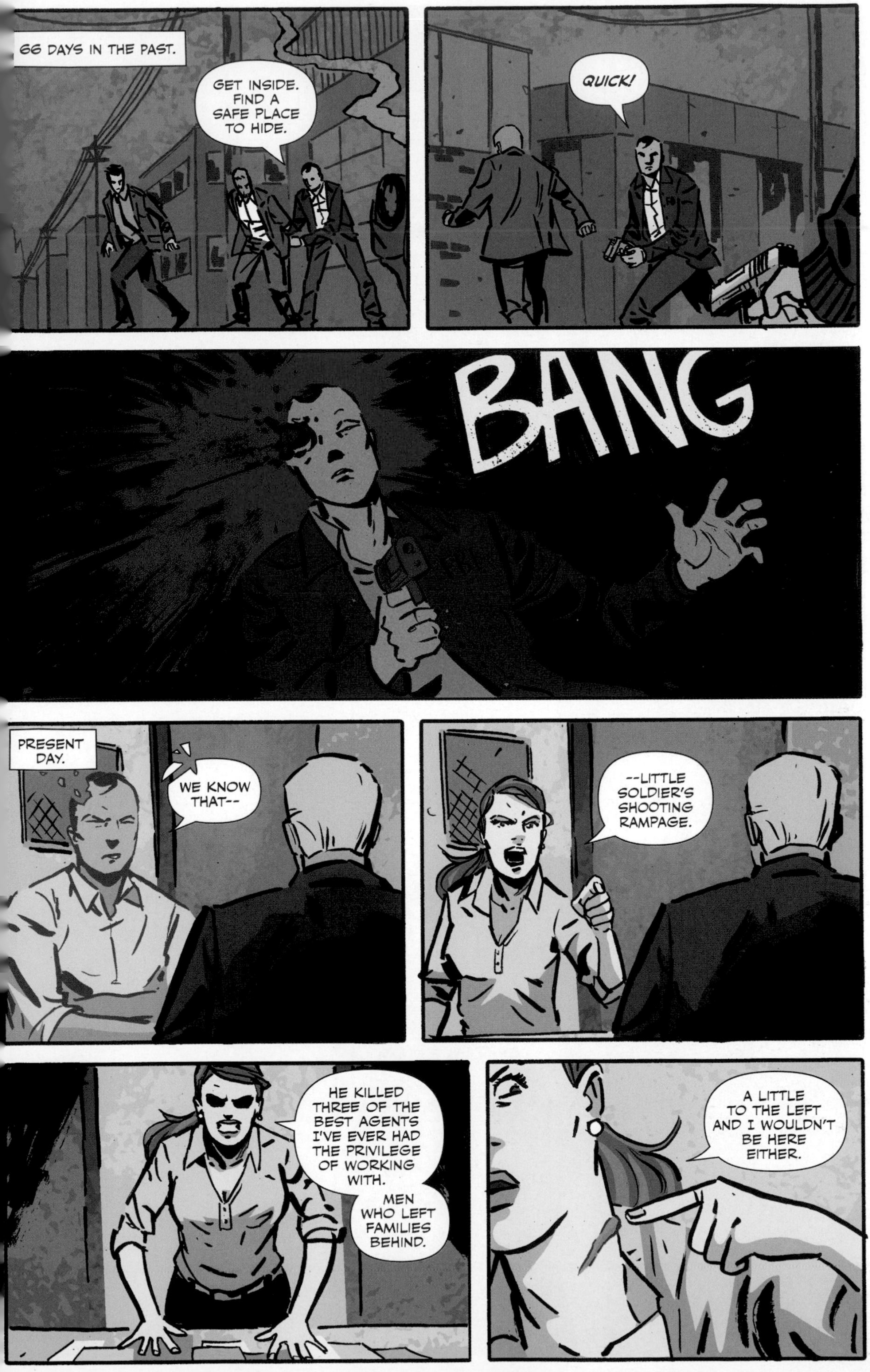
66 DAYS IN THE PAST.
GET INSIDE. FIND A SAFE PLACE TO HIDE.
QUICK!
BANG
PRESENT DAY.
WE KNOW THAT--
--LITTLE SOLDIER'S SHOOTING RAMPAGE.
HE KILLED THREE OF THE BEST AGENTS I'VE EVER HAD THE PRIVILEGE OF WORKING WITH.
MEN WHO LEFT FAMILIES BEHIND.
A LITTLE TO THE LEFT AND I WOULDN'T BE HERE EITHER.

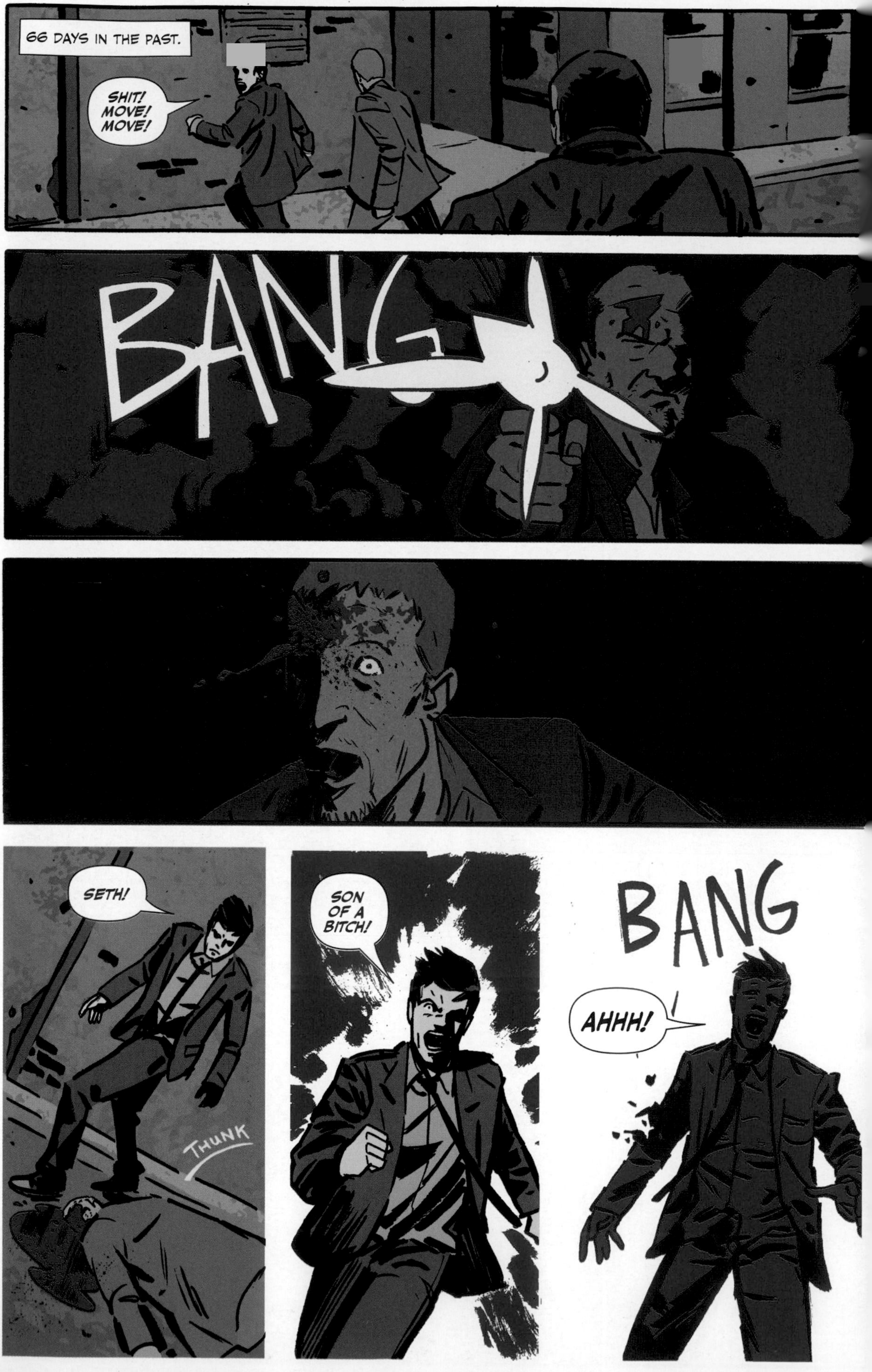
66 DAYS IN THE PAST.
SHIT! MOVE! MOVE!
BANG
SETH!
THUNK
SON OF A BITCH!
BANG
AHHH!

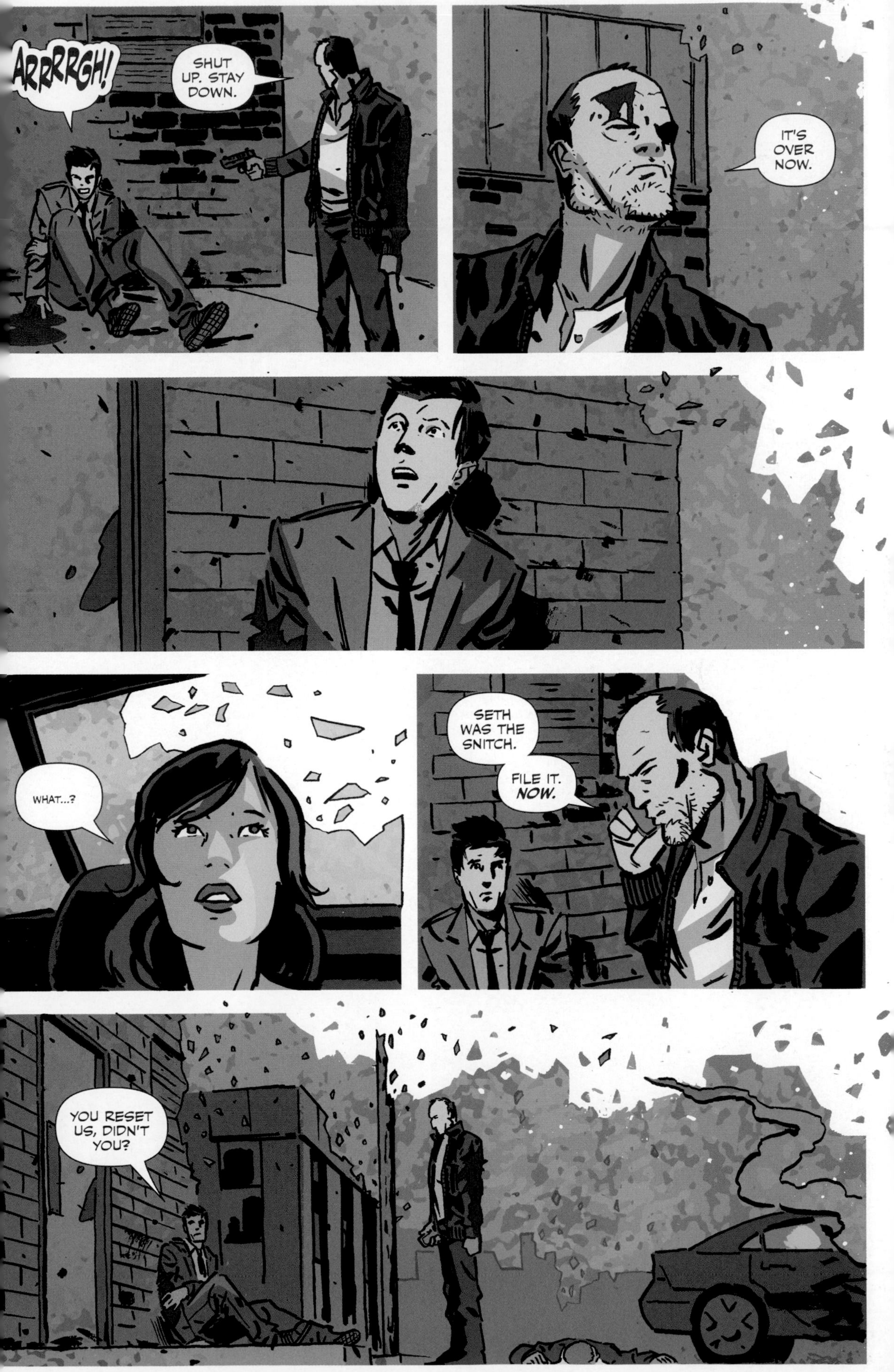
ARRRRGH!
SHUT UP. STAY DOWN.
IT'S OVER NOW.
WHAT...?
SETH WAS THE SNITCH.
FILE IT. *NOW.*
YOU RESET US, DIDN'T YOU?

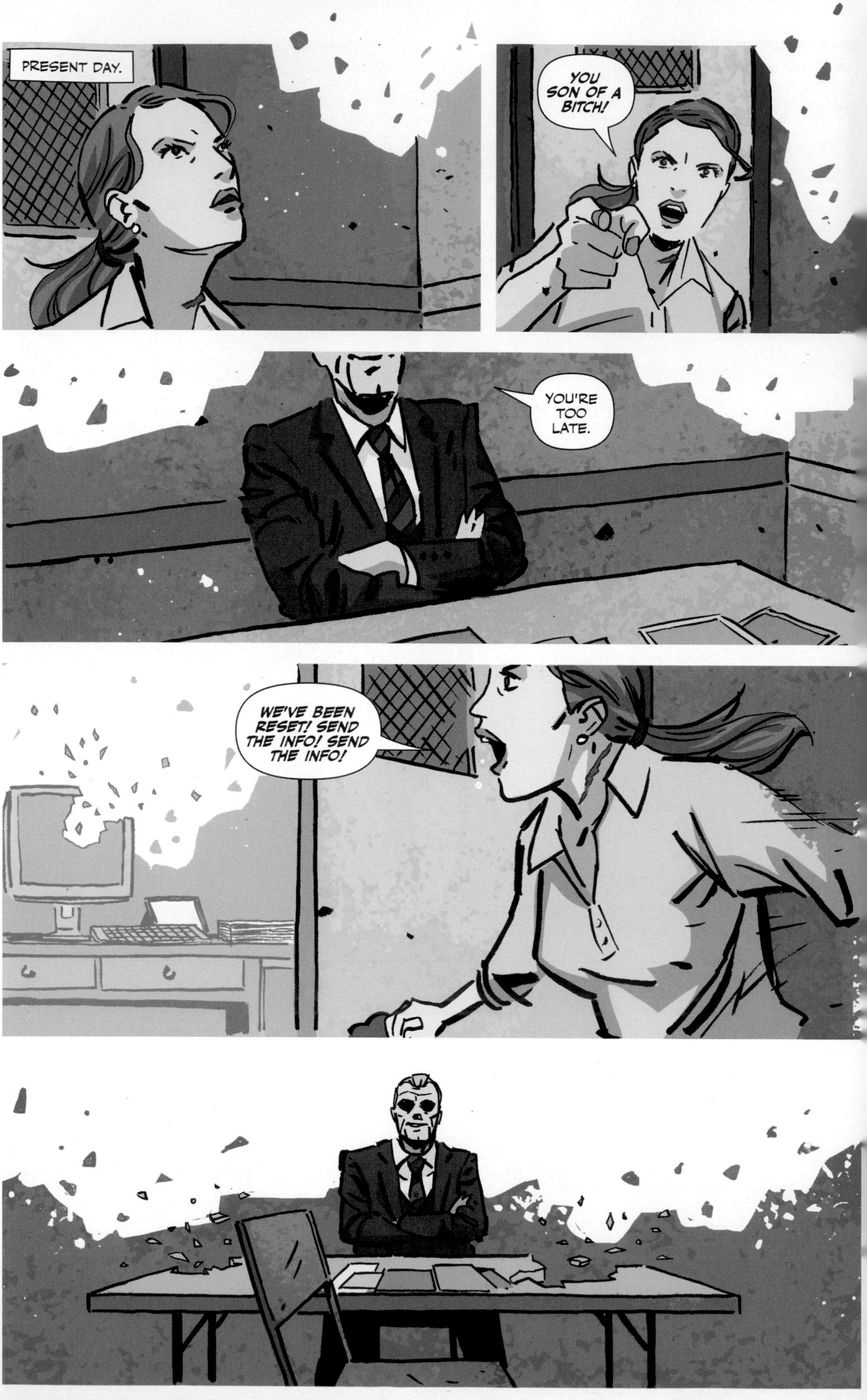
PRESENT DAY.
YOU SON OF A BITCH!
YOU'RE TOO LATE.
WE'VE BEEN RESET! SEND THE INFO! SEND THE INFO!

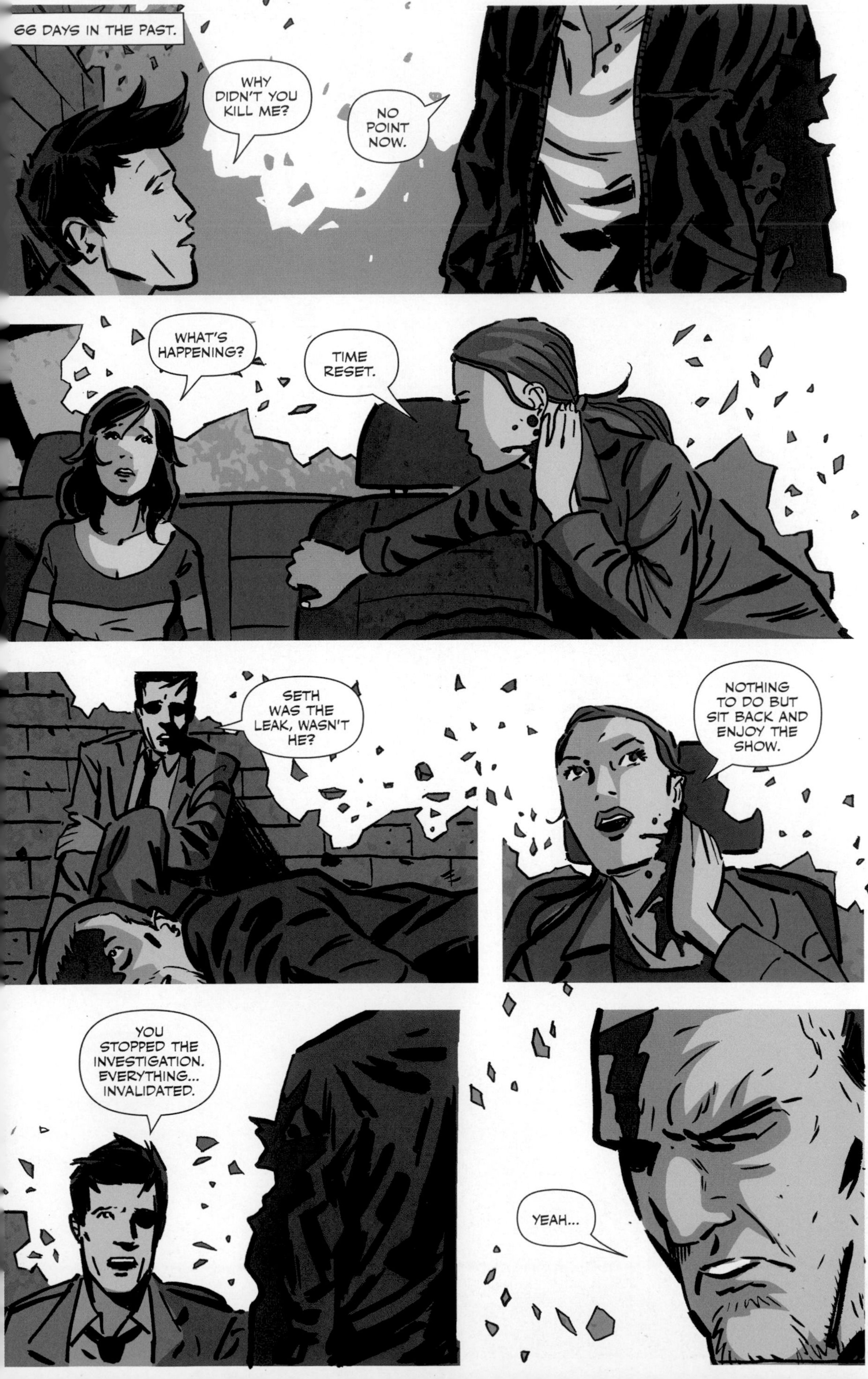
66 DAYS IN THE PAST.
WHY DIDN'T YOU KILL ME?
NO POINT NOW.
WHAT'S HAPPENING?
TIME RESET.
SETH WAS THE LEAK, WASN'T HE?
NOTHING TO DO BUT SIT BACK AND ENJOY THE SHOW.
YOU STOPPED THE INVESTIGATION. EVERYTHING... INVALIDATED.
YEAH...

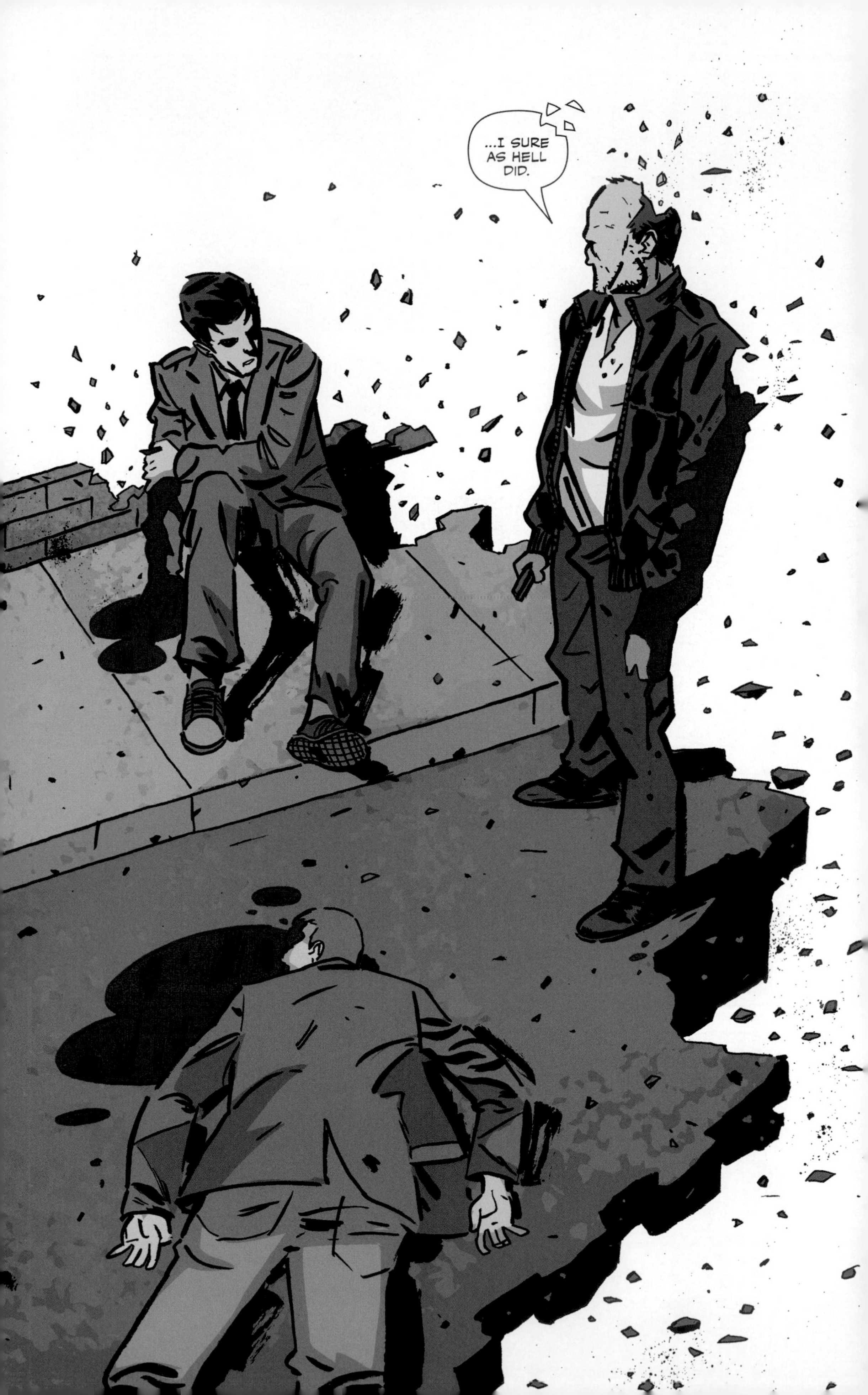
...I SURE AS HELL DID.

CHAPTER FIVE

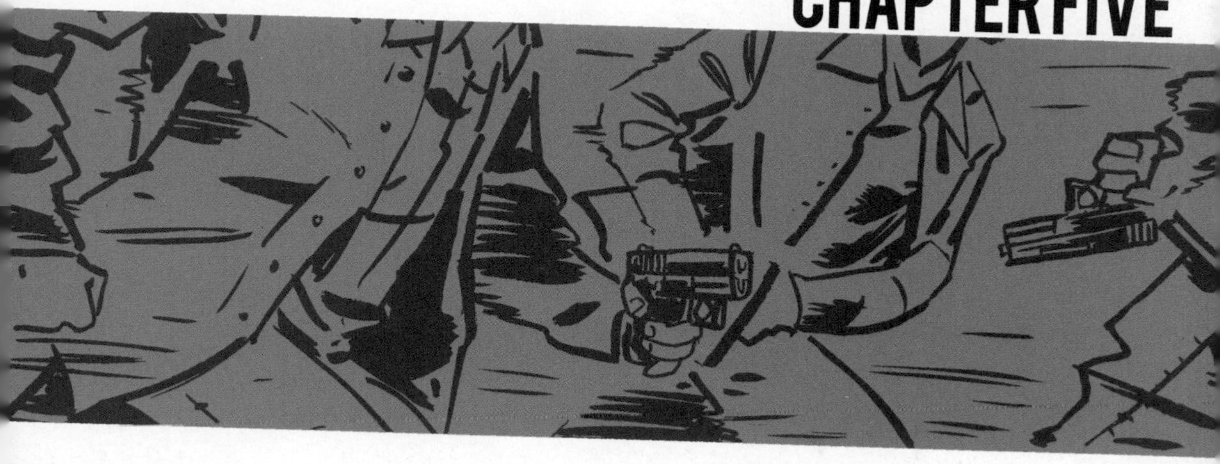

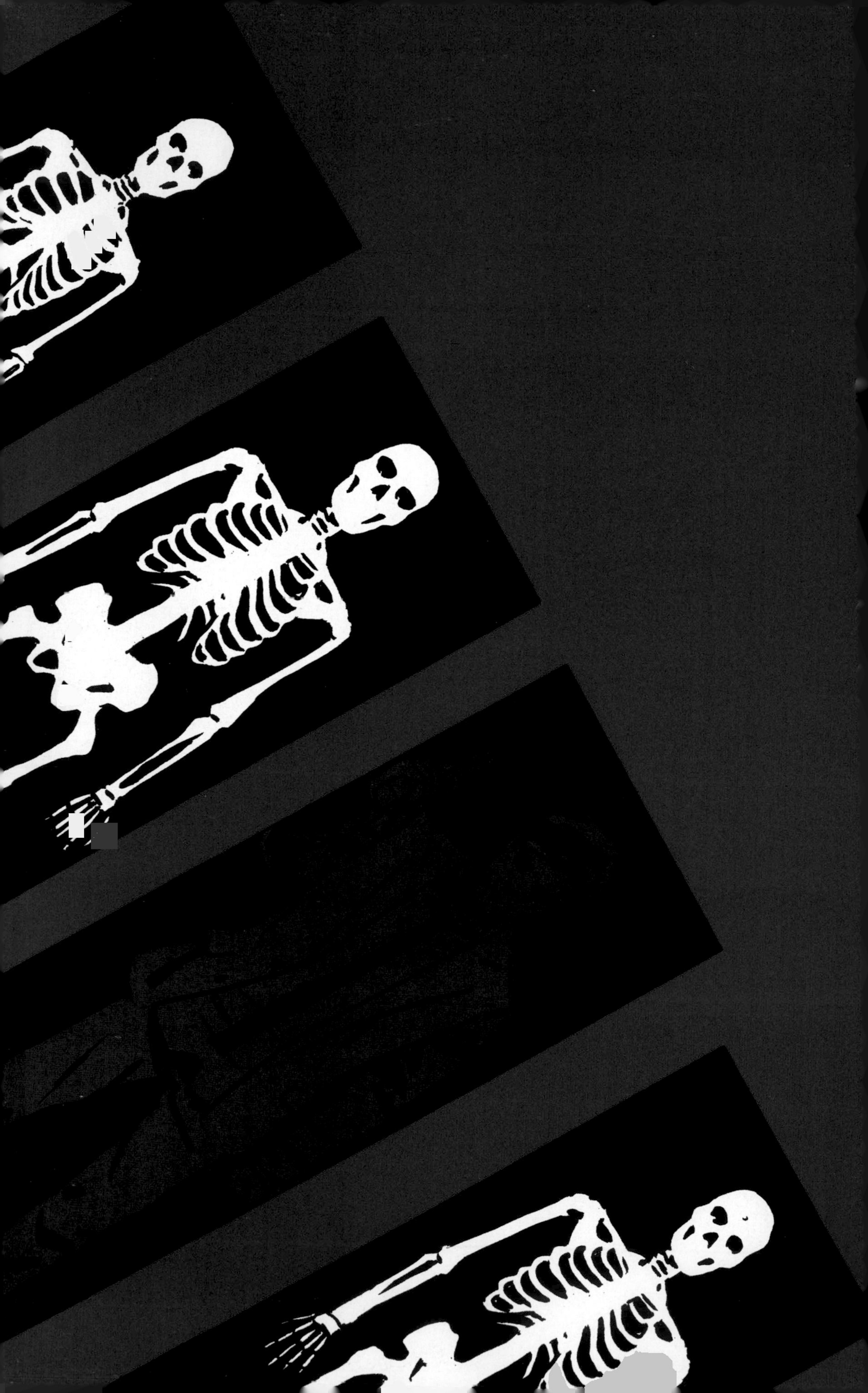

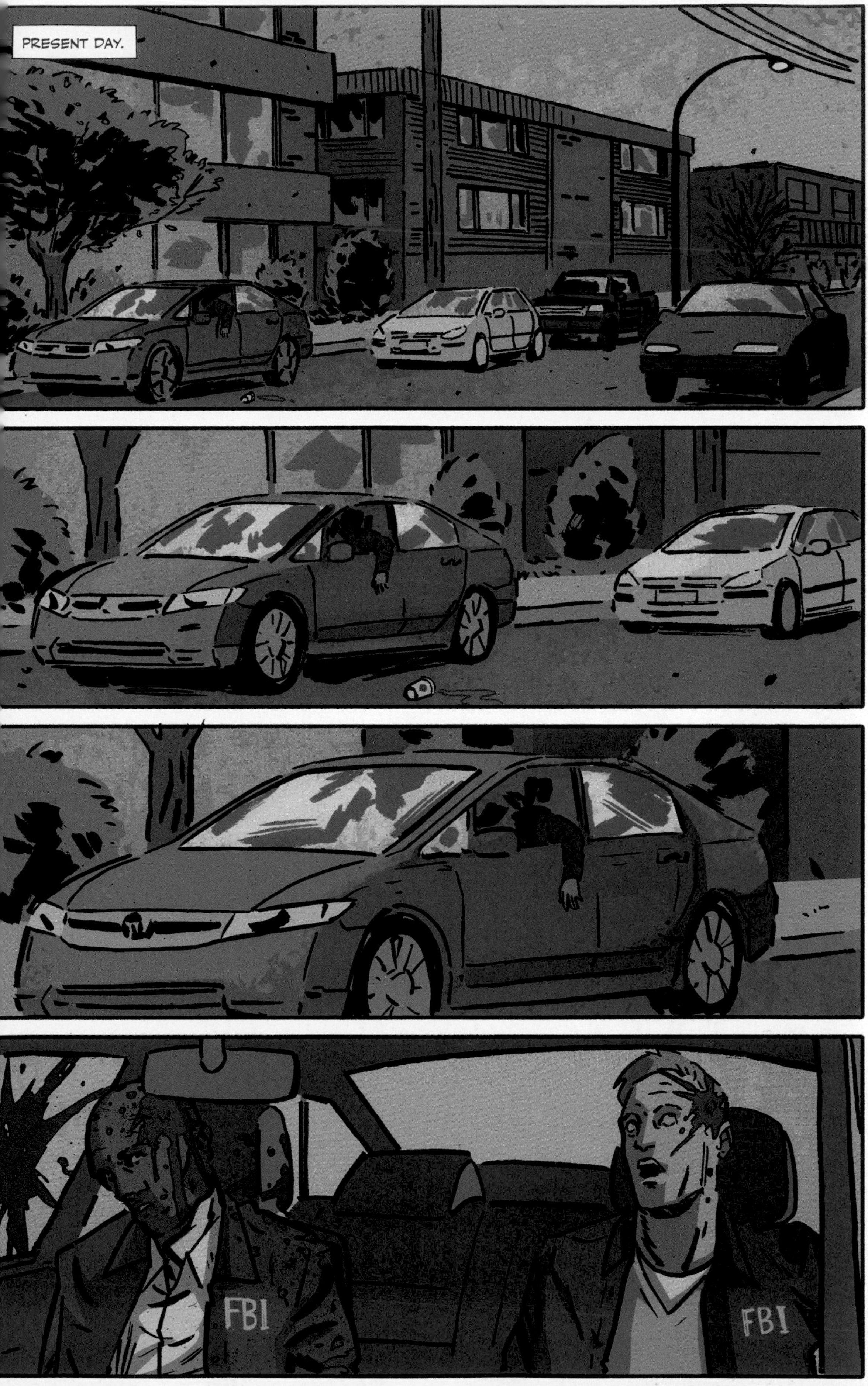
PRESENT DAY.
FBI
FBI

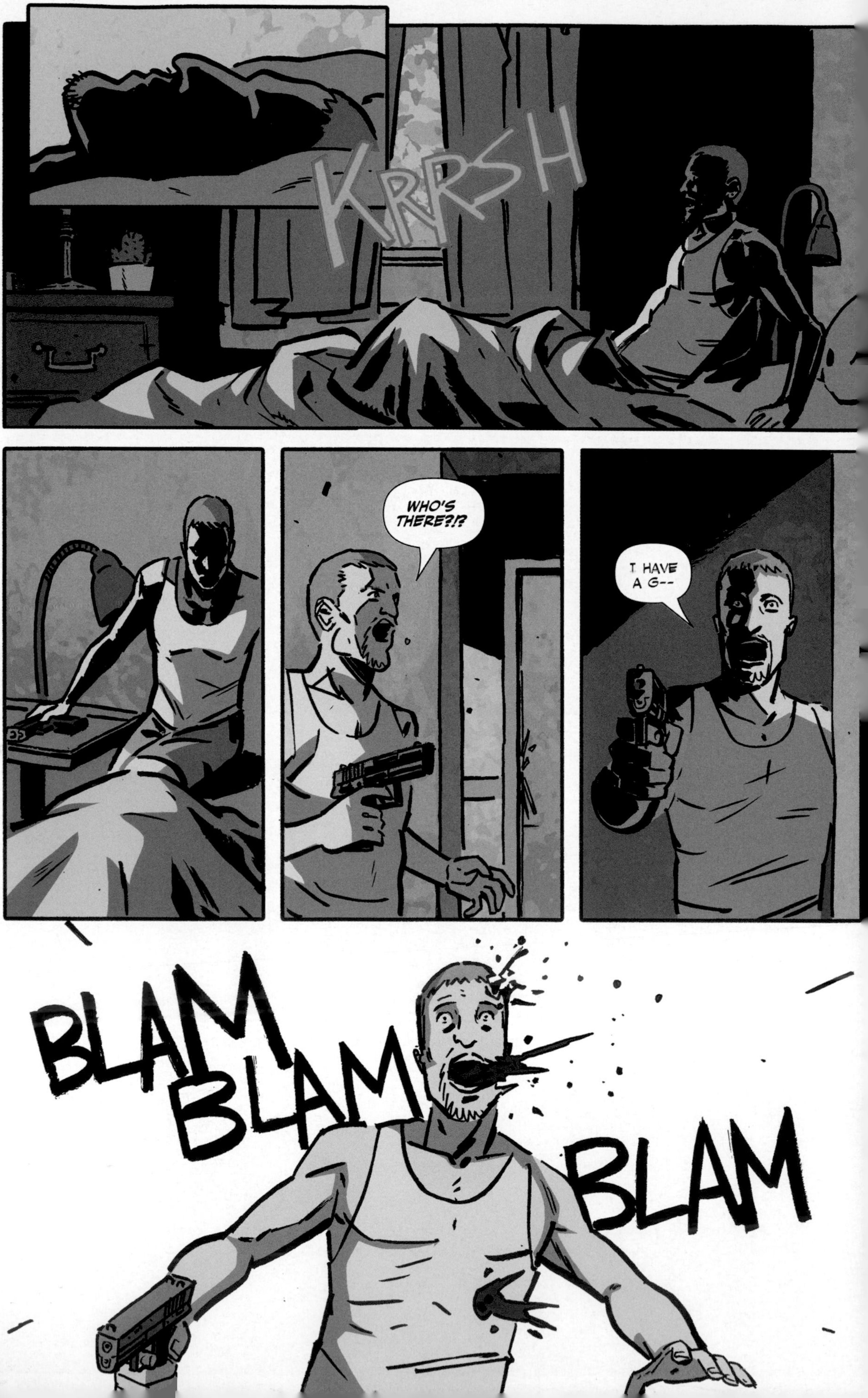
KRRSH
WHO'S THERE?!?
I HAVE A G--
BLAM
BLAM
BLAM

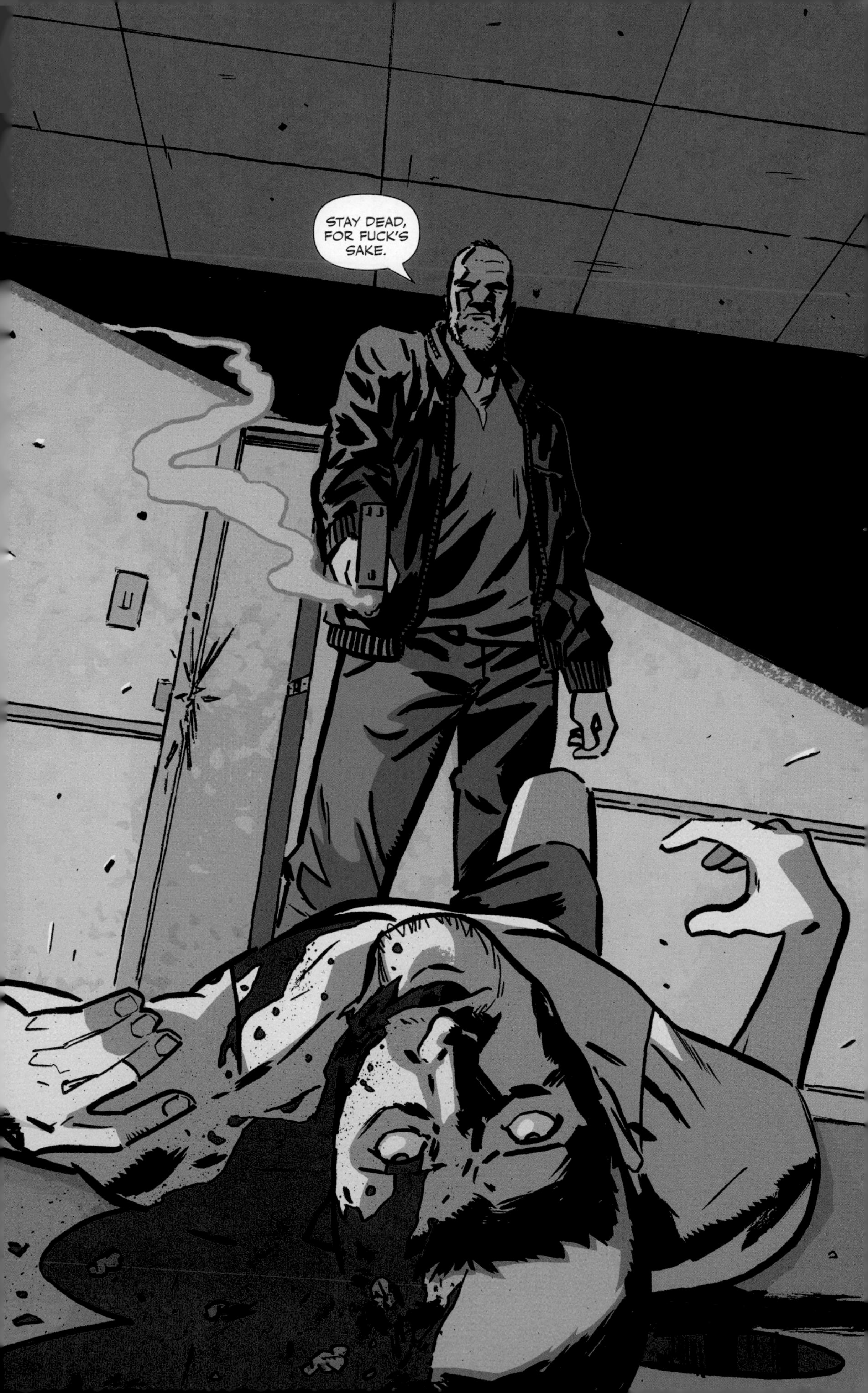
STAY DEAD, FOR FUCK'S SAKE.

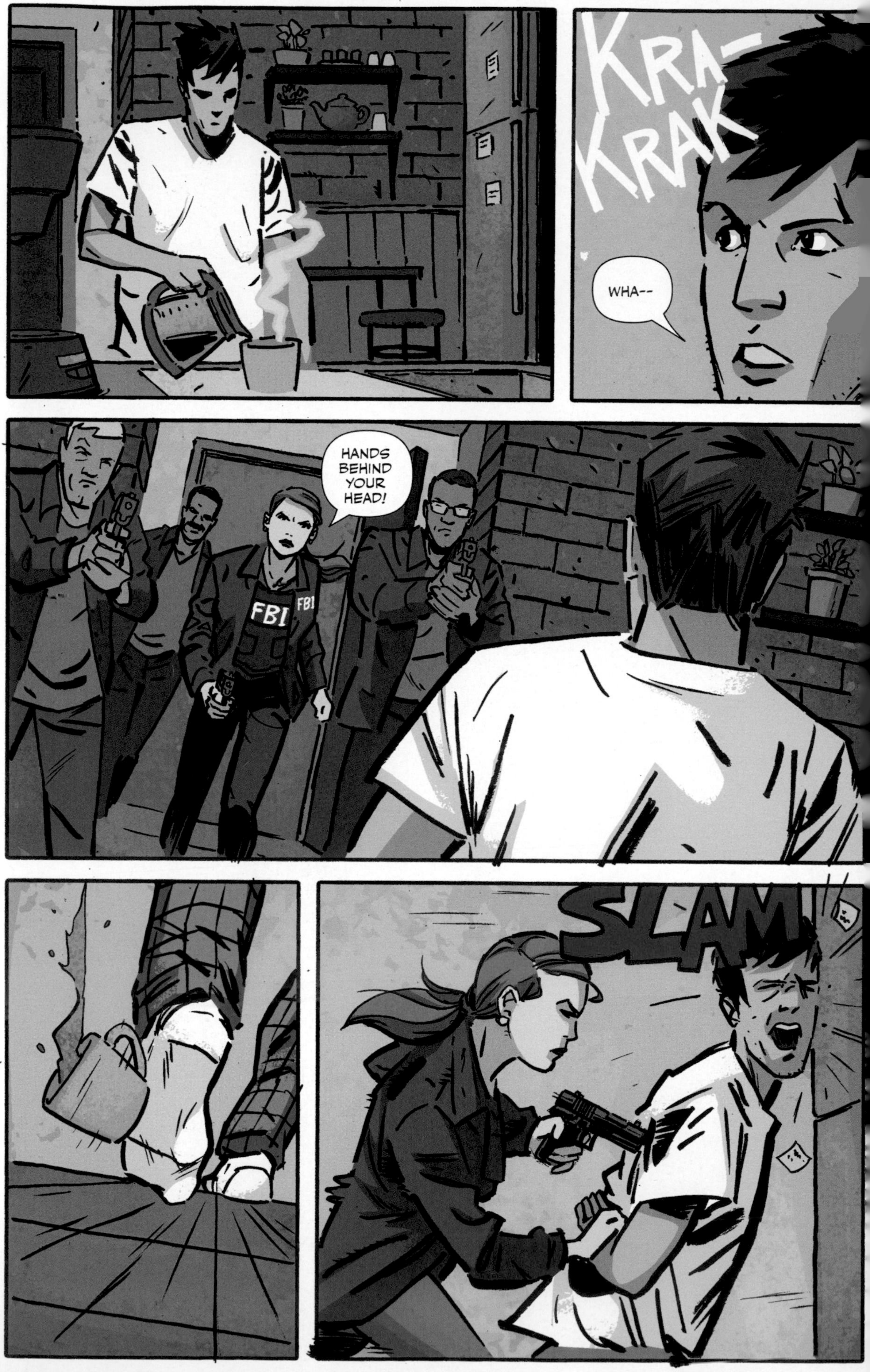
KRA-
KRAK
WHA--
HANDS BEHIND YOUR HEAD!
FBI
FBI
SLAM!

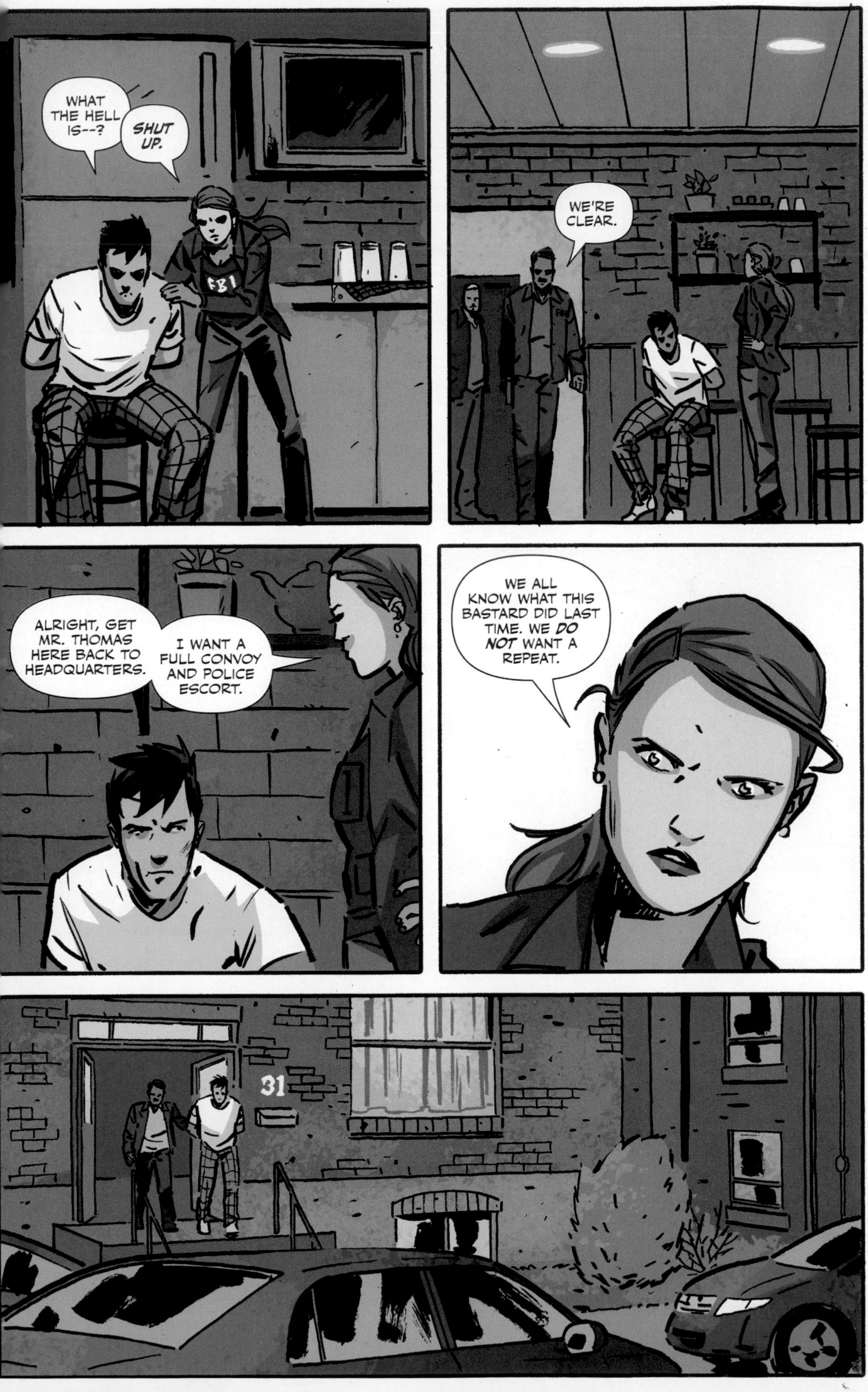
WHAT THE HELL IS--?
SHUT UP.
WE'RE CLEAR.
ALRIGHT, GET MR. THOMAS HERE BACK TO HEADQUARTERS.
I WANT A FULL CONVOY AND POLICE ESCORT.
WE ALL KNOW WHAT THIS BASTARD DID LAST TIME. WE DO NOT WANT A REPEAT.
31

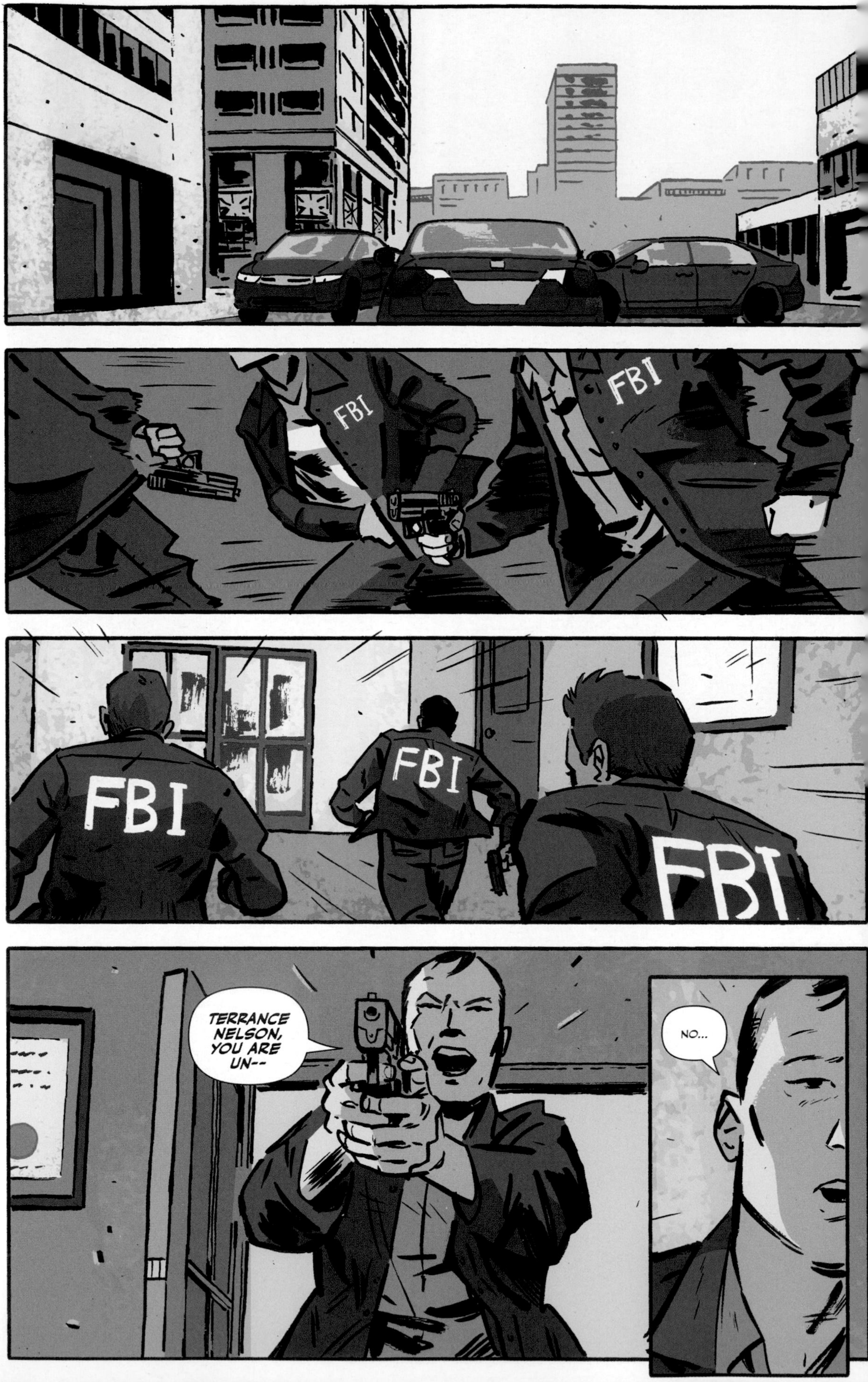
FBI
FBI
FBI
FBI
FBI
TERRANCE NELSON, YOU ARE UN--
NO...

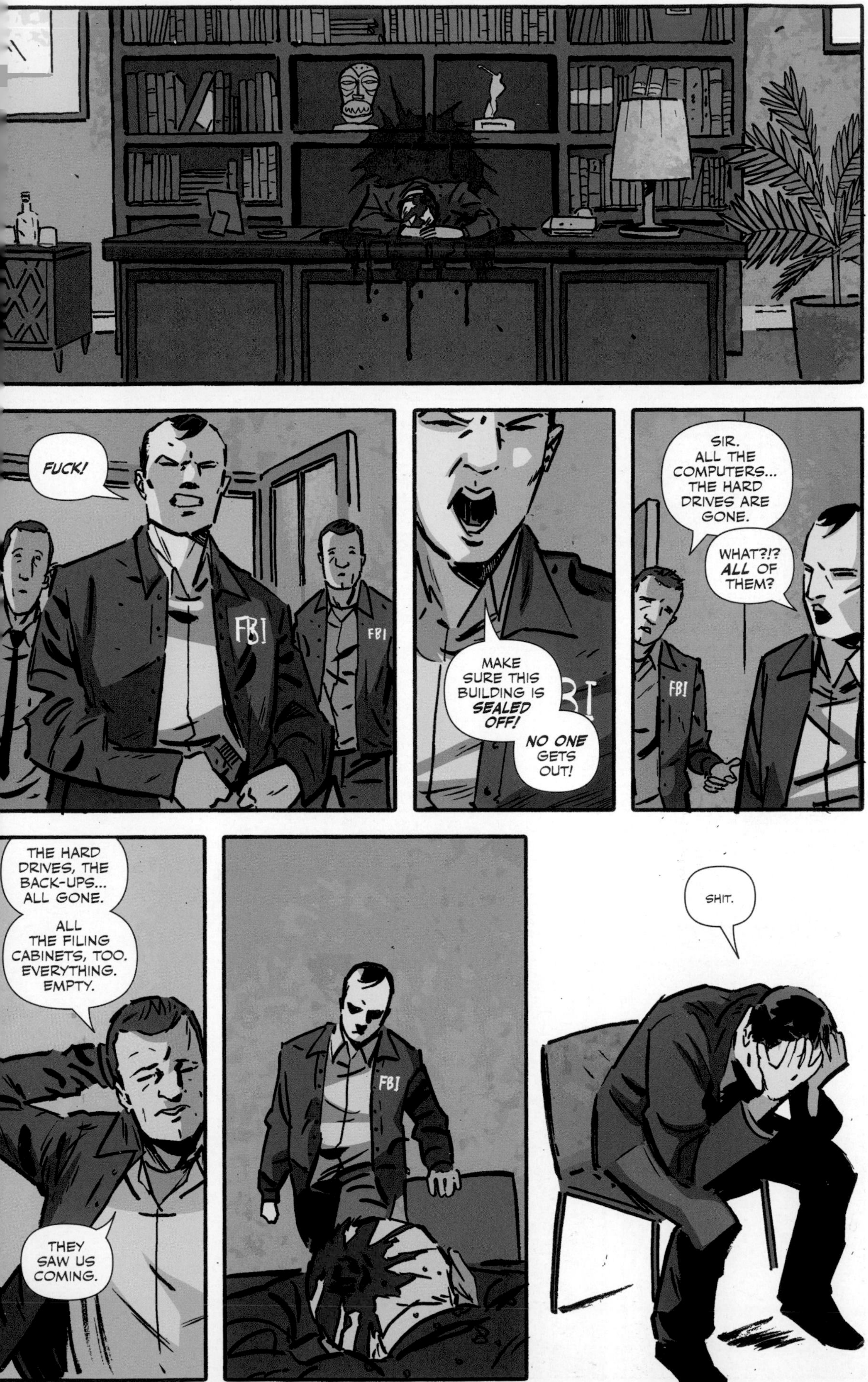
FUCK!
MAKE SURE THIS BUILDING IS SEALED OFF!
NO ONE GETS OUT!
SIR. ALL THE COMPUTERS... THE HARD DRIVES ARE GONE.
WHAT?!? ALL OF THEM?
THE HARD DRIVES, THE BACK-UPS... ALL GONE.
ALL THE FILING CABINETS, TOO. EVERYTHING. EMPTY.
THEY SAW US COMING.
SHIT.

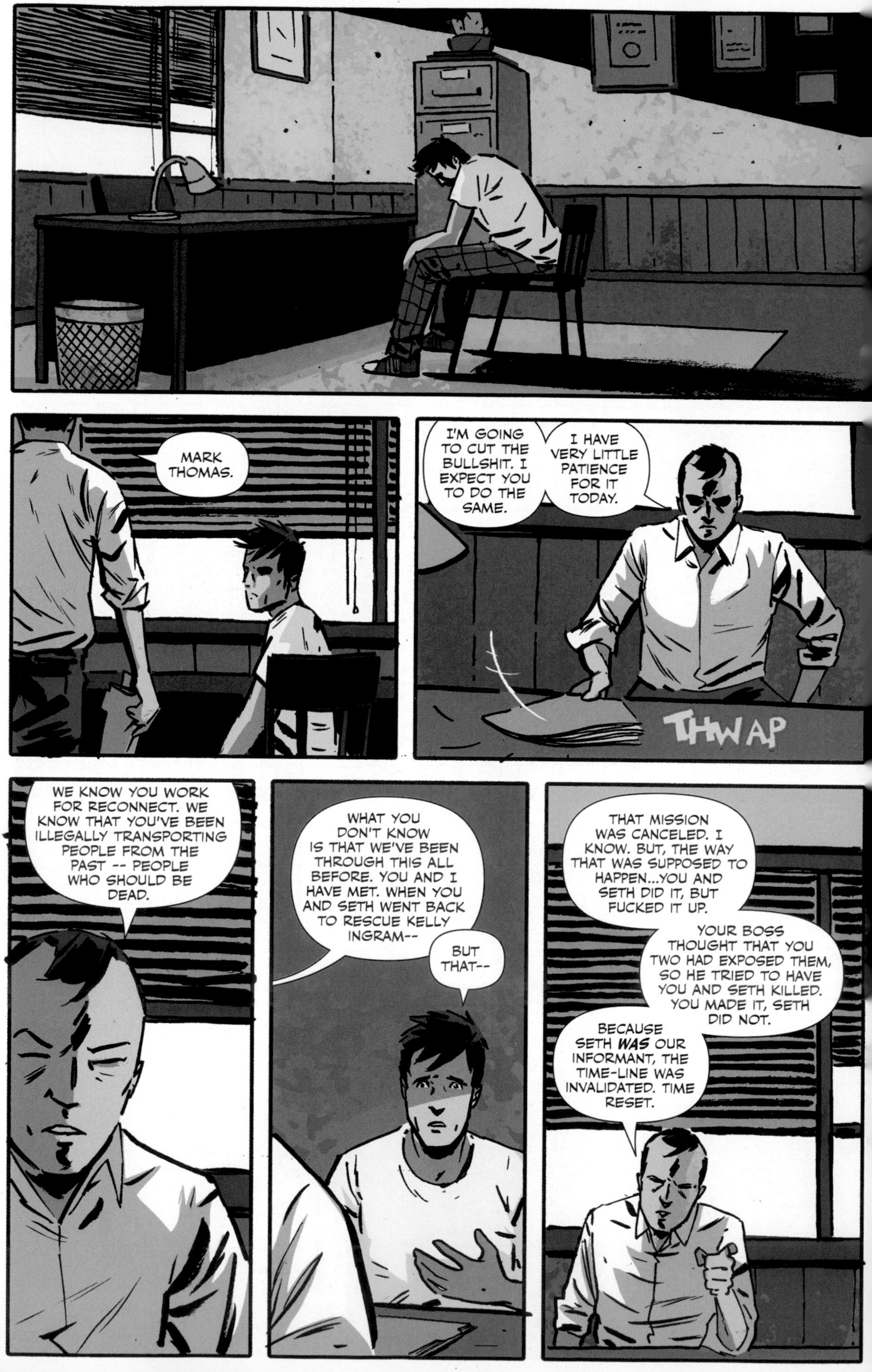
MARK THOMAS.
I'M GOING TO CUT THE BULLSHIT. I EXPECT YOU TO DO THE SAME.
I HAVE VERY LITTLE PATIENCE FOR IT TODAY.
THWAP
WE KNOW YOU WORK FOR RECONNECT. WE KNOW THAT YOU'VE BEEN ILLEGALLY TRANSPORTING PEOPLE FROM THE PAST -- PEOPLE WHO SHOULD BE DEAD.
WHAT YOU DON'T KNOW IS THAT WE'VE BEEN THROUGH THIS ALL BEFORE. YOU AND I HAVE MET. WHEN YOU AND SETH WENT BACK TO RESCUE KELLY INGRAM--
BUT THAT--
THAT MISSION WAS CANCELED. I KNOW. BUT, THE WAY THAT WAS SUPPOSED TO HAPPEN...YOU AND SETH DID IT, BUT FUCKED IT UP.
YOUR BOSS THOUGHT THAT YOU TWO HAD EXPOSED THEM, SO HE TRIED TO HAVE YOU AND SETH KILLED. YOU MADE IT, SETH DID NOT.
BECAUSE SETH *WAS* OUR INFORMANT, THE TIME-LINE WAS INVALIDATED. TIME RESET.

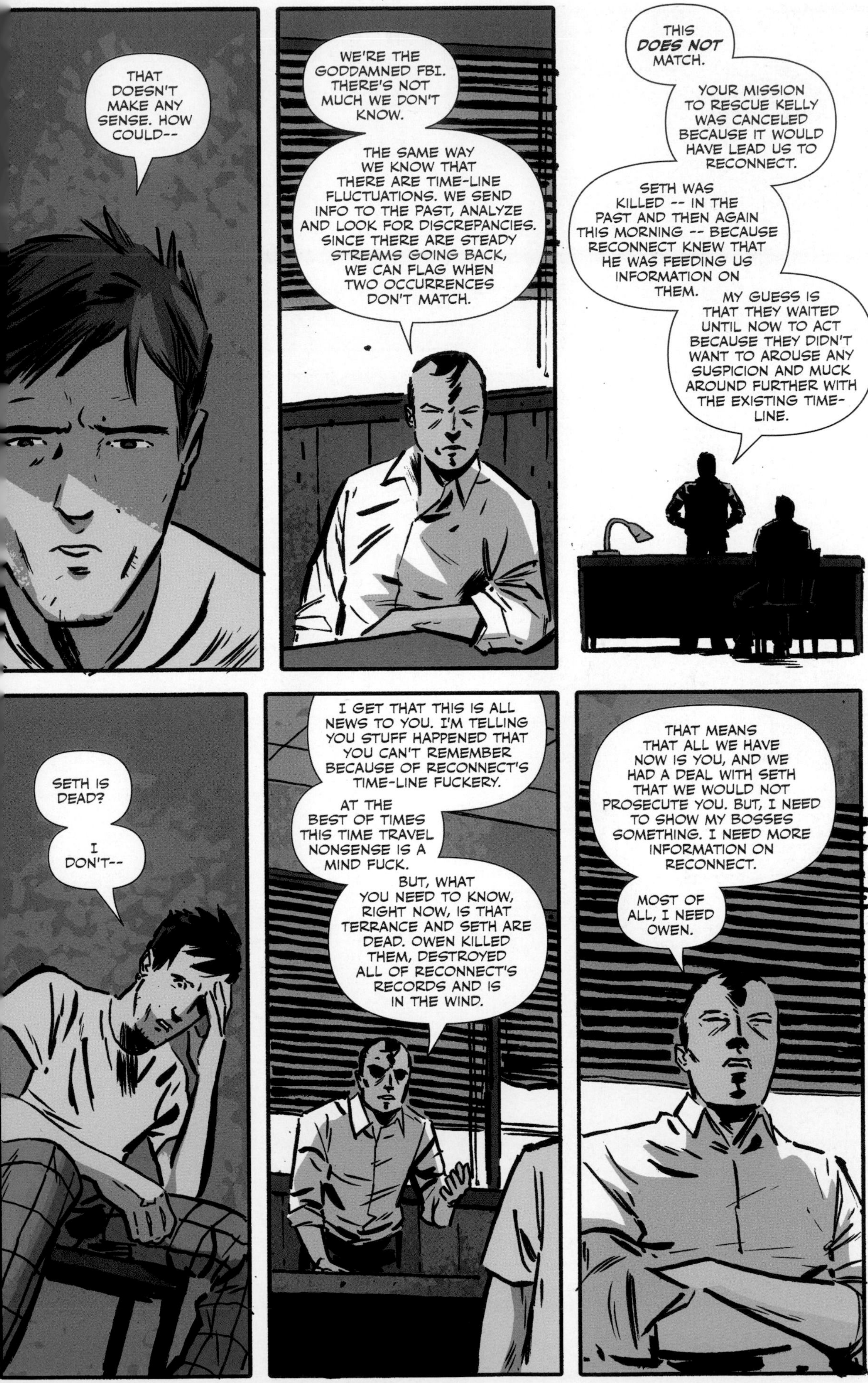
THAT DOESN'T MAKE ANY SENSE. HOW COULD--
WE'RE THE GODDAMNED FBI. THERE'S NOT MUCH WE DON'T KNOW.
THE SAME WAY WE KNOW THAT THERE ARE TIME-LINE FLUCTUATIONS. WE SEND INFO TO THE PAST, ANALYZE AND LOOK FOR DISCREPANCIES. SINCE THERE ARE STEADY STREAMS GOING BACK, WE CAN FLAG WHEN TWO OCCURRENCES DON'T MATCH.
THIS *DOES NOT* MATCH.
YOUR MISSION TO RESCUE KELLY WAS CANCELED BECAUSE IT WOULD HAVE LEAD US TO RECONNECT.
SETH WAS KILLED -- IN THE PAST AND THEN AGAIN THIS MORNING -- BECAUSE RECONNECT KNEW THAT HE WAS FEEDING US INFORMATION ON THEM.
MY GUESS IS THAT THEY WAITED UNTIL NOW TO ACT BECAUSE THEY DIDN'T WANT TO AROUSE ANY SUSPICION AND MUCK AROUND FURTHER WITH THE EXISTING TIME-LINE.
SETH IS DEAD?
I DON'T--
I GET THAT THIS IS ALL NEWS TO YOU. I'M TELLING YOU STUFF HAPPENED THAT YOU CAN'T REMEMBER BECAUSE OF RECONNECT'S TIME-LINE FUCKERY.
AT THE BEST OF TIMES THIS TIME TRAVEL NONSENSE IS A MIND FUCK.
BUT, WHAT YOU NEED TO KNOW, RIGHT NOW, IS THAT TERRANCE AND SETH ARE DEAD. OWEN KILLED THEM, DESTROYED ALL OF RECONNECT'S RECORDS AND IS IN THE WIND.
THAT MEANS THAT ALL WE HAVE NOW IS YOU, AND WE HAD A DEAL WITH SETH THAT WE WOULD NOT PROSECUTE YOU. BUT, I NEED TO SHOW MY BOSSES SOMETHING. I NEED MORE INFORMATION ON RECONNECT.
MOST OF ALL, I NEED OWEN.

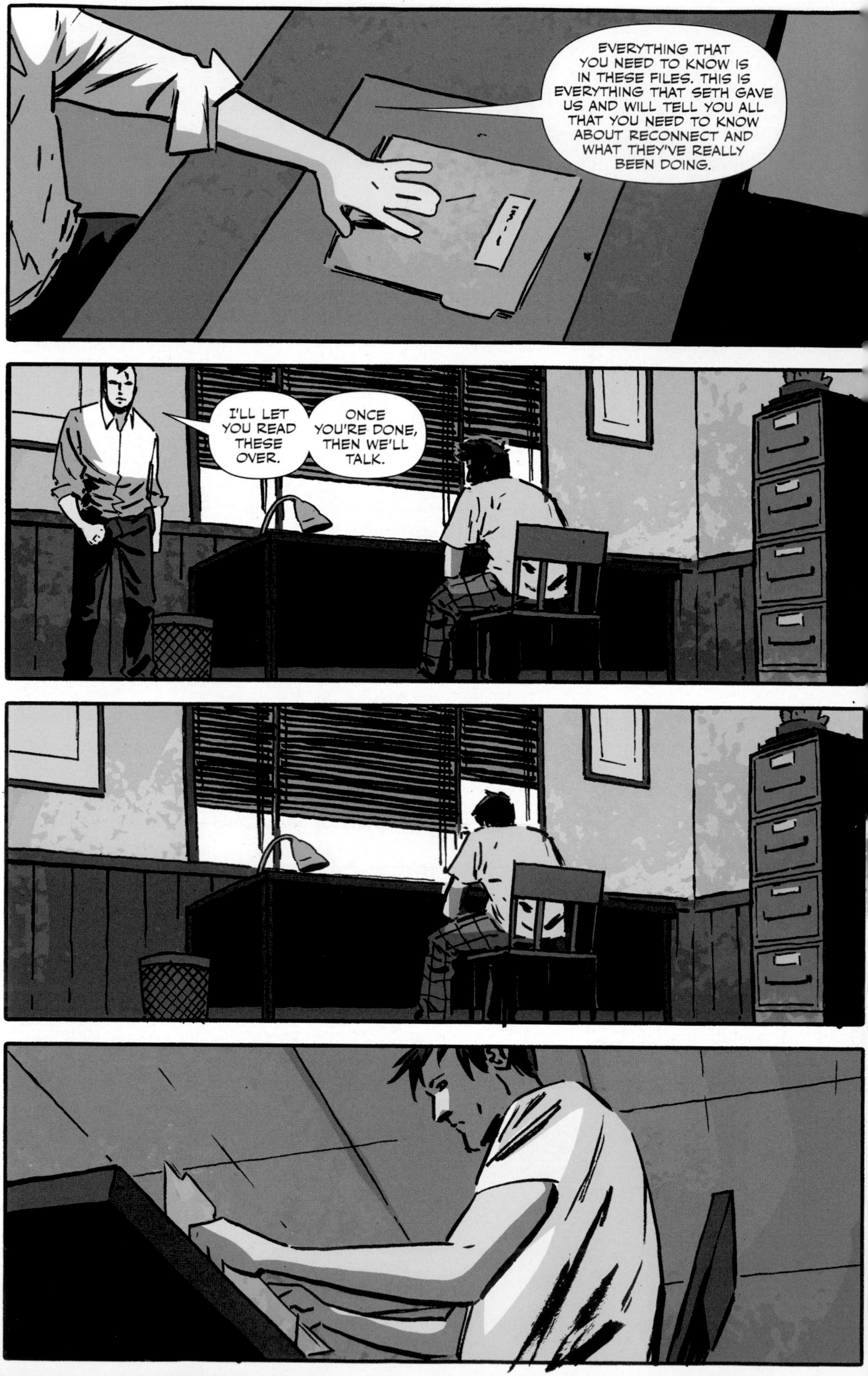
EVERYTHING THAT YOU NEED TO KNOW IS IN THESE FILES. THIS IS EVERYTHING THAT SETH GAVE US AND WILL TELL YOU ALL THAT YOU NEED TO KNOW ABOUT RECONNECT AND WHAT THEY'VE REALLY BEEN DOING.
I'LL LET YOU READ THESE OVER.
ONCE YOU'RE DONE, THEN WE'LL TALK.

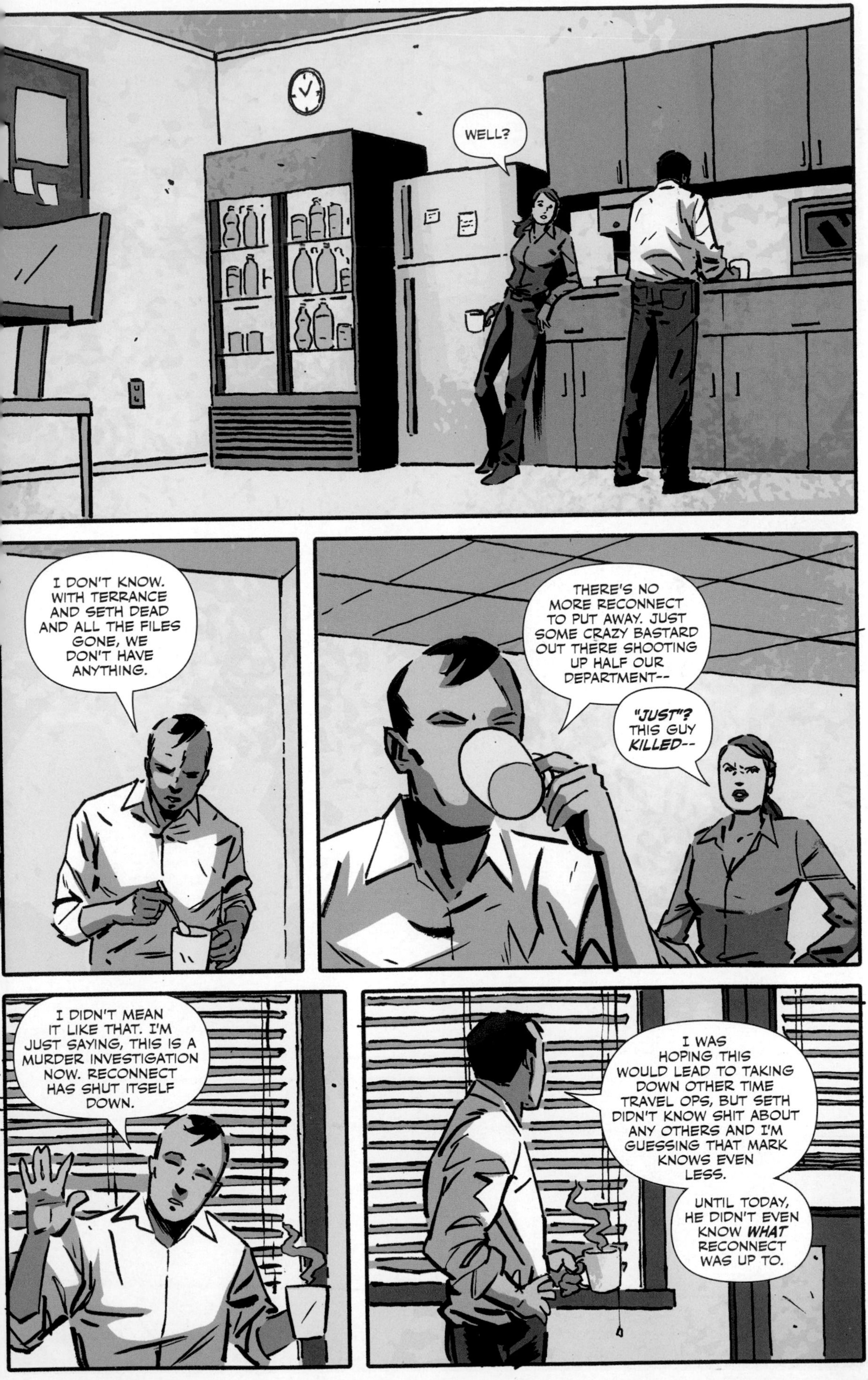
WELL?
I DON'T KNOW. WITH TERRANCE AND SETH DEAD AND ALL THE FILES GONE, WE DON'T HAVE ANYTHING.
THERE'S NO MORE RECONNECT TO PUT AWAY. JUST SOME CRAZY BASTARD OUT THERE SHOOTING UP HALF OUR DEPARTMENT--
"JUST"? THIS GUY KILLED--
I DIDN'T MEAN IT LIKE THAT. I'M JUST SAYING, THIS IS A MURDER INVESTIGATION NOW. RECONNECT HAS SHUT ITSELF DOWN.
I WAS HOPING THIS WOULD LEAD TO TAKING DOWN OTHER TIME TRAVEL OPS, BUT SETH DIDN'T KNOW SHIT ABOUT ANY OTHERS AND I'M GUESSING THAT MARK KNOWS EVEN LESS.
UNTIL TODAY, HE DIDN'T EVEN KNOW WHAT RECONNECT WAS UP TO.

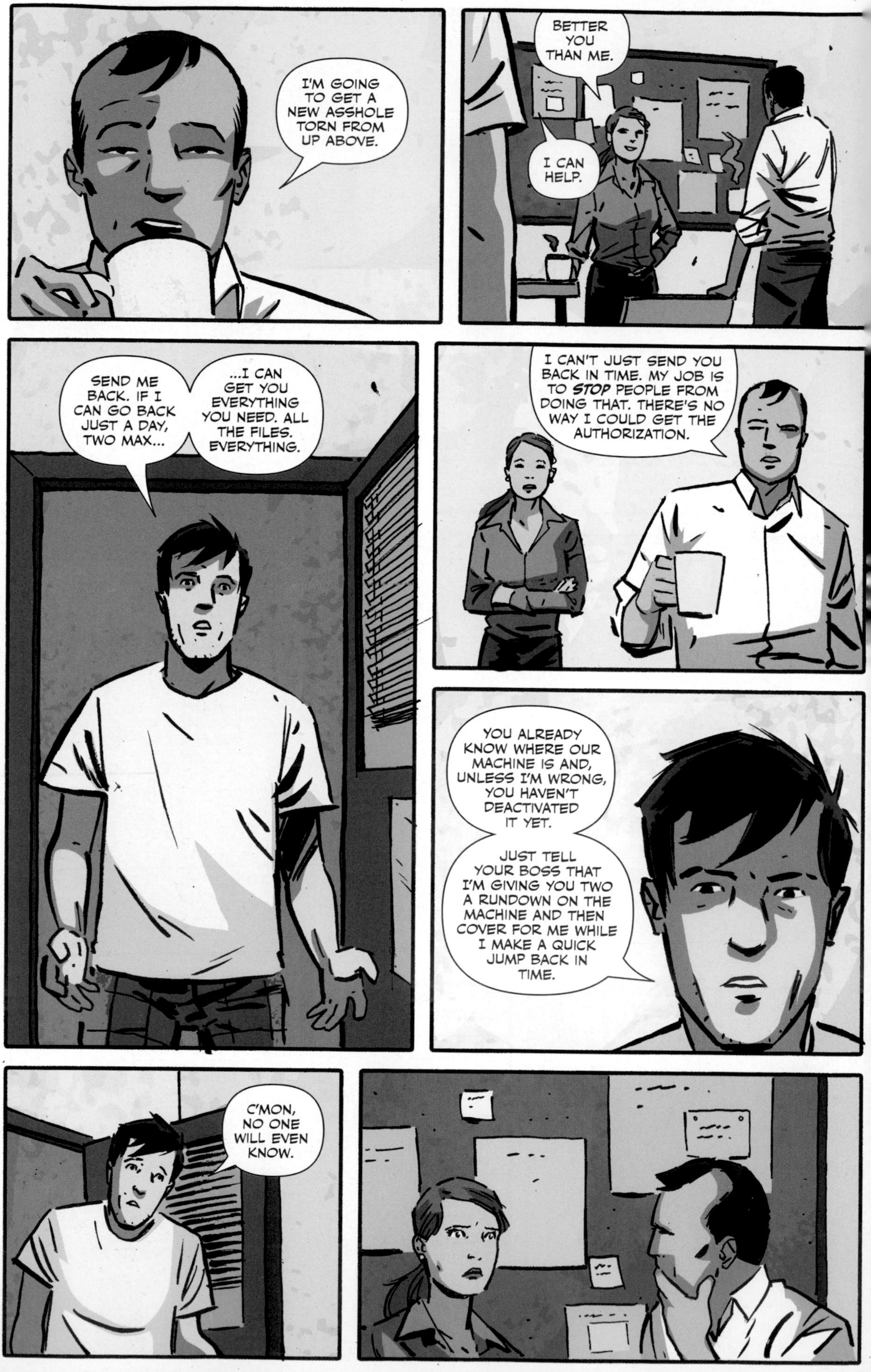
I'M GOING TO GET A NEW ASSHOLE TORN FROM UP ABOVE.
BETTER YOU THAN ME.
I CAN HELP.
SEND ME BACK. IF I CAN GO BACK JUST A DAY, TWO MAX...
...I CAN GET YOU EVERYTHING YOU NEED. ALL THE FILES. EVERYTHING.
I CAN'T JUST SEND YOU BACK IN TIME. MY JOB IS TO *STOP* PEOPLE FROM DOING THAT. THERE'S NO WAY I COULD GET THE AUTHORIZATION.
YOU ALREADY KNOW WHERE OUR MACHINE IS AND, UNLESS I'M WRONG, YOU HAVEN'T DEACTIVATED IT YET.
JUST TELL YOUR BOSS THAT I'M GIVING YOU TWO A RUNDOWN ON THE MACHINE AND THEN COVER FOR ME WHILE I MAKE A QUICK JUMP BACK IN TIME.
C'MON, NO ONE WILL EVEN KNOW.

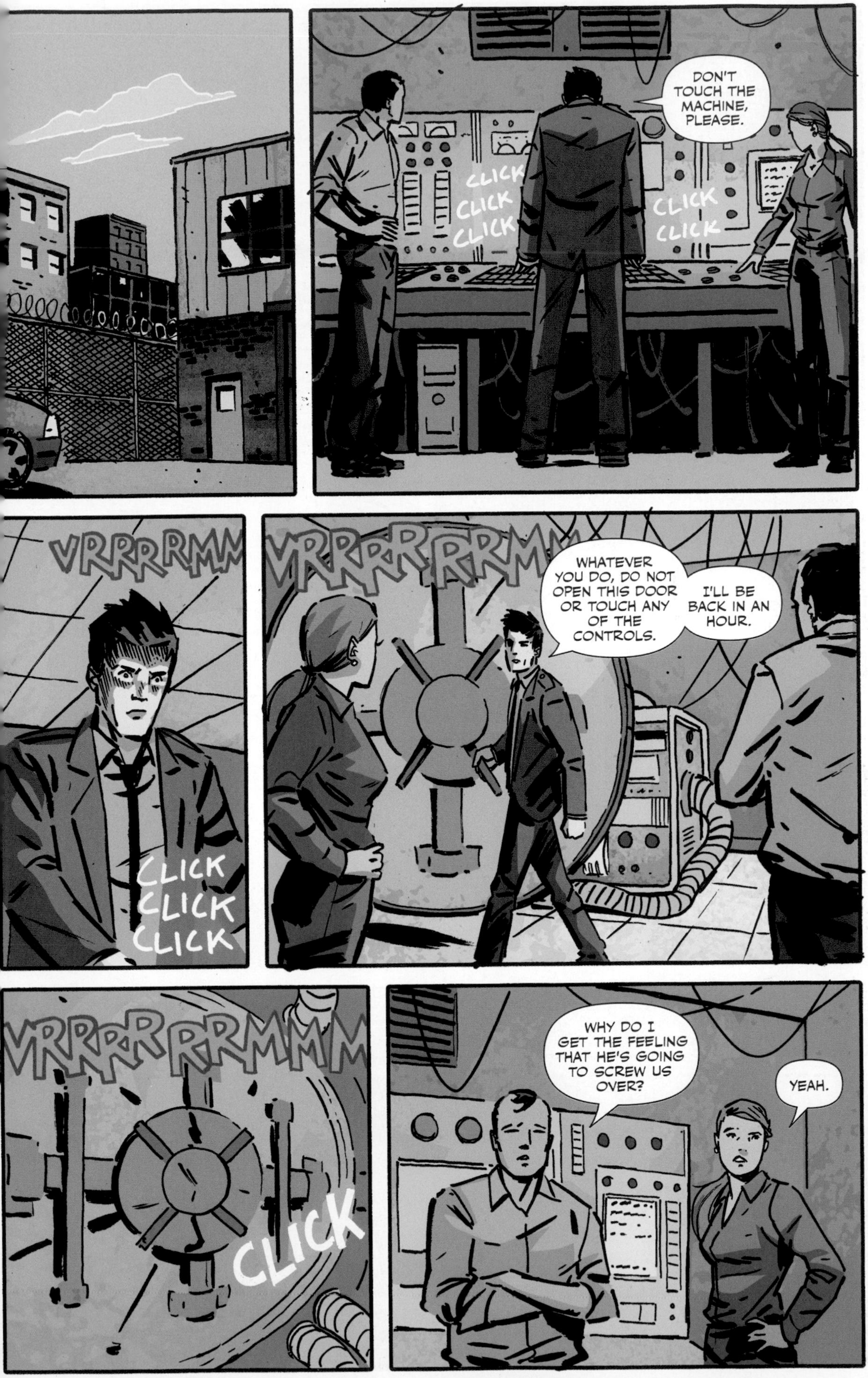
DON'T TOUCH THE MACHINE, PLEASE.
CLICK CLICK CLICK
CLICK CLICK
VRRRRMM
CLICK CLICK CLICK
VRRRRRRMM
WHATEVER YOU DO, DO NOT OPEN THIS DOOR OR TOUCH ANY OF THE CONTROLS.
I'LL BE BACK IN AN HOUR.
VRRRRRRMMM
CLICK
WHY DO I GET THE FEELING THAT HE'S GOING TO SCREW US OVER?
YEAH.

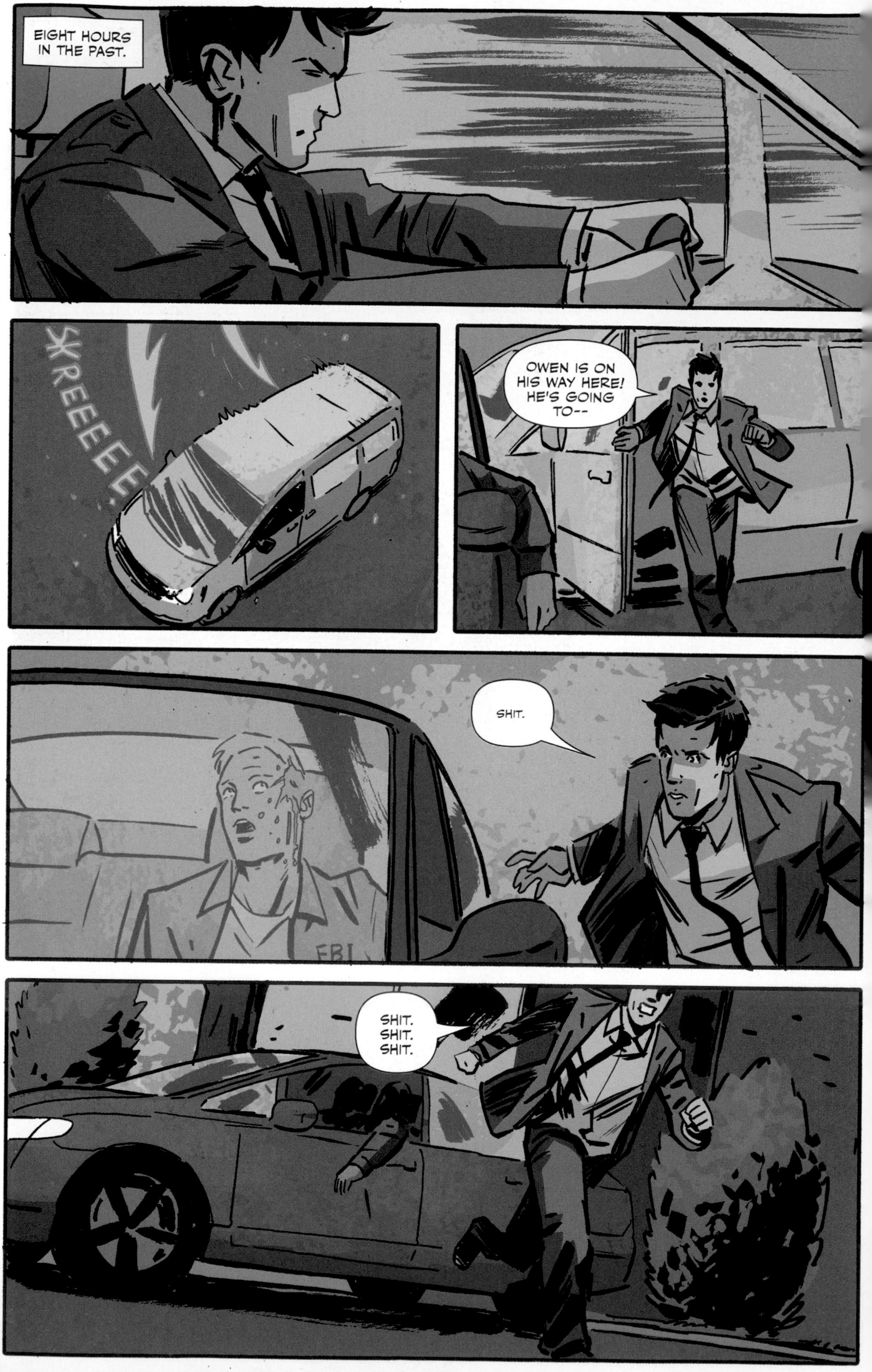
EIGHT HOURS IN THE PAST.
SKREEEEE
OWEN IS ON HIS WAY HERE! HE'S GOING TO--
SHIT.
FBI
SHIT. SHIT. SHIT.

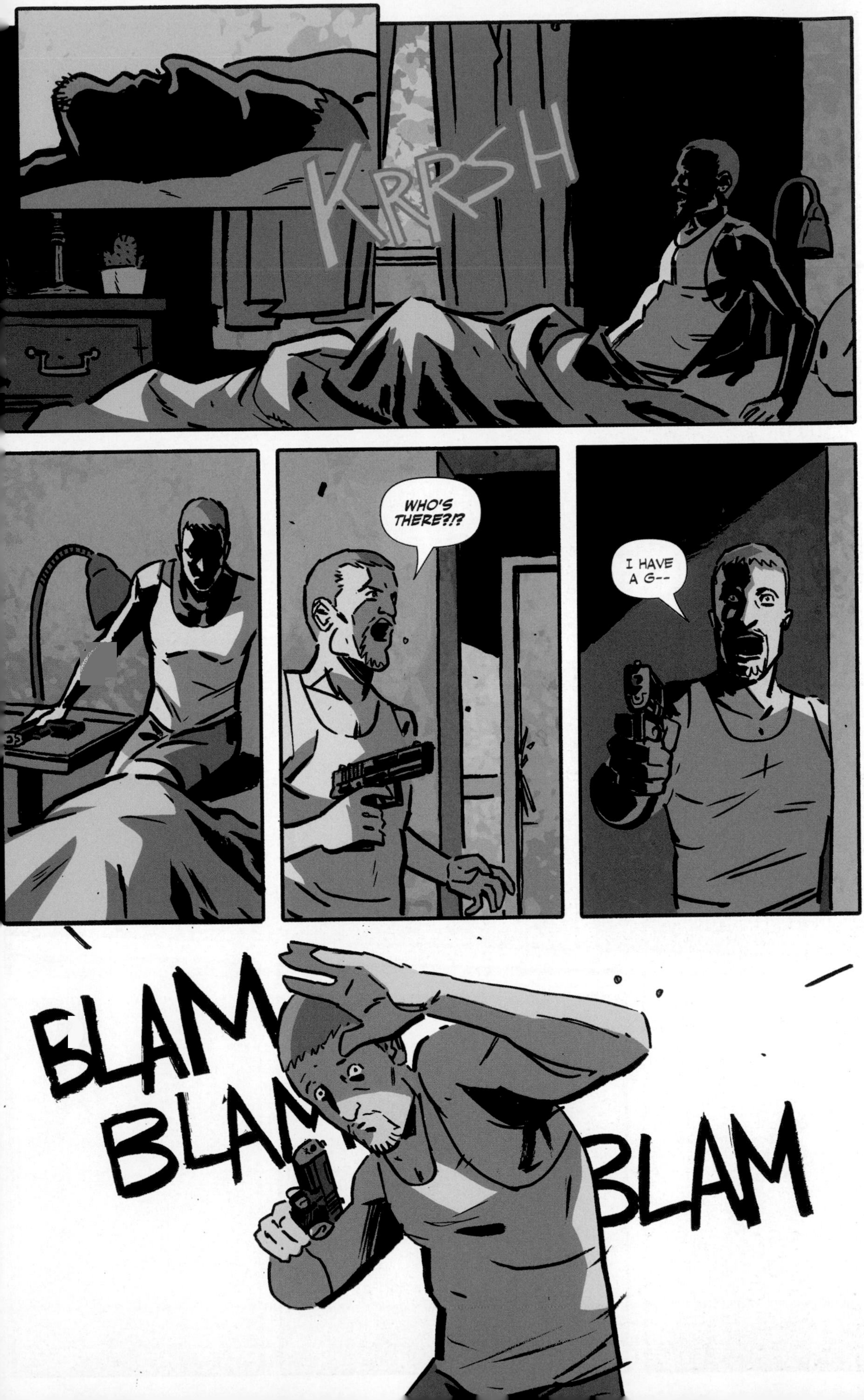
KRRSH
WHO'S THERE?!?
I HAVE A G--
BLAM
BLAM
BLAM

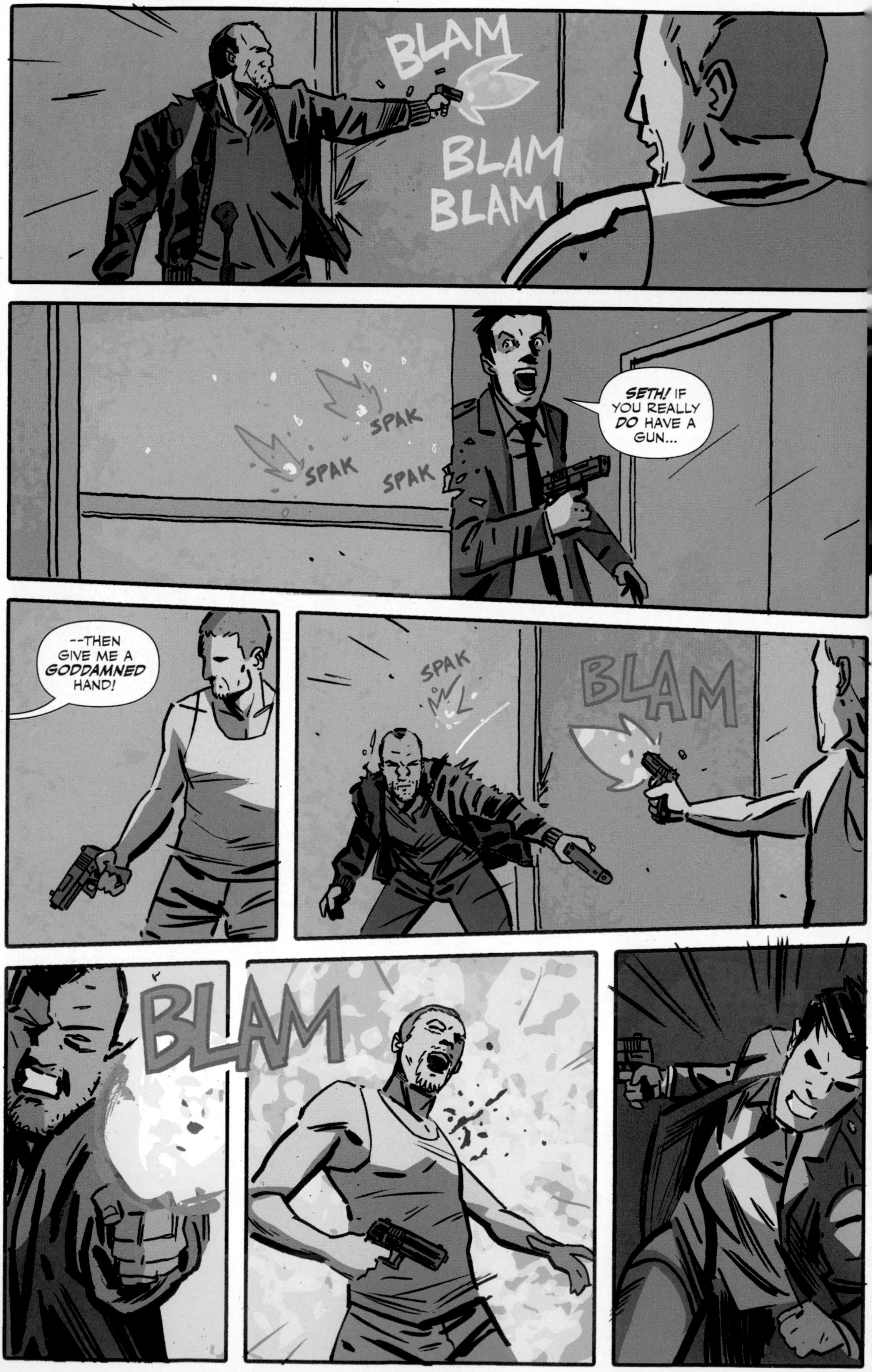
BLAM
BLAM
BLAM
SPAK
SPAK
SPAK
SETH! IF YOU REALLY DO HAVE A GUN...
--THEN GIVE ME A GODDAMNED HAND!
SPAK
BLAM
BLAM

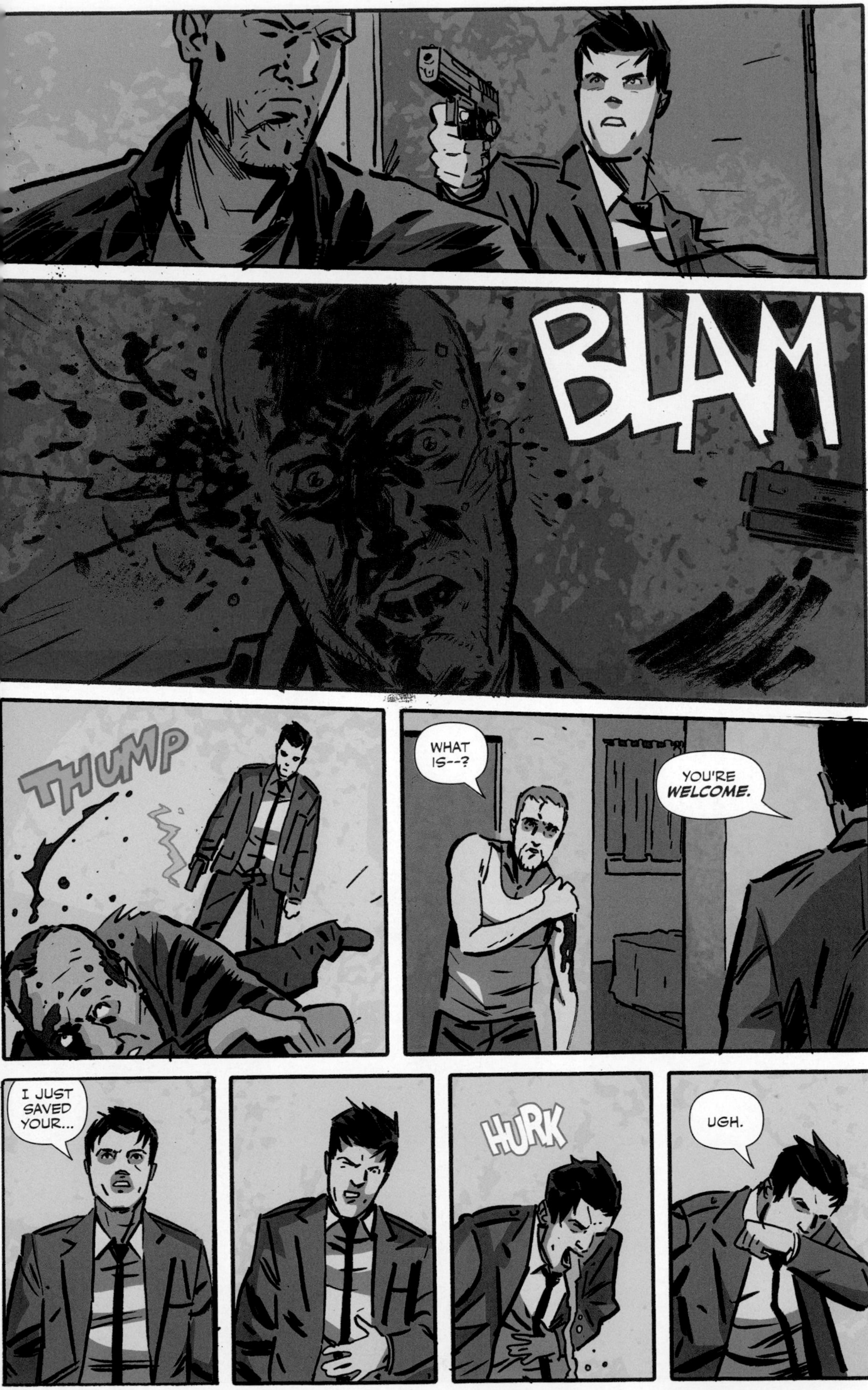
BLAM
THUMP
WHAT IS--?
YOU'RE *WELCOME.*
I JUST SAVED YOUR...
HURK
UGH.

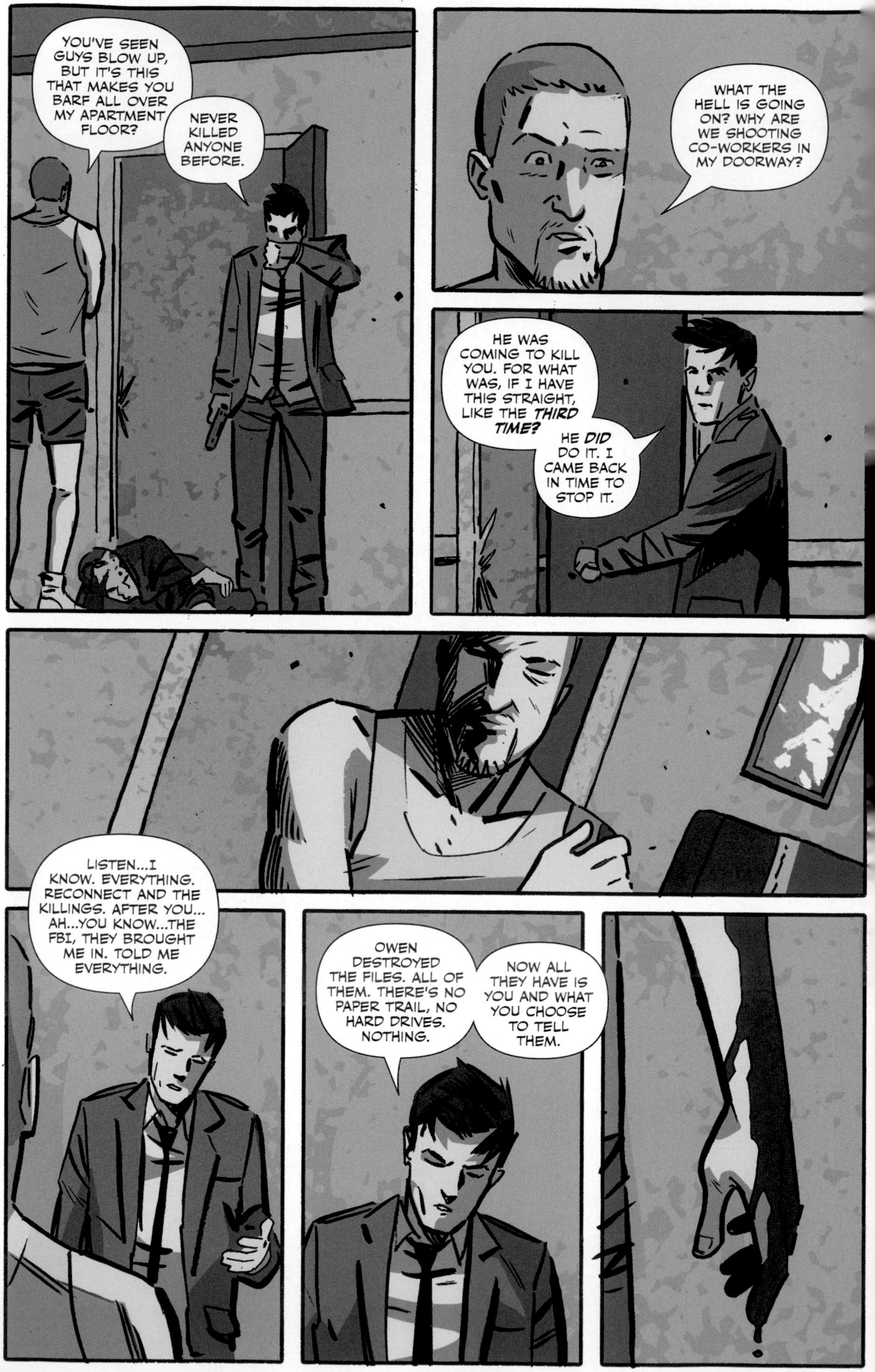

YOU'VE SEEN GUYS BLOW UP, BUT IT'S THIS THAT MAKES YOU BARF ALL OVER MY APARTMENT FLOOR?
NEVER KILLED ANYONE BEFORE.
WHAT THE HELL IS GOING ON? WHY ARE WE SHOOTING CO-WORKERS IN MY DOORWAY?
HE WAS COMING TO KILL YOU. FOR WHAT WAS, IF I HAVE THIS STRAIGHT, LIKE THE *THIRD TIME?*
HE *DID* DO IT. I CAME BACK IN TIME TO STOP IT.
LISTEN...I KNOW. EVERYTHING. RECONNECT AND THE KILLINGS. AFTER YOU... AH...YOU KNOW...THE FBI, THEY BROUGHT ME IN. TOLD ME EVERYTHING.
OWEN DESTROYED THE FILES. ALL OF THEM. THERE'S NO PAPER TRAIL, NO HARD DRIVES. NOTHING.
NOW ALL THEY HAVE IS YOU AND WHAT YOU CHOOSE TO TELL THEM.

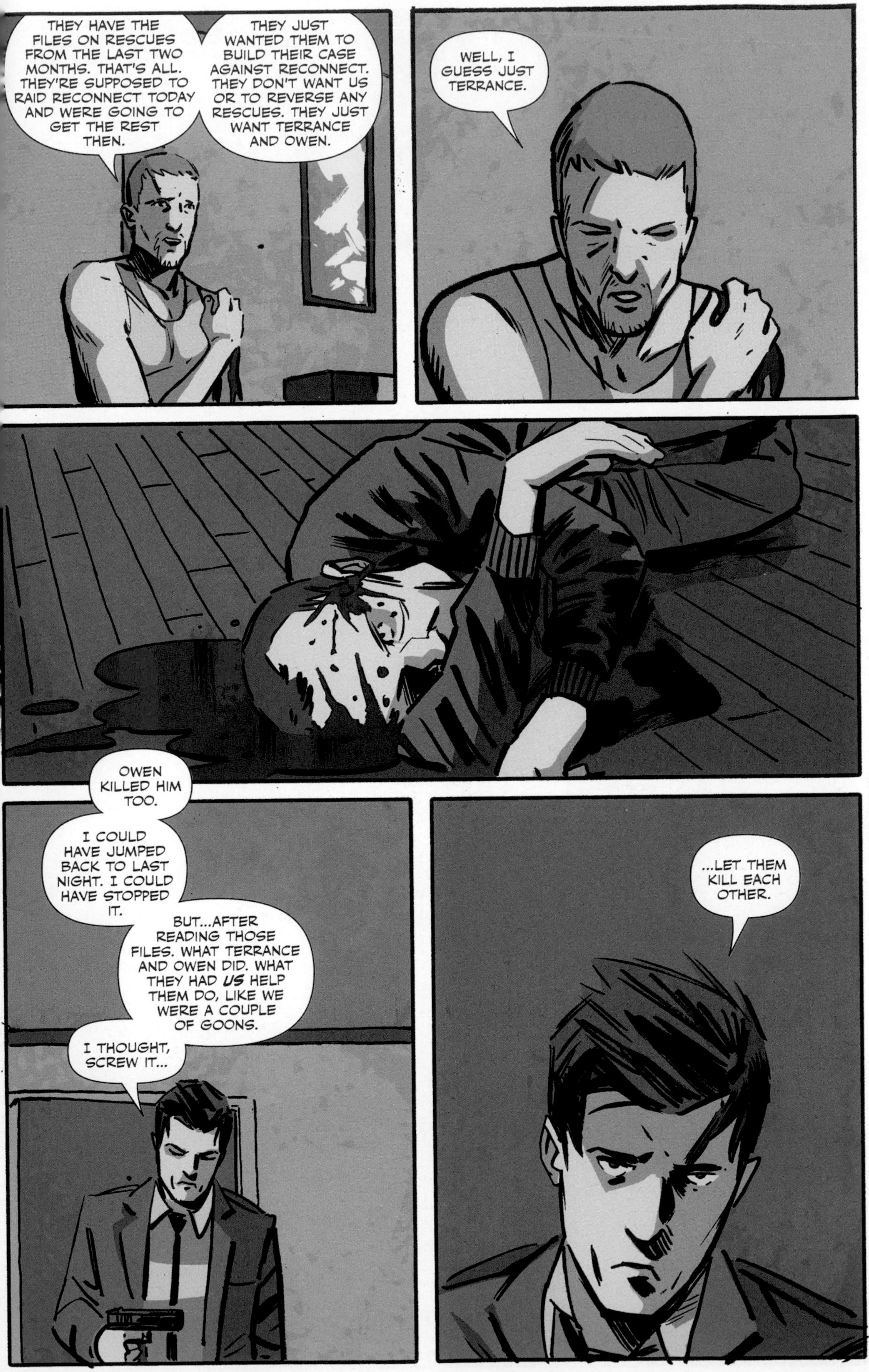
THEY HAVE THE FILES ON RESCUES FROM THE LAST TWO MONTHS. THAT'S ALL. THEY'RE SUPPOSED TO RAID RECONNECT TODAY AND WERE GOING TO GET THE REST THEN.
THEY JUST WANTED THEM TO BUILD THEIR CASE AGAINST RECONNECT. THEY DON'T WANT US OR TO REVERSE ANY RESCUES. THEY JUST WANT TERRANCE AND OWEN.
WELL, I GUESS JUST TERRANCE.
OWEN KILLED HIM TOO.
I COULD HAVE JUMPED BACK TO LAST NIGHT. I COULD HAVE STOPPED IT.
BUT...AFTER READING THOSE FILES. WHAT TERRANCE AND OWEN DID. WHAT THEY HAD *US* HELP THEM DO, LIKE WE WERE A COUPLE OF GOONS.
I THOUGHT, SCREW IT...
...LET THEM KILL EACH OTHER.

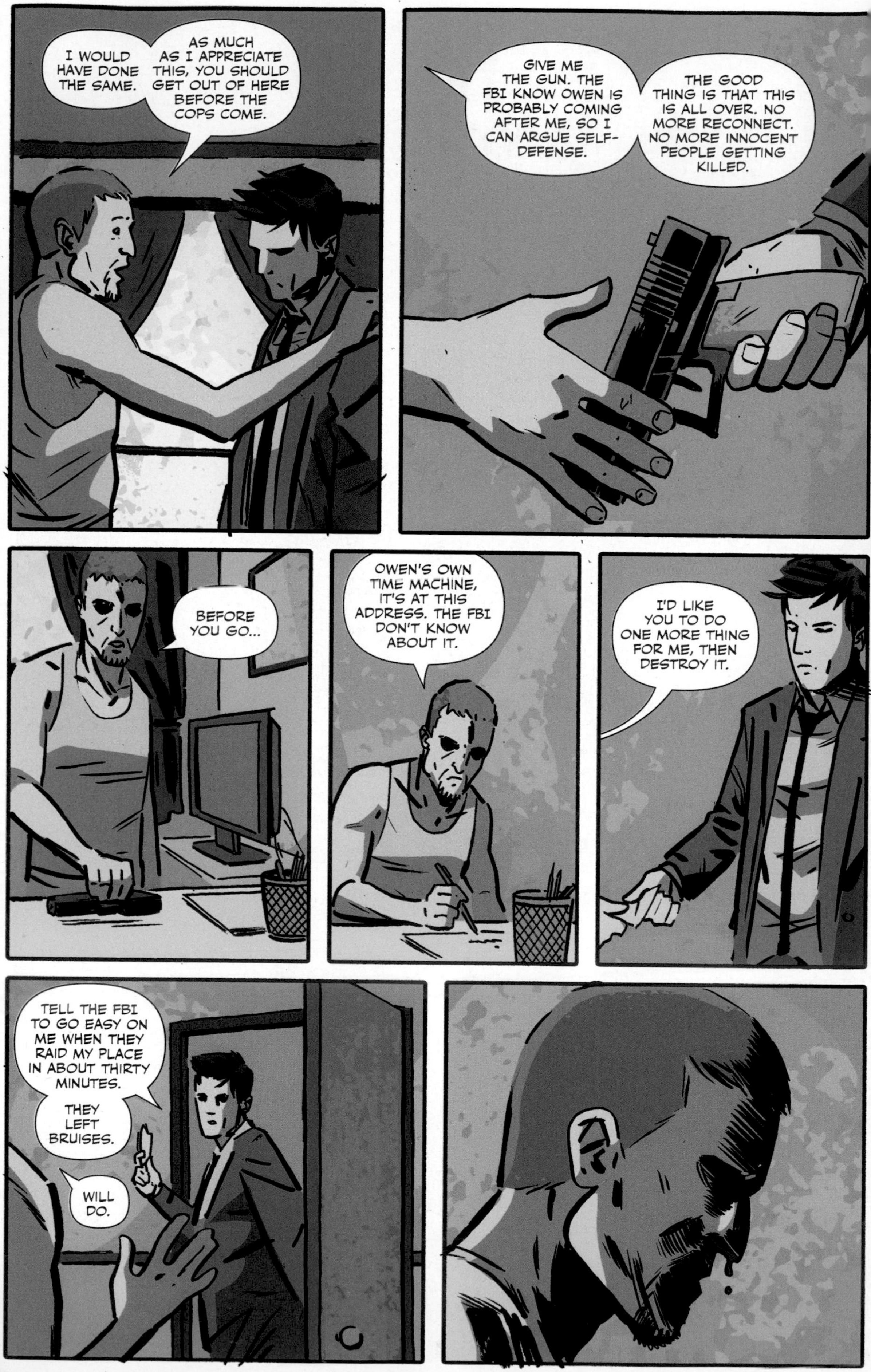
I WOULD HAVE DONE THE SAME.
AS MUCH AS I APPRECIATE THIS, YOU SHOULD GET OUT OF HERE BEFORE THE COPS COME.
GIVE ME THE GUN. THE FBI KNOW OWEN IS PROBABLY COMING AFTER ME, SO I CAN ARGUE SELF-DEFENSE.
THE GOOD THING IS THAT THIS IS ALL OVER. NO MORE RECONNECT. NO MORE INNOCENT PEOPLE GETTING KILLED.
BEFORE YOU GO...
OWEN'S OWN TIME MACHINE, IT'S AT THIS ADDRESS. THE FBI DON'T KNOW ABOUT IT.
I'D LIKE YOU TO DO ONE MORE THING FOR ME, THEN DESTROY IT.
TELL THE FBI TO GO EASY ON ME WHEN THEY RAID MY PLACE IN ABOUT THIRTY MINUTES.
THEY LEFT BRUISES.
WILL DO.

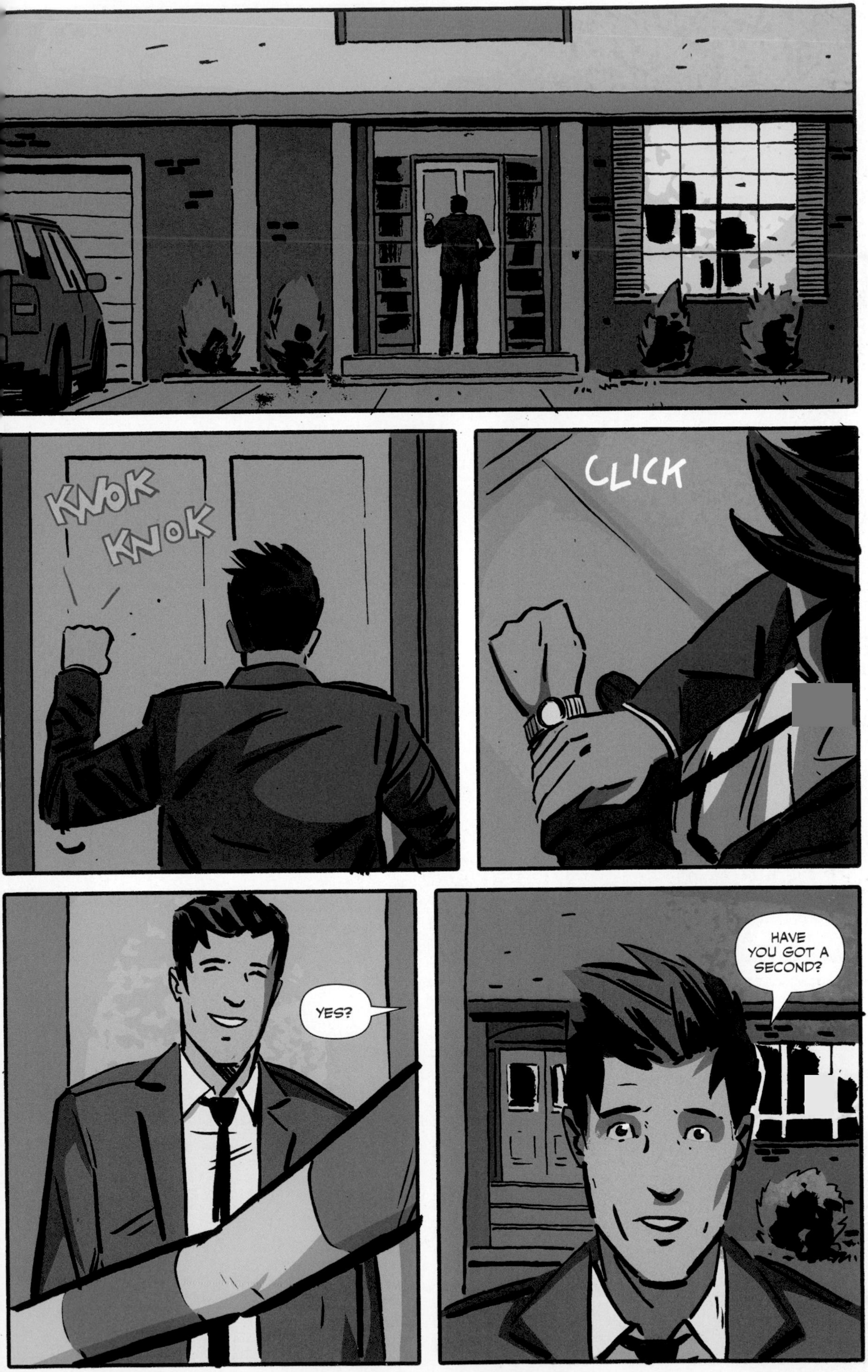
KNOK KNOK
CLICK
YES?
HAVE YOU GOT A SECOND?

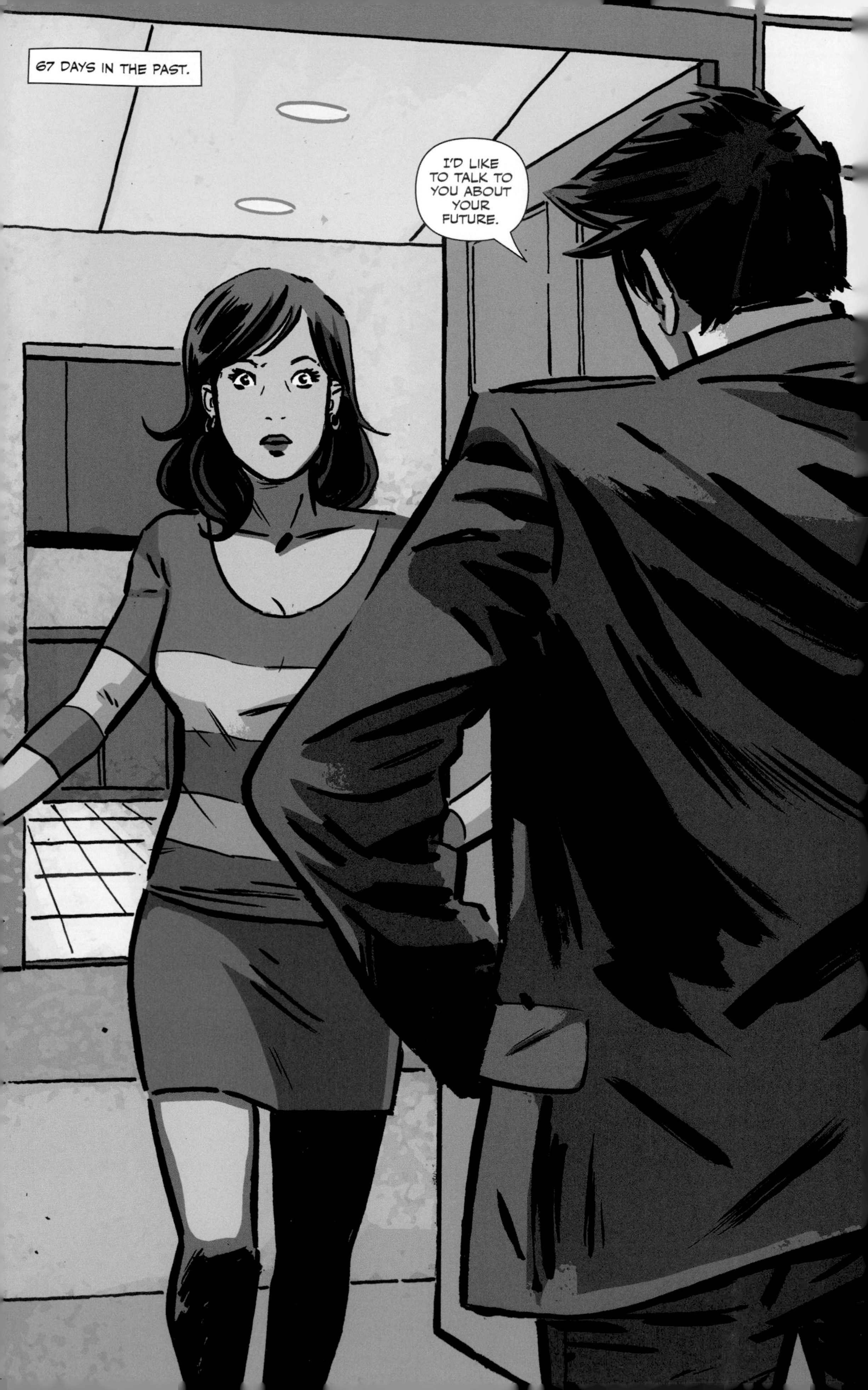
67 DAYS IN THE PAST.
I'D LIKE TO TALK TO YOU ABOUT YOUR FUTURE.

EXTRAS

EVOLUTION OF A COVER.1

Building a cover is no simple task and while pitching COMEBACK we tossed around a bunch of different concepts before settling on a general idea which we would carry throughout the entire five issue run...

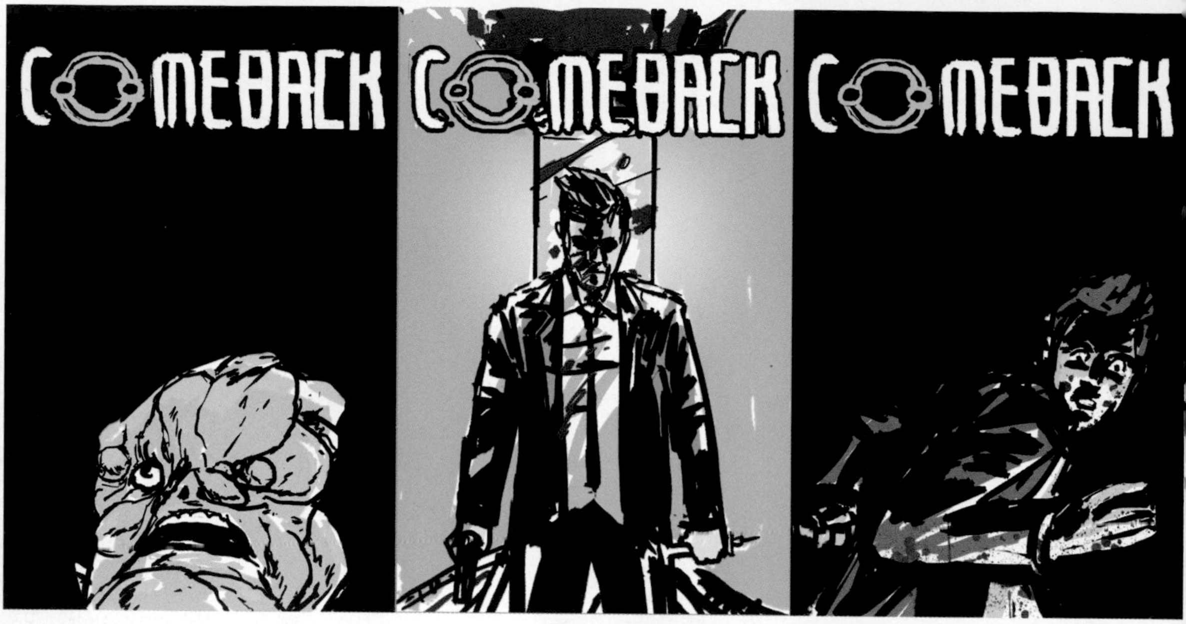
COMEBACK
COMEBACK
COMEBACK

Above: Initially we planned to play up the horror and sci-fi elements from the first issue. Here are some of the original sketches I had, mostly based around the exploding man and time travel scene.

Right: We were actually quite close to going with this cover but we decided to try and come up with a design oriented graphic that we could continue throughout each cover of the series. In this cover you can see the germ of an idea, a hand reaching for a skeleton to bring him back to the world of the living...

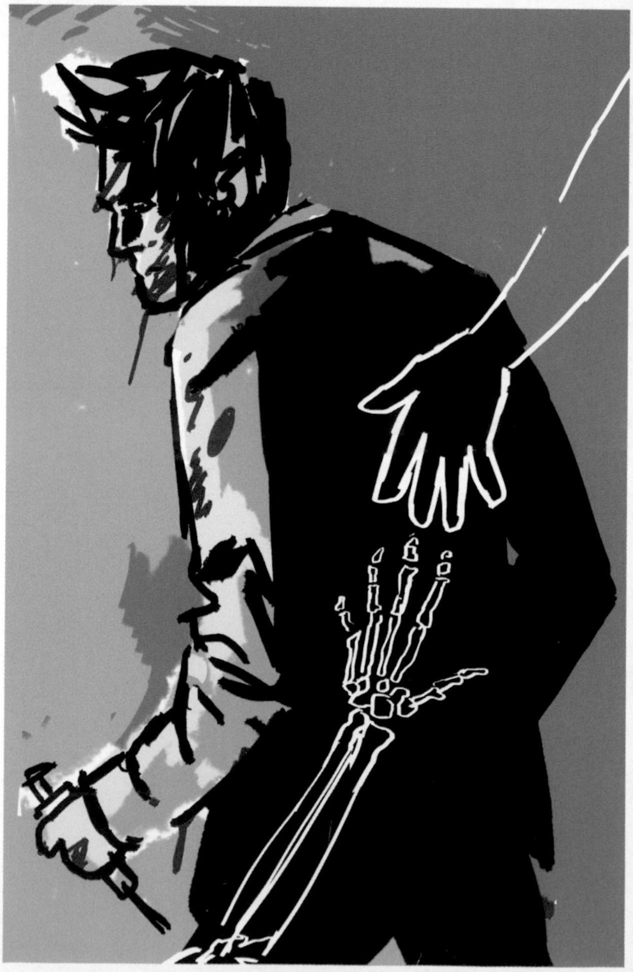

VOLUTION OF A COVER. 2

COMEBACK

COMEBACK

Originally the COMEBACK logo was facing completely forward. When we were initially picked up by Shadowline, we were tossing around some possible adjustments to the cover with designer/writer extraordinaire **Tim Daniel**. He took our original design for the logo and added some slight variations which gave it that much more personality.

COMEBACK

Here are the first tight sketches of a more graphic approach. it was around this point we decided to stick with the insert panel idea through the entire run. It was a nice way to show passing through time in a metaphorical way and to subtly integrate elements of the plot.

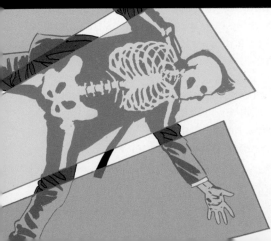

When we pitched COMEBACK, the cover colors were desaturated and dusky, more in tune with Ed's past work on MURDER BOOK. The pitch was accepted with this theme but a few days before the book went to print we went back in and kicked up the saturation to give it some extra oomph and really stand out on the shelves.

Also of note is the color sense that **Jordie Bellaire** brought to the table on all of the covers. She consistently gave us something that popped right off of the shelves and really gave the book a distinct identity.

THE PROCESS. 1

PAGE NINETEEN – 6 PANELS
PANEL 1
Mark is on the ground in a seated position. His back is up against the wall of the building they were just in front of. He's gripping his arm. He's in pain. Looming in front of him is Owen, gun pointed toward Mark.

MARK (screaming in pain): ARGGGGGH!
OWEN: Shut up. Stay down.

PANEL 2
Owen looks up, we can start seeing reality breaking apart. As we talked about before, I think everything flaking off, revealing only white behind it. I think here, it should only be just the top of the panel, barely noticeable.

OWEN: It's over now.

PANEL 3
Wincing, Mark looks up – Just watching as the world flakes away around them. Mark looks up while wincing. The amazement in what he sees overrides the pain he feels. He's still holding his arm. The walls and ceiling, their world, continues to flake away.

PANEL 4
Kelly is in the car. She notices the same.
KELLY: What's...

PANEL 5
Owen has his cell out and is talking into it while still looking down at Mark, gun ready to shoot if he tries anything. The background continues to flake away. Maybe the top 1/3 of where they're at is white now.

OWEN: Seth was the snitch.
OWEN: File it. Now.

PANEL 6
Full tier. The world continues to vanish. Maybe the background is halfway gone (the people are the last to go). Owen is snapping his cell phone shut, putting it away. Mark is on the ground, looking up. Seth and Simon are dead in the background. The smashed car smoulders on the ground.

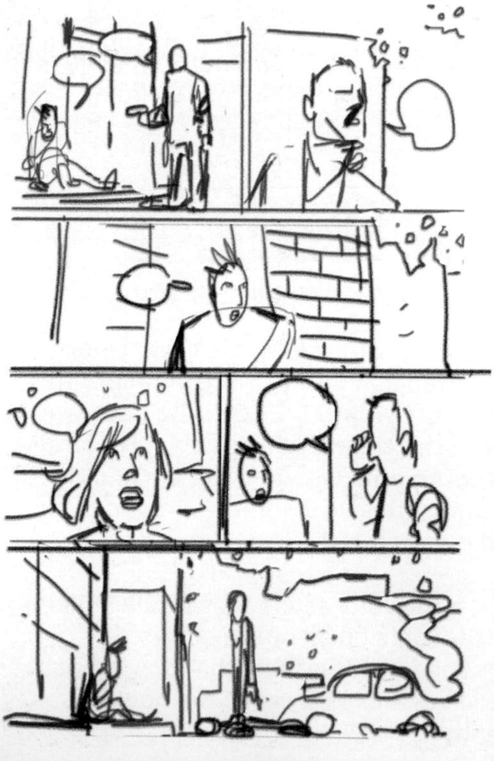

After getting the script I crudely layout a page in photoshop, getting across the general positioning of figures and camera angles. I send this back to Ed and we have a brief dialogue over whether anything needs changing.

Ed and I had been talking about this scene since before the first issue came out, we knew it was the climax of the entire series and was going to make or break it for a lot of readers.

I had done the cover for the issue already so I had somewhat established with Ed how I was going to capture the time deconstruction. We were both excited to get this sequence down on paper.

THE PROCESS. 2

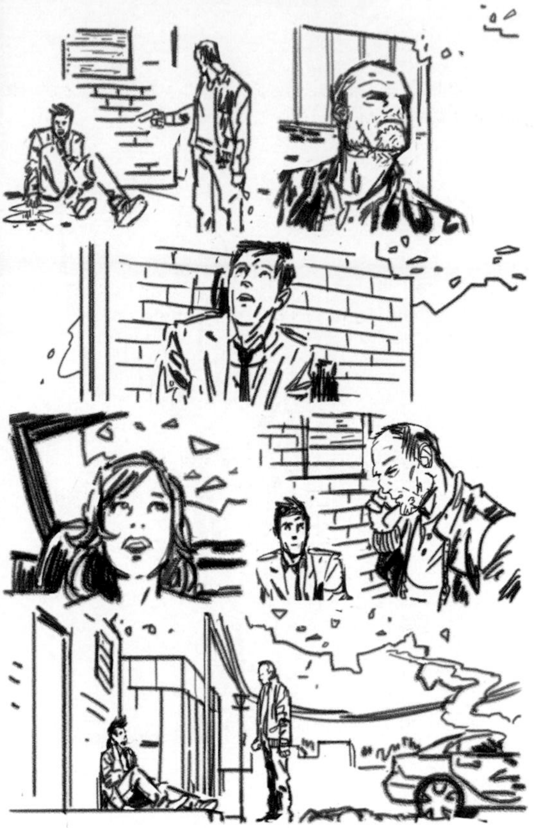

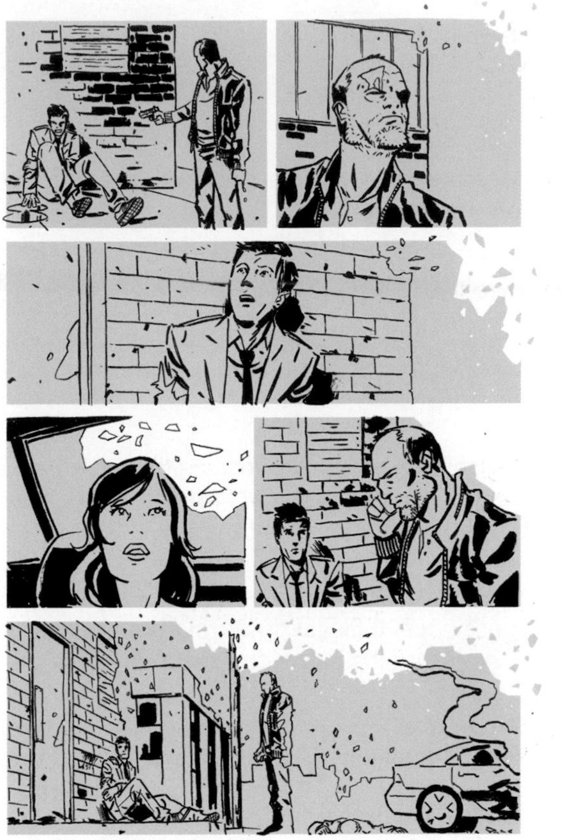

Above: Pencils + Inks. After the layouts are settled on I digitally pencil the pages in photoshop. I then print these in a light, non-photo blue, onto an 11x17 bristol paper. I usually print the panel borders on the paper in black as well but in this case I didn't. I had the idea that when Seth is killed and time is reset, the first sign of that was dropping the panel borders to make things seem immediately different, unstable.

I ink using a mixture of brushes, acrylic based artists ink and brush pens. I wanted to drop any outlines on the parts of the background that were deconstructing so when I scanned the pages back into the computer I threw a grey tone down and separated each panel, including the collapsing bits.

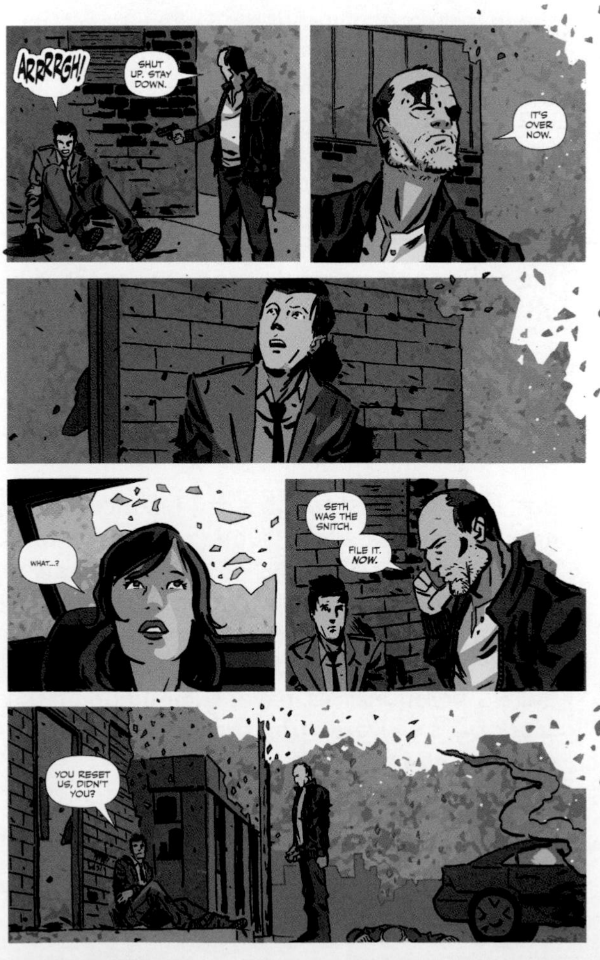

ARRRRGH!
SHUT UP. STAY DOWN.
IT'S OVER NOW.
WHAT...?
SETH WAS THE SNITCH.
FILE IT. NOW.
YOU RESET US, DIDN'T YOU?

Right: Jordie Bellaire is a genius. I said it here and you'll here it from every other collaborator that has the pleasure of working with her. This page came out looking exactly as it was in my mind only better. The muted blue creates a perfect dissonant atmosphere while the bright crimson really pops and grabs the reader.

After this Ed comes in and finishes the entire process by digitally lettering the page, giving the dialogue a pass and sometimes editing the script one final time. It starts and ends with Ed Brisson.

THE PITCH

Reconnect. To Mark, it's more than a company—it's an opportunity for good. Reconnect can reverse tragedy by sending agents into the past to rescue your mother, your wife, your brother or father or child moments before their untimely death. Mark is one of these agents. He brings the rescued from the past to the present, to a blessed reunion with their loved ones. He saves lives.

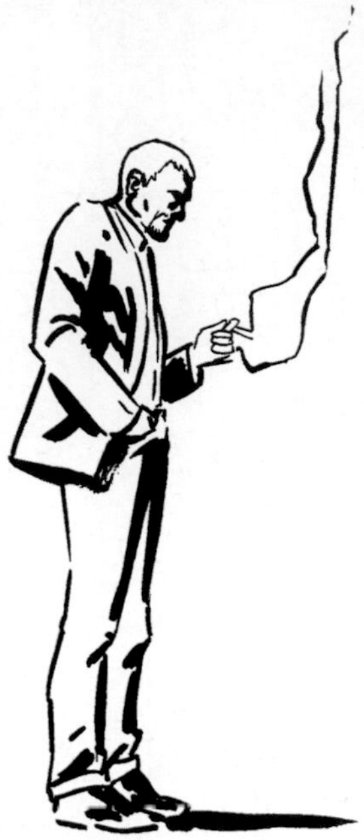

The service isn't inexpensive. Reconnect collects a hefty fee, and Mark is well paid for the risk he takes traveling through time. Because time travel isn't just heavily regulated—it's illegal for private enterprise. To Mark, though, this isn't a question of conscience. If illegal time travel can save lives—and it does—then it's worth the risk. It's worth the cost.

But after an assignment goes sideways, leaving one Reconnect agent dead and Mark with an uncooperative rescue in tow, Mark finds himself stuck in the past. Mark then receives orders to kill a government investigator looking into Reconnect. If Mark ignores these orders, the investigator will shut down Reconnect and leave Mark stranded in the past and, potentially, dead; but if he does as he's told, Mark will be ending a life, exactly the opposite of his intentions. Mark has to make a choice that straddles the difference between what is good, what is evil, and what is necessary. To make this choice, Mark must challenge his conscience and reconsider his priorities. Above all, he needs to live with the decision he makes, as long or as short as his life may be.

In the end, Mark manages to spare the investigator and thwart the investigation before finally returning to the present.

But, in a final twist to the story, his success is not as gratifying as he'd first assumed. Unknown to Mark, not everyone he rescues goes on to live a full life. Instead, Reconnect has its own secrets to hide. After each rescue, an agents assesses the rescued and disposes of those it deems to be a threat to their multi-million dollar operation. This leaves their blood on the hands of Mark, who delivered the rescued to their new, unexpected, and tragic fates.

On the left is the pitch that we used to get COMEBACK picked up.

As you can see, we stuck pretty close to this outline in the story. The only real changes were in expanding Owen and Seth's roles. Hell, they're not even mentioned here. It wasn't until I sat down and started writing COMEBACK that those two characters really started to take on a life of their own.

I'd be remiss if I didn't thank Jeffrey Gerretse for helping me put together this pitch document.

ALTERNATE COVER COLORS

When finalizing the covers, **Jordie** would often toss a few different ideas our way, all of which were brilliant.

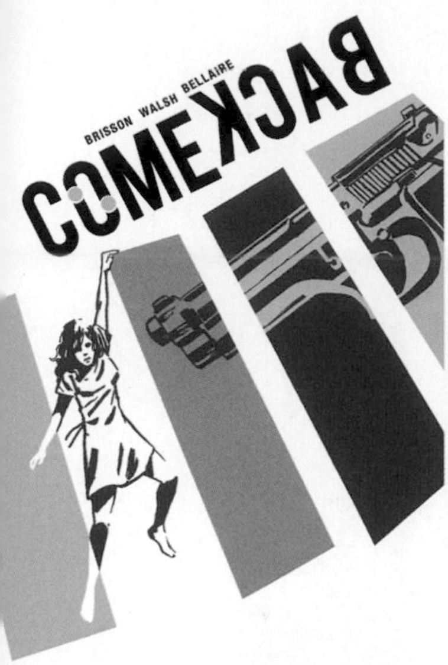
BRISSON WALSH BELLAIRE
COMEBACK

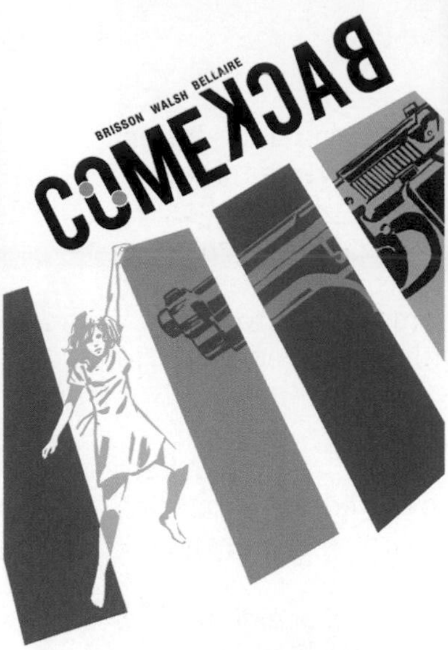
BRISSON WALSH BELLAIRE
COMEBACK

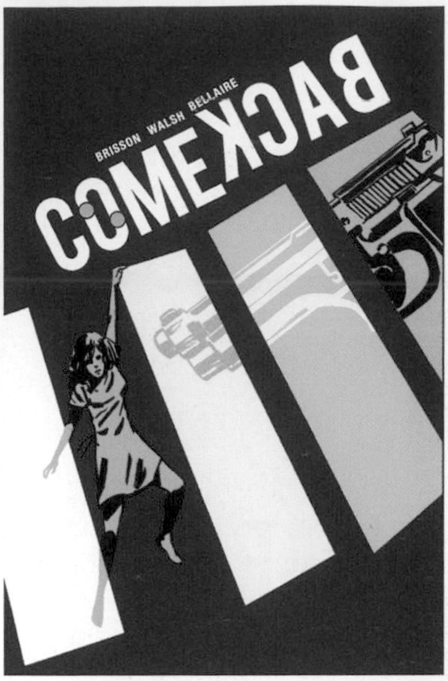
BRISSON WALSH BELLAIRE
COMEBACK

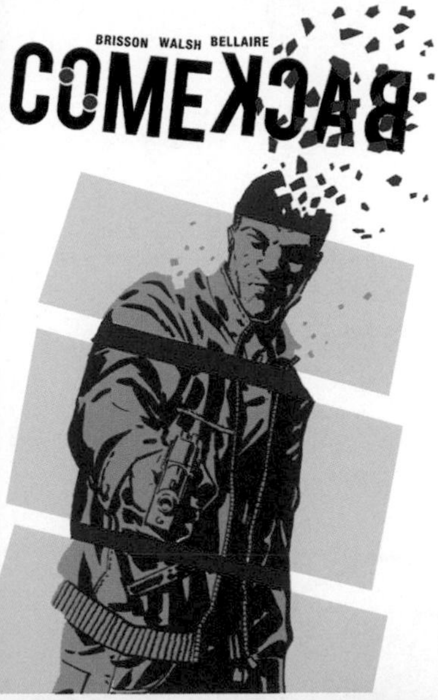
BRISSON WALSH BELLAIRE
COMEBACK

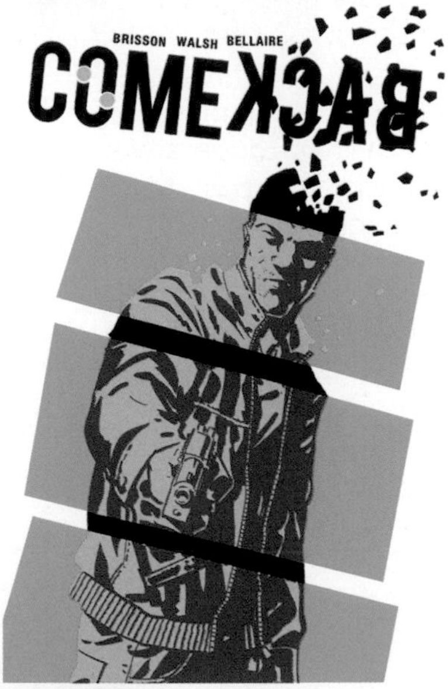
BRISSON WALSH BELLAIRE
COMEBACK

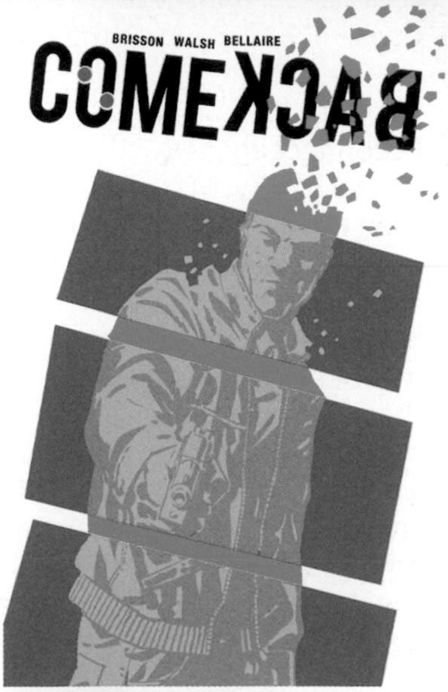
BRISSON WALSH BELLAIRE
COMEBACK

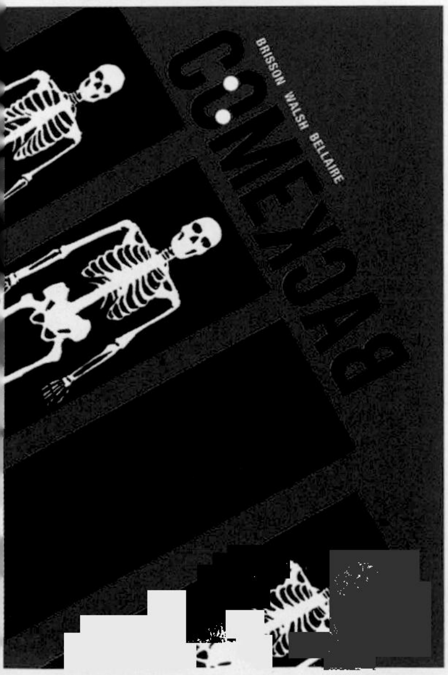
BRISSON WALSH BELLAIRE
COMEBACK

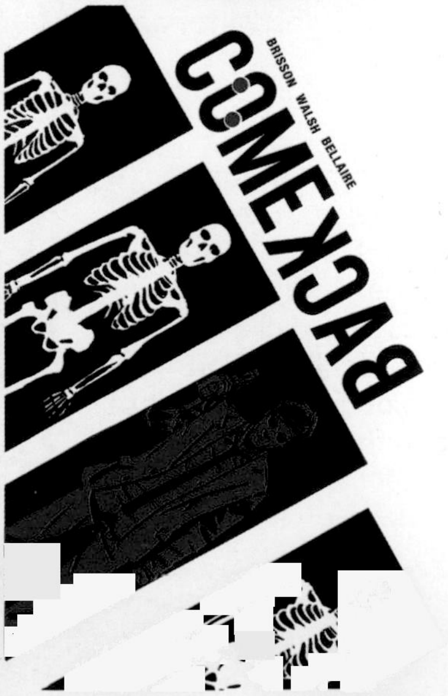
BRISSON WALSH BELLAIRE
COMEBACK

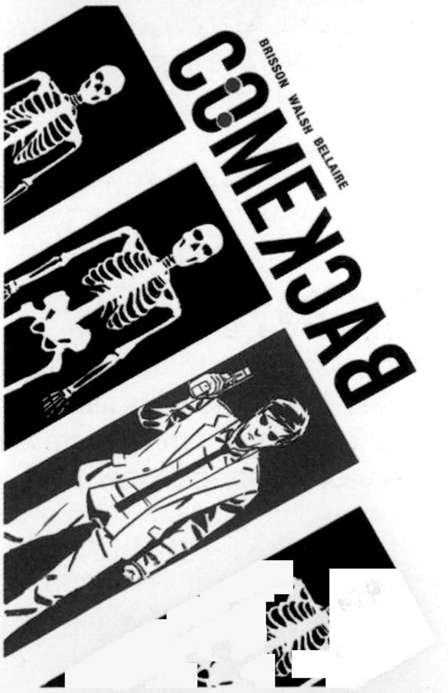
BRISSON WALSH BELLAIRE
COMEBACK

EARLY CHARACTER SKETCHES AND DESIGNS.

MARK

We wanted to make Mark seem casual. He's supposed to be approachable and easy going. His job in RECONNECT is to put the rescuees at ease, so Micheal thought to give him a more casual look.

SETH

It's the stressed out smoker! We wanted him to seem like an intense guy, but still someone that would be good friends with Mark. He had to be likeable. As a side note: I love all of the little cigarette tricks Michael had Seth doing throughout the book.

MR. FIELDS

Poor Mr. Gary Fields. Little does he know that he's about to get kidnapped and then exploded in a time travel mishap.

KELLY

I'd hoped to do more with Kelly in Comeback, but the five issue constraint didn't allow enough time to explore the things I wanted to with her, so, sadly, a lot of it had to be cut. She could have had a whole issue devoted to her.

THE TIME TRAVEL MACHINERY!

Before starting Comeback, Michael and I had quite a few conversations about the tech and how we thought it should look. Because RECONNECT is an illegal operation, we thought that it made more sense to have the tech look cobbled together and just a little junky. More 60s B-Movie sci-fi than the slick white plastic with black rubber that you see in most present day sci-fi.

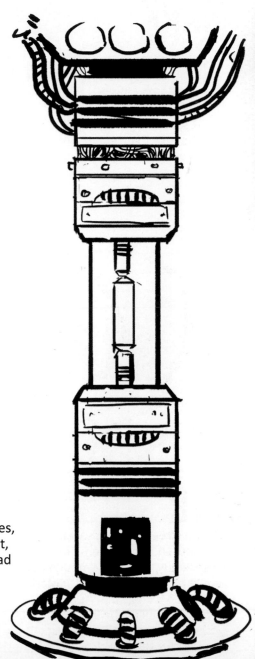

OWEN

Initially, Owen's role in Comeback was pretty small. He was always the guy who was killing off the rescuees, but was originally meant to be behind the scenes. But, as I started writing the book, he became more of a bad ass that was driving a lot of the action. We wanted him to look like a tough as hell bruiser. I will not lie I fell in love with this character and often tried talking myself out of killing him off.

OUTLINING THE SCRIPT

Below is the outline I used when scripting the final issue of COMEBACK. Generally I have a pile of script ideas written in notebooks already. I take that info and put together this very loose outline, which is basically just trigger words or phrases for each page or scene. I keep this next to my lapto[p] for easy reference while writing. As you can see, some scenes changed between the outline and final book -- pages 17-20 were completely rewritten.

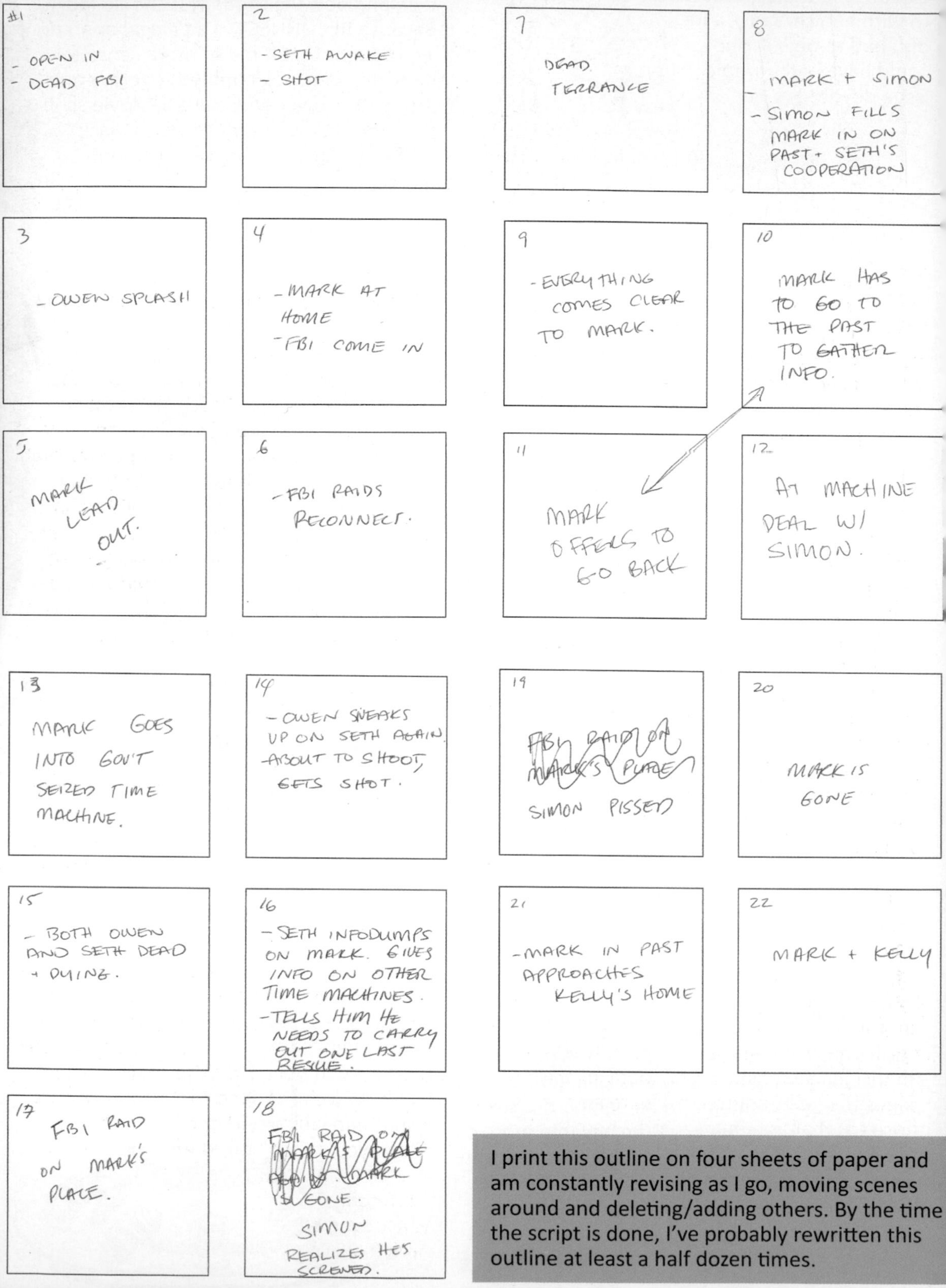

#1
- OPEN IN
- DEAD FBI

2
- SETH AWAKE
- SHOT

3
- OWEN SPLASH

4
- MARK AT HOME
- FBI COME IN

5
MARK LEAD OUT.

6
- FBI RAIDS RECONNECT.

7
DEAD TERRANCE

8
- MARK + SIMON
- SIMON FILLS MARK IN ON PAST + SETH'S COOPERATION

9
- EVERYTHING COMES CLEAR TO MARK.

10
MARK HAS TO GO TO THE PAST TO GATHER INFO.

11
MARK OFFERS TO GO BACK

12
AT MACHINE DEAL W/ SIMON.

13
MARK GOES INTO GOV'T SEIZED TIME MACHINE.

14
- OWEN SNEAKS UP ON SETH AGAIN.
- ABOUT TO SHOOT, GETS SHOT.

15
- BOTH OWEN AND SETH DEAD + DYING.

16
- SETH INFODUMPS ON MARK. GIVES INFO ON OTHER TIME MACHINES.
- TELLS HIM HE NEEDS TO CARRY OUT ONE LAST RESCUE.

17
FBI RAID ON MARK'S PLACE.

18
~~FBI RAID ON MARK'S PLACE~~
~~RAID - MARK IS GONE.~~
SIMON REALIZES HES SCREWED.

19
~~FBI RAID ON MARK'S PLACE~~
SIMON PISSED

20
MARK IS GONE

21
- MARK IN PAST APPROACHES KELLY'S HOME

22
MARK + KELLY

I print this outline on four sheets of paper and am constantly revising as I go, moving scenes around and deleting/adding others. By the time the script is done, I've probably rewritten this outline at least a half dozen times.

AFTERWORD

In the summer of 2011, Michael and I set a one-year goal in which to get a pitch picked up by a publisher. At the time it seemed almost absurd, but we made this deal with one another as though we couldn't fail. We were coming out guns blazing.

Eight months later, COMEBACK was green lit with Shadowline.

While luck played a huge part in this, we hustled hard for those eight months. We were nose to the grind stone, me writing pitches and him drawing them. We were determined not to fail.

What you have here in your hands is the culmination of that hard work. It's the result of more than a year of effort and buckets of blood, sweat and tears. And, hopefully, you think it's a damn good book. We do.

I want to thank Michael Walsh for being a dream collaborator. COMEBACK is the third project that we've worked on together, and by the time we started on this, we were well in-tune with one another – like one of those couples that finish one another's sentences only less obnoxious and much cuter. Many of the pages that Michael created were so close to what was in my mind when scripting that it was eerie. I'm still not convinced that Michael isn't inside my head, so if you see me wearing a tinfoil hat, you know why.

All brain squatting aside, hopefully this is not the last collaboration of ours that you see.

Jordie Bellaire was, from the outset, the only colorist that we had in mind for this project. She was already well on her way to being the comics coloring superstar that she is today, so we had our doubts that she'd have either the time or interest in working with us. But, the comic gods were shining on us and she took pity on these two lowly, struggling comic creators and agreed to come on to COMEBACK. Jordie has been an integral part of the team.

I want to thank Tim Daniel, aka "The Nicest Dude In Comics," for creating the eye-catching Comeback logo.

And, of course, I can't thank Jim Valentino and Shadowline Comics enough for publishing us and giving a chance to show the world our work. Without Jim's support and belief in us, we wouldn't be here. You wouldn't be reading this.

Last, but certainly not least, I want to thank all the readers who took a chance on this book by a new and unproven creative team. There's a lot of comics vying for your hard-earned dollars on the shelves every week, so we're thrilled that you gave ours a shot and welcomed it into your home. Thank you, thank you, thank you.

Ed Brisson
Vancouver, BC
April 2, 2013

A Book For Every Reader...

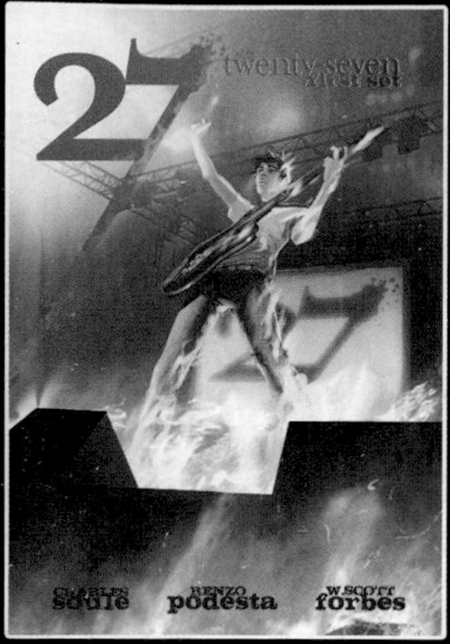
27
twenty seven

SOULE/PODESTA/FORBES

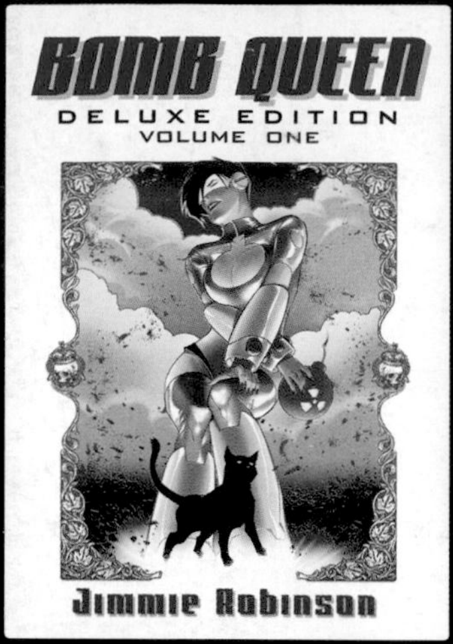
BOMB QUEEN
DELUXE EDITION
VOLUME ONE
Jimmie Robinson

ROBINSON

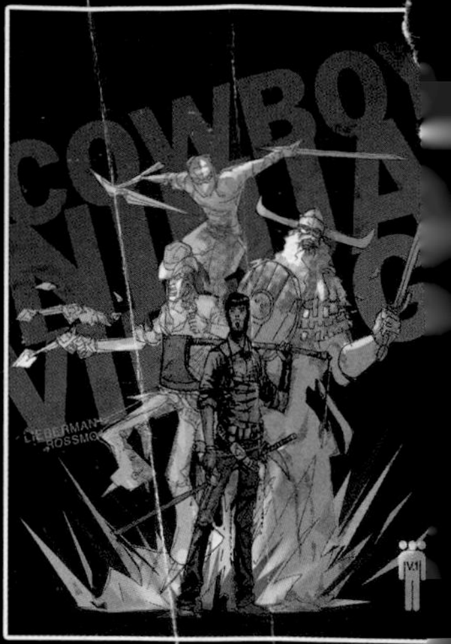

LIEBERMAN/ROSSMO

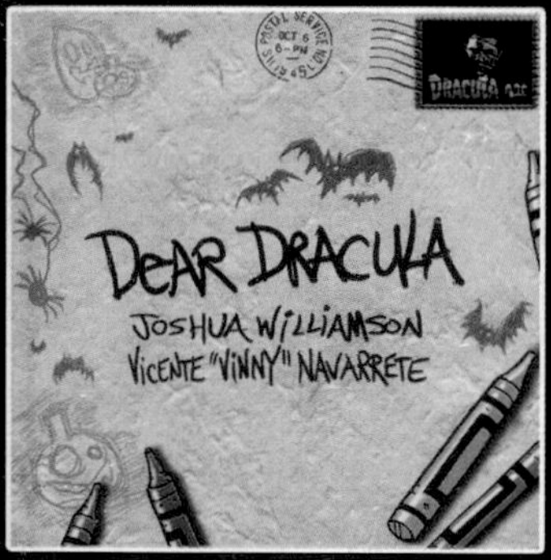
DEAR DRACULA
JOSHUA WILLIAMSON
VICENTE "VINNY" NAVARRETE

WILLIAMSON/NAVARETTE

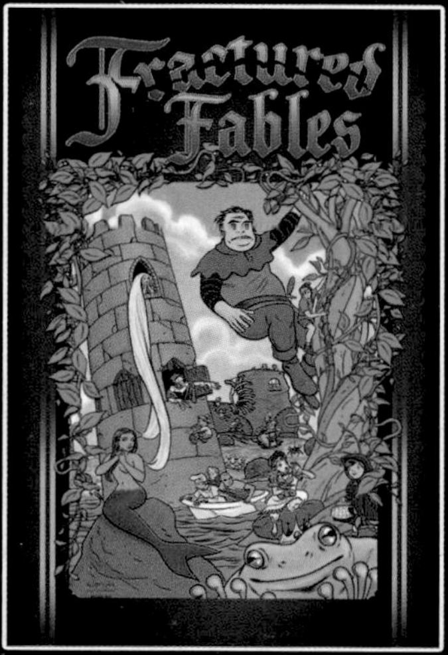
Fractured Fables

VARIOUS ARTISTS

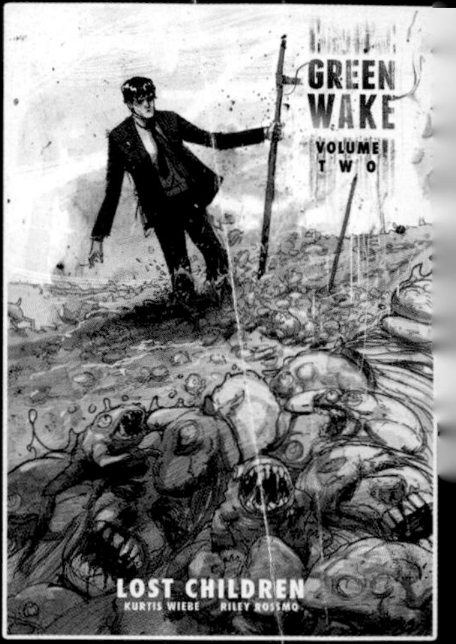
GREEN WAKE
VOLUME TWO
LOST CHILDREN
KURTIS WIEBE RILEY ROSSMO

WIEBE/ROSSMO

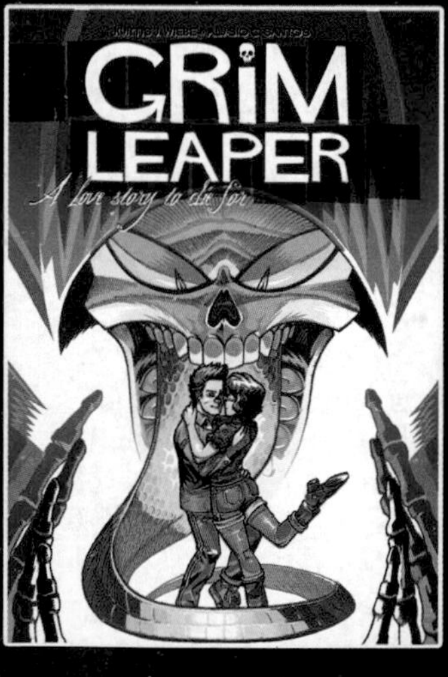
GRIM LEAPER
A love story to die for

WIEBE/SANTOS

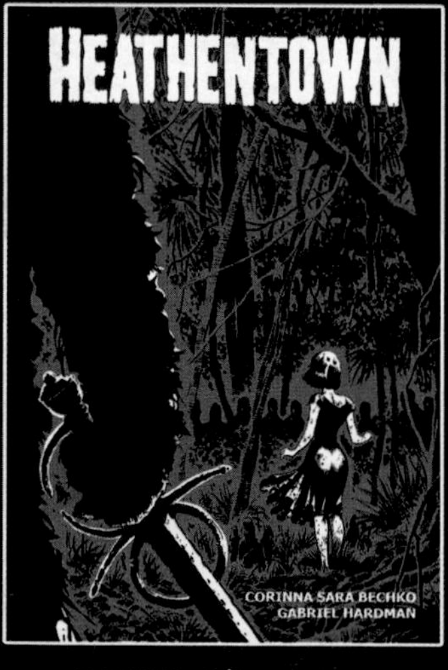
HEATHENTOWN
CORINNA SARA BECHKO
GABRIEL HARDMAN

BECHKO/HARDMAN

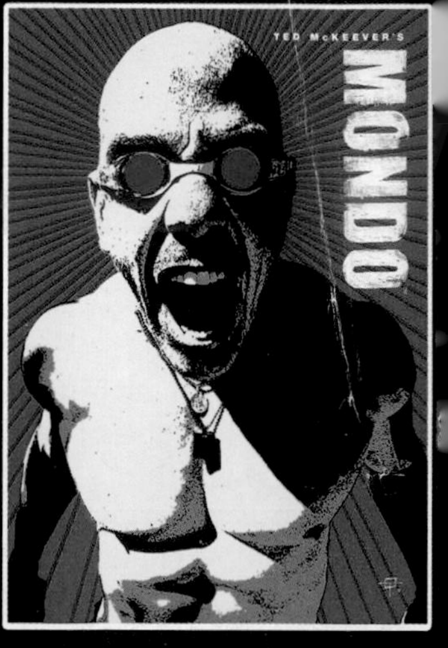
TED McKEEVER'S
MONDO

TED McKEEVER

FOR MORE INFORMATION ABOUT ALL *Shadowline*™ BOOKS AND WEB-COMICS, PLEASE VISIT US AT:

www.ShadowlineOnline.com